THE
INDIA WE SERVED

THE
INDIA WE SERVED

BY

WALTER ROPER LAWRECE

GYAN

Published by

Gyan Publishing House
5, Ansari Road
Daryaganj, New Delhi-110002
Phone: 011-47034999, 9811692060
E-mail: books@gyanbooks.com

Distribution Network
gyanbooks.com
India, USA, Canada, UK, Australia

ISBN: 978-93-6433-133-3 (PB)
First Published, 1928

2nd Impression 2024

Printed at: Gyan Press, Delhi.

THE INDIA WE SERVED
Author: WALTER ROPER LAWRECE

INDIA WE SERVED

THE INDIA WE SERVED

By

SIR WALTER ROPER LAWRENCE, BART
G.C.I.E., G.C.V.O., C.B.

With an Introductory Letter by
RUDYARD KIPLING

CASSELL AND COMPANY, LTD
London, Toronto, Melbourne and Sydney

To

MY WIFE

Dear Walter

Thinking over our talk together, when you showed me your Indian Diaries, I am more than ever certain that you must make a book of them and cover that wonderful time between the post-Mutiny reconstruction and the coming of the New Age.

Everything fits in for the work like a fairy-tale. You began with some years of as mixed service as any man could wish. You had the great good luck to be able to retire before your impressions were blurred. Then you came back as Private Secretary to a Viceroy and saw the whole machinery of Indian administration laid bare.

Finally — when you were on duty with the Prince and Princess — you had the complete panorama and pageant of all India unrolled beneath you as from an aeroplane.

What in Asia more do you need — except the ministrations of a faithful friend who will keep on reminding you of what he knows to be your duty.

<u>I</u> am going to be that friend.

Ever yours

Rudyard

PREFACE

THE letter on the other side is my apology for this book. Another friend,[1] cheering and chiding, bade members of my service observe and leave some record before we died; but most of us were as loath to write as to die.

I see now that I had unusual opportunities for observing, very close, and from many points of view; also from afar, through the wrong end of the telescope, as a member of the Council of India.

These reminiscences may seem to linger unduly in that region of enchantment—the Rájas' land—known to so few, rich in colour and throbbing life. But to me this was always the real India.

Some think that the dreamland of Queen Victoria has gone for ever, and that the old relations between the Indians and the Sahibs are fast passing into myth and memory: even so, they reflect credit on both, and may be recorded.

But I believe that for many generations India will have need of the Sahibs and that the young pilgrim, who goes the road which I took, will find kindness and welcome if he gives the password and the greetings. He must know the language and understand the customs. He will, I hope, admire, as I did, the great men who made the road and prepared the camping grounds with water, food and firing and safe harbourage at night. They knew what the country wanted. I

[1] *See* Chapter IX, p. 168, footnote [1].

have attempted in my tale to tell of all the roads I trod up to the time when they tried to turn India into a Western path.

If these reminiscences help the youth sailing East I shall be richly rewarded, and old Pliny's belief, that "no book was so bad but that some good might be got out of it," will once more be justified.

W. R. L.

Bunce's Farm,
Sussex,
1927.

CONTENTS

CHAPTER I

CHAPTER II

CHAPTER III

THE INDIA WE SERVED

CHAPTER I

Childhood—Gipsies—Dame's School—Review of the Gloucestershire Hussars —Cheltenham College—The Ideal House Master—Home Life—School Friends—Balliol—Arnold Toynbee—Dr. Jowett—With Detective in East End—Rhoda Broughton—The Charm of Oxford—Some Foreigners and an Indian—Outfit for India—Arrival at Lahore.

On entre,
On crie,
Et c'est la vie:
On bâille,
On sort,
Et c'est la mort.
Un jour de fête,
Un jour de deuil,
La vie est faite
En un clin d'oeil.

IF not in the twinkling of an eye, yet in the first five or six years, the sketch is made and the faint, fatal chart drawn of our strange pilgrimage. It all depends on three influences, the mother, the nurse and the governess. I was superlatively fortunate in all three. They were not only good, but beautiful as well. This I learned in later years from my elders. It was to the charm of my young nurse that I owed the welcome I received in the cottages of the lovely village in which I was born seventy years ago. I can remember the lush pastures, the green lawns and the beautiful trees in that slumberous country where the white-faced Herefords grazed, and the apples grew. Years later I thought that the fairest work of nature was the colour of the almond groves, and the iris, of Kashmir. But the apple blossom, when it blushes in the warm clasp of the enraptured sun, almost vies with the delicate beauty of the almond.

To my nurse I owed my visit to the gipsies in the hop garden. I shall never forget the drowsy scent as the gipsies softly smothered me in the hop cradles. Perhaps those warm faces with the brown eyes gave me my first orientation, my first gentle push Eastwards. Certainly I have liked the gipsy folk ever since.

I can remember with freshness the cottages with their little rows of daisies, primroses and sweet-williams, and how I thought the food of the villagers was delicious. Like Effie in "Silas Marner," "I like the working folks and their victuals and their ways." We were on the same level of thought. What we talked about I cannot now recall, but I have a suspicion that my friends of the cottages were against authority, and that they had a sympathy for one like myself, who was being brought up by rule. One rebel, in particular, was old Betty, who was a master weeder in our gardens. She had a dear face, like an apple in March: she was weather-wise and a teller of stories. She always welcomed me in the set words: "Come his ways, the pretty dear!" and when she spoke of governesses and nurses, she would say: "Drat them!" and pull up her weed with a special virulence. This may ultimately have prejudiced my young mind against authority, but in the early days the authority was gentle and impalpable. My mother and my governess taught me to read without tears, and the easy, happy life which I have enjoyed is due to these eight quiet years.

Then a gentle uprooting from the red soil of Moreton-on-the-Lugg to the yellow marl of the Cotswolds. A Dame's school. She wore ringlets, and at noon regaled herself with bread and cheese and ale, a sight that always made me hungry. There was a tall, thin, sallow man who taught Latin. He carried a cane, with which he tapped his desk. And there was a stout lady who instructed us in French. It was not a large school, only eight boys, and I have among my papers a bill dated September, 1866, which shows that for two terms my education cost £9 3s. 9d., and of this, 3s. 6d. was for the "share of carriage to see the Review." Ah, that Review! I have seen many splendid pageants and great arrays of armies, but my young and plastic mind was impressed, as by nothing since, by that march past of the glorious Gloucestershire Hussars, on a warm day in June. One incident affected our School almost to tears. As the regiment passed, glittering in the sun, one of the troopers fell slowly off his horse. We were loud in our sympathy; but a fierce-looking sergeant said things to the prostrate warrior which, being interpreted by our Dame, suggested that beer was the cause of the trooper's downfall.

From the Dame's school I entered Cheltenham College, starting in the lowest form of the junior school. In that junior school they certainly taught one thing most thoroughly: whether it was from fear or affection I know not, but I learnt the Latin and Greek grammars almost by heart, and the rest of my life at school, till I left in 1876, was easy and effortless. It was a good school and I went to an excellent house and was devoted to my house master. He was sometimes sarcastic, but we liked and respected him and would do much to win his approval. One term he was ill and unable to look after the house, and we behaved like angels, all for the sake of "Joe." Like my father, he wished me to become a barrister; but I had heard a naval friend of my family talk about the life of an Indian Civilian, and in a vague way I decided that India should be my goal. One night, towards the end of my school days, "Joe" was remonstrating with me for my lack of industry and energy, and said that I had no chance of passing the examination for the Indian Civil Service. He was very outspoken, and when I left Cheltenham and went to the great crammer, Mr. Wren, I worked hard, just to show my friend and house master that he was wrong. I had the great luck to come out at the head of the list.

Few boys work at a public school unless they are compelled or coaxed. I had been compelled to assimilate the Latin and Greek grammars, and they were my only school asset. But I had another great asset. I was one of a large family, and my brothers and sisters were all clever and accomplished. Their preoccupations were sport and English literature, and my favourite brother, Wyndham, a fine athlete and sportsman, and also a writer of good verse, knew his Chambers's "Cyclopædia of Literature" almost by heart; and though light-hearted and careless, he took a delight in pouring his knowledge of English poetry into me. And as I admired him for his prowess in sport and wished to win his good opinion, I, too, acquired the Chambers habit and the love of English literature.

My father and his two brothers were great sportsmen, but philosophers too, and the patriarchal rule in our home was that everyone must be doing something. So my holiday pastime of lying under a shady tree looking at the sky and thinking the "long, long thoughts" of youth, was often rudely interrupted by my too energetic parent. When I grew to manhood I sometimes missed his driving power. I do not propose to dwell on my home life, though it was delightful and full of incident. We were a Welsh family, fond of music and song, sport and anecdote; sometimes laughter, sometimes wrath, and then affectionate reconciliation.

I look back to my school days with pleasure. I made some dear friends, most of them now gone: but my greatest friend, Endicott Peabody, a splendid American, is still my best of friends, as he was always my best of guides. But the happiest time in England was the life in Oxford.

I went to Balliol in October, 1877. Mr. Jowett, the Master, took a keen interest in the Indian Civil Service, and had written to my father to suggest that I should enter his college. The second term he gave me charming rooms: he advised me to cultivate friendships, to study character, and to observe rather than to work. I followed this advice too literally, and just read enough to scrape through the periodical examinations prescribed by the Civil Service Commissioners. So I had leisure to enjoy the charm of Oxford life. It was all new and wonderful to me—"that city of young life astir for fame." The independence, the carelessness, the glorious companionship and the beautiful surroundings. I knew and liked everyone in college, and I especially admired the two dons who looked after me—Arnold Toynbee and Mr. Strachan Davidson. Their forbearance and patient toleration were astounding. Toynbee attracted me greatly. He was full of enthusiasm, very tolerant, and very stimulating. He always made us feel that there was something in us. He was like Mr. Jowett in that respect.

The Master was most kind to me. I used to stay with him at his house in West Malvern, and at the Master's lodge I met great and unbending men, Dean Stanley, Robert Browning and others. Undergraduates were expected to listen rather than to talk, and rashly one day I struck in. Dean Stanley, who had just come back from America, was saying to the Master that the Americans could not write English. I suggested that "The Scarlet Letter" was English. The Dean snubbed me, and I felt rather unhappy during the rest of the breakfast. As I was walking out of the room, Dean Stanley came up, spoke kindly and asked me to call on him at Westminster. Later he made a great impression on me. I heard him preach in the Abbey on the death of Motley, and I thought it the greatest of sermons: and I thought, as I still think, that if I could choose any office in England, I should choose the Deanery of Westminster. I must add that I do not think I heard a single sermon during my stay in Oxford. I often listened to the divine choirs of Magdalen and New College, but I was an infrequent attendant at Balliol Chapel.

Many terrifying legends clustered round Mr. Jowett. I always found him a most wise and considerate guide. We took up essays to him. I know mine were, in his own words, "poor stuff," but in his talk he was always encouraging, and he kept me close to what was practical. He never sneered. He was impatient of silly remarks, but he loved a good joke, and it was pleasant to hear him laugh. I once asked him, when we were walking in the snow at Malvern, whether Jane Austen was much read at the beginning of the century. "I don't know," he said rather peevishly, "I did not live at the beginning of the century." He was so full of energy and vitality that he disliked any allusion to age. I owe much to that dear Master, who encouraged and helped me, and was my friend till his death. The last time I saw him, before returning to India after short leave, I said, on wishing him good-bye, that I should see him again in three years. He replied: "You will never see me again, but don't forget to write to me about the introduction of tobacco into India." They had told him that his days were numbered, but that did not impair his sacred thirst for knowledge.

Though the Master was interested in the governance of India, he, like all the rest, knew nothing of actual conditions in India, and during my two years' probation I never met anyone who ever mentioned India. We read a certain amount of Indian history and Indian law, but there was no one to tell us of life in India and the work which awaited the young Civilian. Perhaps this was wise, for if we had known the tasks and responsibilities ahead of us, I, for one, should not have been so happy and careless as I was at Balliol. I had the good fortune to find an excellent teacher of Hindustáni. I liked him, and so did a certain amount of work. I learnt the grammar, and this helped me greatly when I arrived in India. The great foundation for a happy and successful life in India is a thorough knowledge of the grammar of Hindustáni, and this knowledge can only be acquired while at home.

By chance I made friends with a detective at Scotland Yard, and when I went from Oxford to the Inner Temple to eat dinners, I used every night after dinner to go down with my friend to Whitechapel. We visited the Mahogany Bars, and the Singsongs of Ratcliff Highway, the Eagle Music Hall, the resort of the burglars, and the Effingham Theatre, much loved by the pickpockets. I saw many curious scenes and made some most interesting acquaintances. In the course of two years I gained some knowledge of the doss-houses of Whitechapel.

My detective friend attributed his apparent immunity from violence to the fact that his criminal clients, lavish in some respects, always disliked expensive lodgings. If a criminal made himself obnoxious by violent outbursts he was a marked man, and his lodging-house received numerous visits from the police. The lodging-house deputy soon realised that one of his guests was unpopular, and moved him on. But the other lodging-houses knew why he had been moved on, and there was no home for him in Whitechapel. He would then migrate to Seven Dials or Westminster; but here, again, it would be difficult to find a lodging for long. So I always noticed that the relations between my detective and the criminal tribes were friendly, indeed intimate, and I was certainly treated with great courtesy.

I danced at the Mahogany Bars, drank excellent sherry at twopence a glass with the old women who chaperoned the girls, and heard from them stories of romance and pathos. I saw a jealous foreigner stab a rival fatally, but my detective took no notice. As the man fell, two policemen in uniform walked quietly in. As we left, the dance went on. They were dancing the Ratcliff Highway Kick.

But there was one man with whom my detective's relations were strained. This was Captain P——, a famous and successful criminal. When I made his acquaintance he was owner of two flourishing gin palaces, and lived luxuriously. One night, as I drove on a bus with my detective towards the East, he showed me by the light of a street lamp the photograph of a man strapped in a chair. He called my attention to a slanting scar on the forehead, and told me that he wished to test my powers of recognition. A few hours later we were at the Eagle Music Hall. I was near the liquor bar, and my detective had left me to find out from a woman the address of a criminal, one Hamer, whom he wanted. As I stood watching the stage, a well-dressed man, whose face was quite unfamiliar, walked up and politely asked me if I was seeing the sights of the East End. He told me who the performers were, and pointed out in the audience some of the leading cracksmen. Then the detective arrived, did not acknowledge the man's greeting, and said we must be moving. However, the woman with whom he had been talking came up and asked him for a drink. He said: "Ask Hamer to give you a drink." She said: "What do I know of Hamer?" "All right," said the detective, "I'll give you a drink," and off they went. The well-dressed, polite stranger came up again and asked me to have a drink, but I declined. We talked some time, when back came the detective. He looked happy, but when he saw my companion he scowled. "Have a drink?" said the polite stranger. "No," said the detective, "I don't drink with murderers and scoundrels like you." "See here," said the stranger, "that's a nice way to accept a gentleman's hospitality: I'll report you to the Home Office." We then left, and the detective said: "Did you recognise him? That was Captain P——, forger, murderer, and capitalist." He then told me the reason of his dislike for P——. It was not because he had forged Turkish Bonds, and had instigated, indeed probably had himself perpetrated, the murder of a woman in Coram Street—an inconvenient witness. P—— had done something still more irregular. My detective liked fishing and enjoyed a day's racing, and a year before, being off duty, went down to see the Oaks. P——, who was in the paddock, had pointed him out to others as a "Copper," and the word went round, and my friend's pleasure was spoiled. But later, Captain P—— had to give evidence at the Mansion House, and my detective asked some of his colleagues at Scotland Yard whether they would like to see the famous man. Eight of them drove off in two four-wheelers to the Mansion House, and my detective grouped them on the steps. Soon Captain P—— drove up in a smart brougham, and my detective advanced to meet him. "Why, this is friendly," said P——, grasping his hand. "Yes," said the detective, returning his grasp. "You gave me away to your pals at the Oaks. Some of my friends from the Yard are taking note of you, your clothes, your brougham, your driver, and lastly," he said, "your scar," indicating the scar with his left hand. "Now, wherever you go, you will have someone who knows you. Good morning."

I learnt much from my association with the detective, among other lessons the importance of quick and ready admission of a mistake, and going right back to the beginning for a fresh clue. This rule is good not only for the Police, but also for Politicians and Administrators. It is a hard, often a very wearisome and disappointing life. My friend used to give information in order to gain more valuable information. He never attempted disguises. He depended greatly on his memory for faces. For instance, he had been for months trying to arrest Hamer, and it was by sudden chance that he remembered that Hamer had been a friend of the woman we saw at the Eagle. He took Hamer the next day. There is a great deal of chance in the work of a detective. I believe that our Scotland Yard detectives are the best in the world. There is very little in our British system which helps them in their work. The Home Office was strict, and did not encourage too much zeal. On one point my detective and all his colleagues whom I knew were very positive, and that was that their work would be impossible if the death sentence were ever abolished.

Now, this is a digression from Oxford, but it arose from my previous mention of Arnold Toynbee. He was working in the East End, and he took an interest in my experiences and persuaded me to tell some of my adventures. So I gave a kind of lecture to my friends in my rooms. One day, Cross, who had won his blue on the river, brought his father, who was then Home Secretary. When I had finished the story of my wonderful detective, Mr. Cross came up and said: "Do you know that you are liable to a penalty for going with the police without my permit, and that S—— (the name of my detective) is liable to dismissal?" I thought at first that he was in earnest, but his son reassured me, and Mr. Cross not only gave me permission to go round with my friend, but also gave me passes for Portland and Dartmoor, as he thought it might interest me to see the inevitable ending of the activities of my acquaintances.

In 1877–79 there were few ladies in Oxford, but I had the great privilege of being a friend of Miss Rhoda Broughton, and I used to go to her charming house, where she lived with a sister. She was a very sympathetic and encouraging friend, and she instilled some sane ideas into my mind. I told her that I had met "Nancy's" father: but she said there was no such person. I happened to know the words of an old song, "Mr. Lobo said to his ugly wife." She had quoted the first line in one of her books, but did not know the context.[1] I met Robert Browning occasionally at Miss Broughton's house. He told many anecdotes of social life, but I never heard him allude to literature.

I do not think that I or any of my great friends ever attended a debate at the Union. Quite wrongly we regarded the orators as "pifflers." But though we did not make speeches, we talked till late hours, and though I cannot

[1] The verse runs as follows:

"Mr. Lobo said to his ugly wife:
'I'm going to the river to fish, my life':
Says Mrs. Lobo: 'You beast, you aren't,
You know you're going to galliwant.'"

now recapture the charm of these conversations, I know that they were full of generous ideas, and splendid, impracticable aims. We did not discuss politics, letters, nor careers. I would give much now to listen again to Cecil Spring Rice and the others, all so delightfully irrelevant, irresponsible and elusive. It was a jocund company "When wits were fresh and clear—and life ran gaily as the sparkling Thames." We met at luncheon, at tea after the river, and at wines in our rooms after dinner in the Hall. There was an admirable college stores from which we bought our wine. We drank claret and port, but I never saw spirits drunk at Oxford.

In 1879 Balliol went head of the river, and we gave a great ball. I was on the small committee which arranged the details. Every week we met in Mr. Paravicini's rooms, decided on Heidsieck Dry Monopole for our champagne, on Veitch for our flowers and on the band of the Royal Marines for our music. Just before the date of our ball, one of our college was drowned at Sandford's Lasher, and the question arose at once as to whether we should cancel the ball; but after the funeral his father begged us to give the ball, as his son would have wished it. It was really the house-warming of the new hall at Balliol, in which the Master took such pride. It was my last night in college, and I was sad to leave.

I cannot define the charm of Oxford, nor can I explain the source of her influence. But I know that the charm was potent, and that the influence was healthy as the sea breeze, and it is still blowing in my face. I would always send a boy to Oxford, as I would send him to a public school; not because they are ideal places for study and learning, but because they both teach in the most convincing manner conduct and consonance. I know what I owe to the example of the men who were my guides at Balliol, and sometimes I think with a kind of horror of what I might have become, if I had spent my two years of probation in London, untrammelled and careless of the compelling power of a competitive examination. Parents are apt to be impatient if a son runs off the rails. It is mostly a question of environment and luck. It was easy and pleasant to run along the rails at Balliol: it would have been as easy and seemingly as pleasant to have run off the rails if one had been living in rooms in London.

There was another charm about Balliol for the comparatively poor man. Many of the men at Balliol belonged to very rich families, but they lived to the ordinary standard, and we were all passing rich on £300 a year. I was a member of Vincent's Club. Among its many privileges was that of being able to have a hot breakfast on Sunday.

I hesitate to give the names of those to whom I owed so much. Of those now living most have become distinguished in every walk except the Church. In my time only one of us was destined for the Church. There was a charming American, a very attractive Frenchman, two Japanese, and one Indian. Just before I came up the two Japanese had quarrelled over cards, and one of them felt so strongly that he rushed into the "Quad" and declared his intention of committing hara-kiri under the Master's window. It was a beautiful summer's night, and the Master, roused from his study of Thucydides, quelled the intending suicide by calling him "sensual Oriental," and so the matter ended. I made great friends with the Indian. He was a Moslem from Bengal, and entertained us by smoking a real hooka, sitting on the floor. He was a charming and most affectionate companion and was very popular. But he told us very little about India, for he lived in a large town and knew nothing about the country. He told us one fact which interested us, though I was never able to verify it when I reached India. He said that when tigers preyed on a village too regularly the people would strew large leaves smeared with a strong gum around the carcass of the tiger's kill. The tiger would endeavour to tear off the sticky leaves from his body, and invariably end by plastering the leaves over his eyes. Whereupon the villagers would approach the blinded tiger and club him to death. My Indian friend and I parted with regret, and he gave me a letter of introduction to one of his acquaintances in Bombay.

Among the many whom I counted as friends at Balliol

were two who profoundly affected my life. The first lived on my staircase, and neighbourship led to a life-long friendship. He tempted me back to England after I had served sixteen years in India. The second lived on a staircase just opposite mine. He it was who persuaded me to return again to India: they were very opposite in character, but both influenced me. And this is the secret of Oxford, this curious and subtle play of diverse characters on one another.

The two years at Oxford passed like an exquisite dream, but they gave me an outlook and a direction which helped and steadied me when—ominous phrase!—I went down. Balliol was for me "the tall mountain."

I still have a great and fresh memory of those early days and would be sorry if I ever forgot the friends and places I loved so well. Yet I would gladly escape one dream, which comes persistently, and shows how the competitive examinations and the long anxious waiting for the result must have affected my young mind. I dream that an order comes telling me that I must pass the examination again. I remonstrate, but the authorities are obdurate. I wake in a fright, for I know that I could never again pass that examination.

I purchased an outfit for India, and in my ignorance I bought clothes which would have been of use in Madras, but were ridiculous in the Punjáb. The only things I found of use were good riding-breeches, a good saddle and a gun. I advise all who go to India to take all the books, prints and household gods they treasure, but to avoid helmets and clothes which the outfitters recommend. It is wisdom to have nice things in India and good policy to convey the impression not of bivouac, but of determined domicile. Servants appreciate the fact that their master means to make a home in India, and visitors, Indian as well as English, like to see something, however humble, which comes from the old country.

I had chosen as my province what was then known as the North-West Provinces, now the United Provinces, but, luckily for me, just before I started for India, I was transferred to the Punjáb. I knew no one in India, but friends gave me letters of introduction to officials in the North-West Provinces. I kept them as a great possession, but I never delivered them, and one cold morning in December I reached Lahore without a friend and without a blanket, shivering in my flimsy garments, and with a purse as cold as my body.

CHAPTER II

"How many goodly creatures are there here,
How beauteous mankind is! Oh brave new world,
That has such people in't."—*Tempest.*

Voyage to India—A Theatrical Company—Bombay—Entertained by Moslem Gentleman—Journey to Lahore—Eurasian Hotel—Stay with Lepel Griffin—John Lockwood Kipling—Fancy-dress Ball—The Zoo—Old Mogul Gardens—Municipal Committee—Nur Din, Chief of the Scavengers—Posted to Peshawar—Adventure with a Ghâzi—His Trial—Become Political Officer to Brigade at Thal, Kurram Valley—The Police Officer of Kohat—Affray with Waziris—Said Khan—Life with 18th Bengal Cavalry—Capture of Village—Linguistic Vagaries of Indians and Englishmen—Camels—The Eurasian Treasury Officer—The Khyber Pass—Peculiarities of Eurasians—Problem of their Future.

IT has taken me twenty-two years to reach India, and I always had a kind of fear that something would prevent me at the last. The voyage out gave me an idea of what the Atlantic, not the much-maligned Bay of Biscay, could do when roused. Our ship, the *Rydal Hall*, from Liverpool, carried only about forty passengers. There was a large theatrical company going to Bombay, and some six young Indian Civilians of my year, and when we buffeted our way into smooth water we enjoyed every minute. I remember how glad we were, after drinking distilled water, to taste the real element at Port Said, a brown, muddy liquid which trickled down to that picturesque but abominable refuse heap of humanity in 1879. It was our first sight of the East, of poinsettias and the desert, and I shall always remember Port Said with affection. The members of the theatrical company were charming and we became great friends. Some of the men were famous afterwards in London. In those days it was rather a daring experiment to take a large company to India. I hope they succeeded, for they worked hard at rehearsals, and they were a fascinating and friendly people. I told one of them that the Indian word for theatre was "*Shaitán Khána*," or Satan's House, and am afraid that this was regarded as a gloomy omen.

At last we reached Bombay; it is beautiful, and the curious fact is that nothing surprised me, and I seemed to have seen it before. The palms: the splendid blue of the sea and sky: the colours of the shops, the dress of the people, and the very smells, all based on Turmeric,[1] seemed familiar. Even the Indian porters, with nothing on them but a slight crupper, gave me no pause. But what did surprise me when I landed was to be greeted by a well-dressed Indian, who spoke perfect English. He had brought his carriage to meet me and would drive me to the hotel. The carriage turned out to be a smart coach and four-in-hand. He had heard from my Indian friend of Balliol that I was coming. Having settled in at a hotel, and having reported my arrival to the Home Department of the Bombay Government, I was sitting in the spacious veranda, watching the passing crowds and the jugglers, who showed me the mango growing from the smooth stone, and the way the mongoose dealt with the cobra, when up drove my kind friend on his coach, and took me for a delightful drive through the town and out to the suburbs, over Malabar Hill. He explained the various groups of Indians to me, and in about two hours I think I saw men of every nationality in the East. Only one place in India rivals Bombay in diversity, and that is Peshawar bazaar. We drove back to my friend's house, which seemed to me magnificent, standing in a fine enclosure full of flowering trees and crotons. There seemed to be an army of servants, all Moslems, like my host. He gave me refreshments, served just as in England, and everything in the house seemed of English origin. He invited me to dinner that night. I found about ten guests, all Indian. There were two Hindus and one Parsee, and the rest

[1] Sometimes when I use an Indian word and try to explain its meaning in a footnote, I turn to that most fascinating of glossaries, "Hobson Jobson," the work of those genial scholars, Colonel Henry Yule, C.B. and A. C. Burnell, C.I.E. It is a magic t, which can carry those who have never left England into the busy bazaars of ia. The book takes us back to the times "when Vasco sailed for Calicut and Camoens sang his praise." Turmeric is at the bottom of everything in the East and was the bait which tempted the English adventurers to India. They went for the spices. Turmeric is the tuberous root of *Curcuma longa* and, when bruised, forms one of the ingredients which, with other spices, gives zest to the curries and cereal foods of the Indians. It has been called the Indian saffron.

Moslems, a very pleasant party. They were all clever men; several barristers, a well-known doctor, a Judge of the High Court, and a singularly charming man who came from Haidarabad. He was the secretary to the great Sir Salar Jung. He wrote excellent poetry, and I have seldom heard any man talk more brilliantly. None of us ever mentioned India, or the weather. There was no gossip, no personalities, no criticisms of the Government, and no allusion to the Civil Service. They brought me into the conversation, but never asked me for my impressions of India. They did, however, allude to Oxford, and Max Müller, and they spoke reverently of Queen Victoria. I came away rather puzzled. If this was an average Indian dinner-party, and this the ordinary standard of Indian thought and culture, I did not quite see where I came in. I slept badly that night, pondering.

I was to leave the next evening for the Punjáb. In the morning my friend brought me a fine Arab horse and we rode out to a race-course, and in the afternoon he again drove me round the town. We passed a sports club, where the English were playing lawn tennis. I suggested that we should go in, but he said: "You can go in. I cannot." "Why not?" I asked. "Because I am an Indian." We drove on, and when we reached his house, we talked. He said at the end: "You seem to know very little about India. In two years' time you will know why we cannot go into your clubs, and I doubt whether you will even remember my name. You will certainly not dine with me and talk to my friends as we talked yesterday." I protested that nothing would change me, and he quoted some Persian poet. Four years passed before I again visited Bombay, and I at once called on my friend, and all went happily and he seemed as pleasant as ever. I reminded him about his prophecy, but he only said: "Wait." Two years later I was again passing through Bombay and I called, but was stopped at the gate by an armed sentry. I said I was an old friend. "Yes," said the man, "but he cannot see his friends. He is mad."

I found the journey to Lahore via Allahabad long and very cold. I wish I had talked to some Englishmen and had asked advice. I should then have provided myself with bedding and blankets, for the nights in Northern India are bitterly cold. The winter nights and dawn in the Punjáb were colder and more piercing than in England or even in Kashmir. The winter days were divine and exhilarating. At Allahabad I spent the day with Mr. Douglas Straight. He was then a Judge of the High Court. In a few minutes he brought England back to me.

As I drew near Lahore I asked the guard of the train where I should stay. He advised me to go to the Victoria Hotel. It was on a hill, near the station. The name and the situation appealed to me, and I arrived there at dark. After a shivering night, I came down to breakfast and found about five guests eating a bony fish, which is caught in the river Ravi. They were all dark of visage, all Eurasians, as the descendants of European fathers and Indian mothers were called in my time. They were all in the railway service. One of them kindly addressed me: "Are you come here to get work on the railway?" I replied, quite truthfully, that I did not exactly know what work I should get. "Well," he said, "you'll find it difficult to get any work. It's India for the Indians these days." His companions bore him out and told me of the evil times on which we had fallen, and I felt greatly depressed. The hotel was dirty and slovenly, the table-cloth was stained and smeared, and the men spoke strange English in strange accents. Life was expensive, life was hard, and malaria took the stuffing out of a man. We sat for quite an hour, and I think they saw how depressed I was. But happily there walked into the room a glorious figure in scarlet and gold, and he handed me a letter. It was from Lepel Griffin, the secretary of the Punjáb Government, asking me to come at once to his house with my baggage. No more depression, but weeks of charming and delightful hospitality in the house of the best known Civilian of his time, able, brilliant, and scornful.

I used to ride in the morning with him, and at noon I would go round leaving cards on the English officials in Lahore and on the military officials at Mian-Mir. The *Khálif*, as the tailor was called, sat sewing on the veranda, and would take in the cards. But there was a merciful system of "not at home" boxes into which cards could be dropped. However, I soon made the acquaintance of the whole Civil station, for we used to meet at tennis in the Lawrence Gardens, and dance every evening before dinner in the fine Montgomery Hall. People were always kind to the new recruit, and most hospitable. But the older ones told me that I had come twenty years too late. The golden age of Anglo-Indians was before the Mutiny. Since that awful storm all had changed for the worse. And the wiser old folk spoke with emphasis on the fact that the good relations between the Indians and us could never be restored.

I learned much from Lepel Griffin, but he never mentioned the subject of work until just before Christmas, when he asked me whether I had any idea of making a start. I told him that I was most anxious to begin. So he posted me to the District Staff of Lahore, and I went off to live in the Punjáb Club. My room was next to the room of one of the sweetest characters I have ever known, John Lockwood Kipling. He would call me "young Lawrence," and poured his kindly wisdom into my callow mind. He helped me in many ways, and later when I became an Under-Secretary of the Punjáb Government, I was able to help him. When I think of the lines "His little, nameless, unremembered acts of kindness and of love," I think of wise and gentle John Lockwood Kipling, "the Mr. Kipling." [1]

He helped me in the *Pogley Nautch* (fancy-dress ball), of which I was secretary. It was a subscription ball, and a wise and motherly lady warned me not to give the ball till I had collected all the subscriptions. Another, a wise man too, said: "You are sure to be landed whatever you do, but don't give champagne between the suppers, and don't give out champagne until they give you the empty bottles." However, John Lockwood Kipling cheered me up; he worked hard at the decorations and the lighting, and the ball was a huge success. Of course I had my troubles, but my chief trouble was a man who was tutor of a great Indian Chief. He was splendidly dressed as King Charles II;

[1] When his famous son came to London, a friend of mine, a journalist, hurried to call on him, and as he entered the room in which Rudyard Kipling was writing, said: "Are you the Mr. Kipling?" "No," was the answer, "the Mr. Kipling, my father, is upstairs."

he looked and acted the part. He burst into tears between the suppers when he was told that there was no champagne, and sent off a servant to summon me to the presence. He was elevated by drink, and haughty by costume, and he told me what he thought of me and my service. I offered him claret cup or tea. At the very name of tea he bellowed aloud, when luckily John Lockwood Kipling came into the supper-room and pacified him. In the early hours, in the cold dank dawn, I found the dissolute monarch, his plumes nodding over his face. He had made up at the second supper with a vengeance, but he recognised in me an enemy who would be a friend. So with the help of some of the servants we lifted him into the bathing-machine conveyance which we called a *tikka-gari*. But he jumped out by the opposite door and ran back shouting for "*Simpkin sharâb*" (Champagne). Honestly there was none, for the *ábdár* (the water-bearer) and his lieutenants had finished it. Eventually we got "Charles II" to his hotel and made him over to his servants. I never saw him again, but as a tutor he proved a failure.

I was very fortunate in securing an excellent servant, Imam Khan. He was my valet and table attendant, and he was also an excellent cook. He was of a Delhi family and spoke good Hindustáni. Later on Mahomedans told me that he was an intensely religious man, but he never obtruded his religion on me. In my ignorance, when he came to my room in the club, I offered him a chair. He gently said this would be unbefitting. When he had been with me some weeks, I suggested that he should wear a pink or blue turban in the place of the very clean white head-dress he always wore. This would also be unbefitting. I asked why, and he told me that it was only the lewd fellows of the bazaar who wore pink. How ignorant I was in those days! But it was blissful and happy ignorance.

I bought for a small sum, fifty rupees, an excellent pony, and I took over for 250 rupees a buggy that had seen good days, and an old horse not destined to see many days more. But the buggy was useful for going out to dinners, and I was out almost every night. It was impossible to walk, as the roads were deep in dust, and even the "cold road," as the Mall was called, was only sprinkled with water in the evening. Lahore is different now, and is well laid out with good roads, but in those days the dust, the whitened, ugly tamarisk trees, and the squat ugly bungalows below the level of the road, made the civil station as gloomy as its inhabitants were gay. As a "griffin"[1] I made the usual mistakes. One night I was dining with one of the Judges of the Chief Court, most venerable and handsome. He showed me a portrait and asked me if it reminded me of anyone. I said it was like himself. "Oh, yes, of course," he said, "but does it remind you of anyone else?" "No," I said. I was driving a friend home to the club, and he asked me whether our host had questioned me about the portrait, and when he heard my answer, he laughed and said: "Well your chances in the judicial line are gone. The old Judge expected you to say that the picture reminded you of Our Lord."

As a matter of fact, though I was keenly interested in judicial matters in England and attended assizes whenever I could, and was always thrilled by the drama of the Law Courts, I at once took a dislike to judicial work in India. As a young assistant without full powers I was only entrusted with trifling cases of assault and very petty civil suits, but the lying and exaggeration sickened me, and I was thankful when my Chief, the Deputy Commissioner of Lahore, encouraged me to look after the old Mogul gardens, the Municipality and the District Board. I was also curator of the Zoological Gardens. Moti, the tigress, caused me anxiety, and at night I could hear her roars from my room in the club. Once Moti had walked out of her cage into the gardens. Her keeper, an old, attenuated Indian, hurried after her, cast his turban at her feet and made an obeisance. Moti purred her approval, and the old man put his turban round her neck and led her gently back to her cage.

As far as I remember there was no meeting of the District Board in my time, but I had real work on the Municipal Committee. A crisis had arisen and the hot

[1] An ignorant new-comer. The origin of the word is unknown. Prof. Skeat says that "griffin" was an early word for Welshman, and the suggestion is made in "Hobson Jobson" that the word was used abroad to designate a raw Welshman.

weather was approaching. The market gardeners who lived around Lahore, removed the night soil from the city evening and morning, and put it on their land. They were thriving, well-to-do men, and as the Municipal Committee wanted money, it was decided to charge the market gardeners so much a cart. On this they struck, and when I took up the proud position of secretary, the narrow blind alleys of the City of Dreadful Night were deep in horrid ordure.

The chief of the scavengers was one Nur Din. He called himself a Pathán, and could, on occasions, assume a truculent demeanour. He wore fine clothes, with gold braid and little gold chains. His head-dress was a magnificent *lungi* from Peshawar, stiff with gold thread and worn in the Pathán fashion. He rode an active white mare with a pink nose and points painted pink. He used a thorn bit, and was a cruel, fine horseman—I rather think that he must have been a trainer of processional horses. In my ignorance of Indian character and of Indian physiognomy I thought Nur Din a fine fellow, which he quickly saw. He was always punctual when I rode out in the early mornings; always ready with an answer, whether right or wrong, and had a wonderful way of getting me through crowds in the city. I once or twice thought I saw smiles or gestures from the women in the open windows, and indeed Nur Din on his Jezebel of a mare made a meretricious appeal to the women of the bazaar. He showed great zeal when the strike came, and backed me manfully when I took a shovel and insisted on some of the Indians of my Committee doing likewise. Of course, Nur Din ought to have warned me that my conduct in encouraging high-caste Hindus to act as scavengers would be, in Imam Khan's words, "unbefitting." However, it was a grand gesture, and by some miracle we got abreast of arrears, and for a time we beat the market gardeners: and on looking back I think the Hindus were good fellows for not reporting my sullying action. I imagine that they knew that I was ignorant, but at the same time recognised that the time had come to sweep, or to die malodorous deaths.

The weather grew hotter. The mimosa blooms made the air heavy, the birds of harsh notes became insistent, and the sky was as brass. One night a letter came from Lepel Griffin, who had been up to Simla. He was going to Kabul as our envoy, and had asked the Government of India to let me go as his personal assistant, but they refused, as I did not speak Persian. So, wrote the kind Lepel Griffin, "as the next best thing I am sending you to the Frontier." So off I went to Peshawar. I was sorry to leave the kind people at Lahore; but as a place it had no attractions, and I was always glad to escape to the beautiful gardens of Shalimár, or to Sháhdara, across the Ravi river.

The railway to the Frontier only ran as far as Jhelum; the rest of the journey was by road, a road crowded and blocked by all the camels and bullock carts of India. It was war time. Stores were creeping up to Kabul and to the Kurram, and the whole country was out of joint.

I was fascinated by Peshawar, by the peach blossoms and by the picturesque city, in which I spent much of my time. I was not of real use to anyone, but did odd jobs and set to work to learn Pashtu, the language of the Patháns. I did not like my "*Munshi;*" but he did his best. For a short space I was in nominal charge of the Militia Forts, and used to ride out to the Frontier to see whether the men on the pay-roll were actually in the Forts. My custom was to drive about five miles out of Peshawar, and then get on my horse and ride hard to reach the Fort before nightfall. When night approached there was danger, especially when passing a white stone, as the patient sniper would lie out for hours, covering the white stone with his matchlock, and when a foreign substance came on the target, he would fire. One afternoon, as I drove across a bridge near Peshawar, a man rushed at me with a petition in his hand, but as the pony was going hard and I was late, I did not pull up, and the man was swept aside. I reached the Fort, slept the night there, and returned to Peshawar in the afternoon. I was having a bath when I was summoned urgently to attend a trial of a Ghází[1] under the Frontier Outrages Act. I rode over to the bungalow of the Sessions Judge, a man of great learning but unaccustomed to Frontier methods

[1] A Moslem fanatic who believes that he will win Paradise by the slaughter of unbelievers.

and ignorant of the Pashtu language. Other Civil officers were present. The Judge told us that about ten minutes after I had passed the bridge, a stout Commissariat Conductor[1] was leisurely driving over the bridge in a low two-wheeled cart, when a man jumped into the conveyance and stabbed the Conductor in seven places. The man declared that he was a Gházi, bound for paradise. I am sure that the Sessions Judge disliked the Frontier Outrages Act, and wished to deal with the offender in the ordinary way of the Criminal Code. He reminded me of the attitude of Mr. Dennis, the hangman in "Barnaby Rudge." The accused was brought in and I recognised him as the man who had tried to stop me, and I think he recognised me. The Sessions Judge, after reciting the statement taken in the Hospital from the wounded man, said to the accused through an interpreter: "You stabbed this man, but you do not wish to claim that you are a Gházi?" I never saw a man more furious and more contemptuous. "Tell him," he said to the Civilian, who was interpreter, "Tell him to unbind me and give me a knife and come out with me on to the road, and I'll soon show him whether I am a Gházi or not!" That ended the matter, and the man was hanged that evening with a pig-skin round his shoulders.[2]

It was very hot in Peshawar, and I used to ride in the sun to a large reservoir which had been made for the water supply of the cantonment. Unfortunately, though the water was ample and pure, there were no pipes, so we all drank from the *diggis*, as we called the little rivulets which ran to every house and garden. It was most refreshing to swim in the reservoir, but I noticed that I was the only one in the cantonments who seemed to have discovered this glorious bath. The others were right, for after about five days' bathing I felt very queer. My servant shampooed me, but it was fever, with ague.

After a short stay in Peshawar, I was sent to act as Political Officer to a Brigade at Thal, at the bottom of the

[1] A British non-commissioned officer employed in the Supply Department of the army; often a man of some affluence.

[2] This was the practice in those days. Hanging in itself was sufficient to make paradise very uncertain, but the pig-skin closed the door of hope.

Kurram valley. One hot day I rode from Peshawar through the Kohat pass to Kohat. How the heat came off the rocks and stones, and how delicious it was at breakfast in the cool house of the Magistrate of Kohat to drink gin sling through a straw! With the Magistrate, who was a Military Civilian, there lived another military officer who was District Superintendent of Police. They were both very able and experienced, but the Policeman was a man with a past. He had been in a local regiment in Rajputána. These local regiments are recruited from criminal tribes, and there are three English officers, Colonel, Second-in-Command, and Adjutant. It was a sleepy, happy existence, far from the madding crowd of Inspectors and innovators, and there was the best of big-game shooting. As a rule promotion went in the Regiment, and if the Colonel died of old age or cholera, the Second-in-Command would succeed. Now in this particular Regiment, both Colonel and Second-in-Command were fond of their cups, and one night at mess, the Policeman, who was then Adjutant, induced the Second-in-Command to place the Colonel under arrest for unseemly conduct. When the poor Colonel had left the mess for his bungalow, the Adjutant placed the Second-in-Command under arrest for being in a state of intoxication, and forthwith reported the deplorable incident to Headquarters, adding that he had taken over the command of the Regiment, that all was well, and that he awaited orders. Orders came, frustrating his young ambitions. The two senior officers were removed, but the Adjutant was sent to a penal station, where he decided that he would do better in the Police than in the Army. He was certainly a most efficient Police Officer and most charming to me. But then I was not his Colonel nor Second-in-Command.

I arrived next day at Thal, leaving Kohat long before dawn. I found Najaf Shah, a Police Officer, waiting for me in a state of frenzy. There had been a lethal affray over the river, and I was wanted. I had no horse, and he obligingly offered me his, a big Waler, up to great weight and a magnificent goer. He was a caster from the Artillery, but I never rode a better horse. He went down the hillside, over water courses and terraced rice fields with unerring skill.

Up the mountain on the other side of the river our camels had been sent out to graze, when marauding Waziris pounced on them. When I reached the place, I saw two dead men, just killed: one had his dress burnt, as though he had been shot at very close quarters. It was the first time I had seen death caused by violence and it excited me. I stupidly imagined that the two dead men were our men, and I ordered my companion, a fine Pathán, Said Khan, to seize a man who was gesticulating and dancing in front of me, saying he was the slayer—to seize him and hang him. A silence fell on the crowd, and I got off my horse. Then Said Khan drew me aside and, half whispering, said: "Sahib, excuse my seeming impertinence, but we ought not to hang this man, but rather reward him, for he is my nephew and in the Border Police." So we all laughed; but it might have been no laughing matter for me if I had been alone, or with someone an enemy of Said Khan and his family. I suppose killing is infectious, for when I saw the two dead men I had a kind of impulse to blood my hitherto innocent revolver. In honour of the victory over the marauders, I gave a feast of "fat things"—two sheep, rice and *gur* (molasses)—and joined them at the end of the meal. They disgusted me by loud and continued belches. I did not know that this was manners, and later I found that some of the ruling Princes were great sticklers for this form of politeness, which was to evince appreciation of the viands. Said Khan was a giant in stature, a fine horseman, straight and good. He was second son of an important Khan.[1] His elder brother was clever, and was really the man from whom I was supposed to obtain intelligence and spies. But I always stuck to Said Khan, and he never failed me. He was very silent, but he was a tremendous fellow with his sword, and everyone respected him and called him "the trustworthy one." They called his brother *Chalák*, which may be translated "slim."

> "If only the good were the clever,
> If only the clever were good."

[1] Head of a tribe.

If only Said Khan had had his brother's brains he would have gone far. But he was not ambitious, never asked for anything, rather shunned the General and the high officials, and would sit quietly by me when I was working, or ride silently by my side when we were looking up our news agents. I felt secure with Said Khan.

The Brigade was a strong one. I lived at the General's mess outside the camp in a kind of mud fort looking over the Kurram river. Down below was the village of Thal. But I spent most of my time with what I still think is the finest regiment in India, the 18th Bengal Cavalry. Splendid men, fine officers and excellent horses. The Colonel had gone on leave, and his temporary successor was eccentric. I received orders to proceed with the regiment one night to surround an enemy village of some size before dawn, and to bring back the men and cattle. I borrowed the police horse and off we set by faint moonlight. We forded the river without loss of horse-shoes, marched in silence and reached our place well before dawn. Our foe was taken by surprise and made no fight; we gathered the men and the cattle, and I imagined we would breakfast and march back to Thal. But alas! the eccentric Commandant said that this was an opportunity for exploring a new country, and he would march the regiment back over the slopes of the mountains and strike the Kurram river some fifteen miles above Thal. Said Khan at once told me that there was no road and no water, and that if the Waziris heard that we were on the mountains, they could pick us off at their leisure. I spoke to the officer next in rank to the Commandant, and he agreed that it would be madness to attempt the unknown way. I told the Commandant that my instructions were to guide the regiment to this village, and I assumed that I was to take them back by the same route. He asked me to show him my instructions, but I had left them at Thal. "Well," he said, "you can go back with my men escorting the cattle and prisoners. I command this regiment and I go back by the new route." There was no answer to this.

So we started, and it soon grew hot as a furnace. The horses slid on the shaly slope, and there was no water.

We came to one pool full of horrid green, liquid mud, and some of the most maddened of the cavalrymen just tried it. An elderly trooper said: "God made the water." But one of the subalterns said: "No, camels made that water." As we rode on I would canter ahead to get rid of the eccentric Commandant, who told me that if I was a real Christian, I should not feel thirst. But he would catch me up, and among other things he said was, that if I once had killed a man I should not care for any other form of big-game shooting. Of all the days of my life I look back to that day as the most horrible and loathsome. How we got through I cannot tell, but we reached Thal the next day. The regiment was rewarded by being turned from cavalry into lancers, and is now known as the Tiwána Horse.

There was an Indian clerk in the regiment who longed for civil work, and he wrote to me. He opened with the words, "Spanking Sir." I showed the letter to the Adjutant and asked him to introduce me to the clerk. I had a talk and asked him whether he had any English book. He produced with great pride a small book, "Letters from a Gentleman in Town to a Young Friend in the Country," and skimming through it I came to a passage where the writer said: "thanks to industry and assiduity I am now in a position to drive a pair of spanking steeds." We used to laugh at their English, but it was perhaps better than our Hindustáni. I saw a letter from an Indian asking for assistance. He mentioned as one of his reasons for desiring an appointment that his mother was "tight." He meant to say that she was in reduced circumstances. He was translating from the Indian word *tang*, which means "tight" in the sense of fastening. Once a man described a rival as a "flickering fellow." I understood his meaning. But such mistakes are trifling compared with some of the translations used by us. Thus, a British soldier wanting to purchase a sheep's head in the Bazaar asked: "Kitna baje for that there sheep's topi?"—literally; "What o'clock is it for that sheep's hat?" The dealer understood at once. Lord Dufferin was talking to an Indian and said that he liked the Indian music and the minor key. The young civilian who was translating, translated minor key into *chota chábhi*, a small key of a box.

I learned much about the Army—enough to make me a devoted admirer of that grand service. I became acquainted with questions of fodder, food supplies and camel transport. This last branch of knowledge was painful. The food went up the Kurram Valley mostly on camels. If the camel thought his load more than just, he would sit down and die, and a dead camel poisons the air. The Officer in charge of a kind of Militia known as the "Catch 'em alive Oh's," fell sick, and I was asked to do his work for him. I gladly agreed, as I liked riding up the Kurram Valley and calling in at the roadside Forts. But I little knew that the chief duty was the cremation of dead camels. The smell was sickening, and there was no fuel. The road Militia did their best, and we scorched the camels and trusted to the eagles and vultures. High officers coming down from the cool heights to our heated hole of a place would chide me for neglect, but they were going on leave, and on the whole rather disposed to spare my youth.

But Said Khan discovered something which was important. He asked me to go with him on foot before dawn, and he took me down a rough path to the river and then upstream for about a mile. He then put me behind a big rock, and said: "Wait till the Camel Convoy goes up the road, and watch." The Convoy came, escorted by soldiers, when suddenly two laden camels left the string and were led down the path which runs along the river to the village of Thal. "This happens every day," said Said Khan. "Twice before, I have seen it, and you should see it twice." But once was sufficient for me, and giving the camels a good start, we followed. As we entered the little bazaar, the two camels were leaving it at the other end, unloaded, and we saw in the shop of the leading trader four sacks full of grain, with the Government mark on the sacks. "How did you get these?" I asked. "They are mine," said a *Márwári*.[1] "Government marks," said I. "Oh, yes," he replied, "all

[1] The traders and moneylenders of India known as Banyas or Sowkars originally came from Márwár in Rajputána and are called Márwáris. Márwár means "the land of death," and sometimes the moneylender was deadly.

my sacks are marked thus. Please look at all the sacks." "Permit me," said Said Khan, "to take him down the river for a talk," and he put his great paw on the trader's wrist. "Certainly," I said. "Take him away; but no talking will get over the fact that I saw the camels leave the Convoy and followed them here." "I'll talk here," said the prudent trader, "and will tell your Honour of the bad thing the camel people are doing. They are rich and I am poor. It is they who should talk to the noble Khan Sahib by the river." And he turned Queen's evidence.

I told the General of the fraud at breakfast, and he desired me to go into the case. "There is one man in the Camp in whom I have profound confidence. He was in my own Regiment, quite first class, Conductor——. He will assist you." Now Conductor—— had a big tent on the side of the road which ran through the Camp, and the tent was full of good things to eat and to drink. I used to say "good morning" to him as I rode through the Camp, and he was always smart and pleasant. Indeed, one hot afternoon he had suggested that I might be thirsty, but I had declined his invitation.

After breakfast I bethought me of the Eurasian Treasury Officer, known as "Yellow-belly." He was a delightful character, full of imagination, poetry, kindliness, and cowardice. I think he knew he was a coward, for whenever I talked to him, he always dragged in a story of his attacking and killing a tiger on foot in the mountains of Kulu. Friends in Camp assured me that there were no tigers in Kulu, but I had not the heart to tell this to the Treasury Officer. Every night he would sleep on the roof of his hut, with his sentries around him, and men assured me that whenever a raid on the Camp took place, there would be hot firing from Yellow-belly's fortalice. He loved Kulu, and told me of its cool streams, its luscious fruits and its lovely women; and if he had not been a Treasury Official I think he might have been a poet.

But I wanted to know about Conductor——. Did he remit money to India through the Treasury Office? "*Wah, wah tauba*" (shame), said Yellow-belly, unconsciously relapsing into the mother tongue. "But," he added, "for every hundred he remits through me, he remits thousands by *hundi*,[1] through the Bazaar." Ahead of me loomed a Departmental examination. I was not afraid of any subject but one, and that was Treasury work. I saw a chance of gaining some practical experience. "Do you understand *hundis?*" I asked. He smiled. "Then come down to the Bazaar with me and help me to read *hundis*." Most reluctantly he came, and it was clear from the trader's books that Conductor—— had remitted thousands of rupees to India.

I felt sad to tell the General, and so held the news over till the next day. When I told him, he at once sent a message to the officer in charge, to suspend Conductor——. But luckily for the Conductor he had taken French leave the day before, and gone off by the mail cart to India. Just then came the bad news of the reverse at Maiwand, and as everyone in the Kurram Force expected to be off to Kandahar, there was no time for looking into Commissariat frauds.

Towards autumn I was ordered to the Khyber Pass, where the Political Officer had fallen sick. We burned the villages of a troublesome tribe, and I noticed that the villagers themselves joined in the work with great goodwill. They had somehow or other removed their grain and did not care much about mere mud huts. I used in the evenings to sit above a crater near Lundi Kotal, where dead camels were bestowed, and watch thousands of golden eagles circling in the golden sunset. I realised then that dead camels have their use.

I ought to add that the Commissariat Conductor who was stabbed on the bridge, recovered from his wounds. But the flamboyant Nur Din of the Conservancy Department, Lahore, was hanged for murdering one of those who smiled from the open windows. I never met the Eurasian Treasury Officer again, but he survived the hardships of the war and went on counting and weighing the bags of rupees.

I always felt a sympathy for the Eurasians. They were a kindly and gentle people, some very fair in feature and some very efficient. In most of the offices of Government

[1] A *hundi* is a bill of exchange, a banker's draft, and one can remit money safely to any part of India by means of the Marwári's *hundis*.

there were Eurasians, but their chief field of employment was on the railways. They had a curious accent known as "chee chee," acquired perhaps in the convents and schools, but, however acquired, difficult to throw off. They use English words in a peculiar manner. A Eurasian girl says she has "broken" her dress, and "will" she "break" you some flowers? They are fond of ejaculations such as "oh my" and "my man," and seem to prefer long words. They will talk of the "temperature" of a horse, when "temper" would have been more appropriate. A Eurasian once described his pretty cousin, to whom he was engaged, as a "most opalescent young miss," and I once heard a mother say of her two daughters: "She is a dull, and she is a naughty." They cling to European fashions and standards, and their future is difficult and indeed perilous, for the growing competition of the Indian makes the life of the Eurasian a hard problem. Perhaps emigration from India might solve some of their difficulties, for the Eurasian often makes good when he has left India. Very little has been done for them as a community, and any concessions to the Eurasians would be fiercely resented by the Indians, who dislike the *karáni log*[1] as much as the latter dislike the Indians. "Ali Baba," whose shrewd observations on India are as true to-day as they were when Aberigh Mackay was writing forty-six years ago, says of the unhappy Eurasian: "The native papers say 'deport him'; the white prints say 'make him a soldier'; and the Eurasian himself says 'make me a Commissioner, or give me a pension.'" They are no longer called "Eurasians," but "Anglo-Indians;" but I fear that the change of name will not improve the hard lot of this luckless and unprotected people.

[1] The half-caste people. All Europeans who are not "Sahibs" are known as *Gora Log*, the "Fair-skinned" people.

CHAPTER III

"This world, where much is to be done, and little to be known."

—JOHNSON

Fever—Nathia Gali—Adventure at Murree—Bonfire in Forest—Gain further knowledge of Hindustáni—Denzil Ibbetson and his census of the Punjáb —Census work in Peshawar—Ibbetson's Methods and Personality—Life in Hazára—The "Snake"—Jail Work—Executions—Appointment to District of Merwára (Rajputána)—Colonel Dixon—Officials—Methods of my Predecessor—The German Police Officer—Officials of Old School—Life in Beawar—Begin to understand Indians—Episodes of Indian Life—Case of Illusion—India is Illusion—Frequent change of High Officials—Ajmere—Dacoits—Pea-chicks—Pranks of Colonel and German Police Officer—Raising body of Mers to hunt Dacoits—Thagi—Datura Poisoning—Bráhman Murderer—Chits—Act as District Officer, Ajmere—the Snake Charmer—Cholera Epidemic—Street Dogs in Ajmere—the Jains—To Pushkar Lake with Edward Buck—His character—Methods of Indian Servants—Camp of the Viceroy comes to Ajmere.

FOR some time I had had constant fever. The Commissioner of Peshawar most kindly sent me up for ten days to his delightful chalet, at Nathiâ Gali in the Himalayas, beyond Murree. I travelled from Rawal Pindi to Murree in an *ekka*, "in shape like a meat safe placed upon the axle trees of two wheels with hanging curtains at the sides." It was like heaven to feel the cool air and to smell the resin of the pines. As I drew near Murree the fever and the shivers came on. There was no room at the hotel, but the manager kindly promised me a bed on the landing. What I wanted was a hot bath, but this he could not give. I was desperate, so entered a bath-room from the veranda and called for hot water. The water carrier brought tepid water, which did me more harm than good. As I sat with teeth chattering, in the wooden barrel used then for baths, in walked the real owner of the room. He was a General, and a fiery one. He naturally cursed me, for I might have been a loafer or a deserter; but, when he saw my condition, he was most compassionate, and insisted on my using his bed until mine was ready.

I went off the next morning on a hired pony, with a boy guide. I must have been demented, for I drank at breakfast, not tea, but gin and quinine. The path came to a small opening in the forest, a circle of red soil blackened by a generation of bonfires, and here was the best bonfire I had ever seen, just pine chips, which the woodcutter had kept as a titbit. He sat there on his heels, gazing at the white thread of smoke which trailed up through the tall pines to the blue sky and almost tickled the grey beard of the venerable monkey on a high branch, seemingly come to see what they were doing with his timber—man and monkey both silent, both enjoying the exquisite air and sunshine, inhaling a perfume which Flores of Jermyn Street after two hundred years has never captured. It was so good that I would have lingered till the fire was low, but the boy with the laden mule fretted at delay. So I gave the woodman some coins—a few pence in our money—but to him a rich and unexpected windfall, and we passed on. The golden mists of autumn were lifting, and we looked through the tall trees to the radiant snows sparkling and smiling through the veil of the sapphire dome.

My ten days at Nathia Gali were worth a cycle of Cathay. I tried to read for my Departmental examination. Soon after I went to Lahore and scraped through. They must have treated me with lenience, as my roving existence did not tend to technical knowledge.

As I look back, I cannot imagine a worse training than mine. No one taught me my work. In war time civil codes are forgotten, and every Civil officer found it difficult to do his own work and had no time to instruct recruits. So I had learned nothing of the work of a Civilian. One thing I had acquired, a good knowledge of Hindustáni. I had been thrown on my own resources, had no English-speaking clerks, and so was forced to learn the Lingua Franca of India. However, my time was coming, and the great instructor was on his way. Denzil Ibbetson was appointed to be Census Commissioner of the Punjáb, and I was to conduct the census of the District and City of Peshawar. It may not sound exciting work, but to me it was full of interest. I visited all the villages, the frontier forts, and, occasionally, though it was against rules, saw some places of note beyond the Frontier. At first the people were suspicious at the numbering of houses—it meant, perhaps, some new form of taxation, or conscription for the Army, or collection of brides for the soldiers. But these suspicions were soon allayed, and I found that the inquiry into the occupations of the people was full of surprises, and was a great education to me. Indeed, in the city there were occupations, openly admitted to me as Census Officer, which would have startled the great Burton himself. I made the acquaintance of all the leading men of the district, frank, jolly men of great authority, most hospitable, as all Pathans are, good friends, but deadly and unsleeping foes. But the great virtue of this work was that Denzil Ibbetson came up to inspect, and was pleased with my efforts. He was the greatest of the Indian Civilians of my day. Even at that early period of his service, men recognised him as unique. He had spent most of his time doing the "Settlement" of the Kurnal District: and I believe that the Government fretted at the time he took. But it was his way. He was an artist and was not satisfied with anything short of perfection. He made up his mind when there was urgency, and he told me that sometimes in India it was better to make a decision, even a wrong one, than to delay in making a decision. I was never tired of listening to him. He was a full man, of enormous industry, and of infinite wit. He saw fun in everything. He was tall and handsome, with a twinkle in his eye. He was a good musician and a good sportsman. His report on the census of the Punjáb stands out as a classic in the large library of Indian official books. It was a book of reference for the officers of the Indian Army. I have been often asked by travellers and others for a book which would explain some question of religion, race, or custom in India. And I always refer them to Ibbetson's report. This, and Aberigh Mackay's "Twenty-one Days in India," will carry one far.

When the work of the census was finished, I was transferred to the Hazára District, a lovely country on the confines of Kashmir. My life in Peshawar had been very pleasant, and I owe much to the kindness and influence of the wife of the Commissioner. I cannot describe her charm, but all of us felt it. She had great grace, was a perfect horsewoman, was sympathetic and laughing. She was so wise, and inspired us to do the best we could, and used to persuade us that we had the best in us. She seemed unconscious of her power, and her charm worked without effort or intention on her part. She never touched official matters, never belonged to a clique, and never listened to gossip, and we, all of us who had the privilege of her friendship, adored her.

Hazára, with its pretty, almost English, headquarters at Abbottabad, would have been a paradise for me, had it not been for "the snake." He was an Indian Extra Assistant-Commissioner, and in the eyes of the Head of the District, who was a Military Civilian,[1] he was perfect. The really important and interesting work was given to "the snake," and the routine jobs were made over to me. Now, I should say here that I was, and am still, devoted to Indians. I learned most of my work from them, and in my twenty-one years' residence in India never came across an Indian whom I absolutely detested. But "the snake" was detestable and detested by every Indian and Englishman in Hazára. I should not have cared, but unhappily the Head of the District used to blame me for trifles, and used to add that "the snake" had noticed with regret my faults and omissions. My real fault was that I lived at the mess of the 5th Gurkhas, a very distinguished regiment of the Punjáb Frontier Force, and the Head of the District was rather shunned by the officers of the Gurkhas, the First Sikhs, and the Mountain Battery, the garrison of Abbottabad.

As the weather grew warmer the Head of the District used to go up to Nathia Gali, but he told me that I must not come up, as the station could not be left without a British Civil Officer. I quite agreed, but a new man had been appointed Commissioner of the Division, and he also came

[1] In the non-regulation provinces in those days a certain number of officers of the Indian Army were appointed to civil work.

up from Peshawar to spend the hot weather at Nathia Gali. I went down the road to meet him. He was a great Greek scholar, a famous racquet player, and one of the most delightful of men. We became friends at once, and he said I must come up to stay with him in the hills, and play lawn-tennis and whist. I told him the difficulty about an Indian Civilian being left in Abbottabad. He smiled and said nothing. Next week I received a letter from him telling me to come up at once. He said: "I agree with the Head of the District, and have ordered him to go down to Abbottabad till further orders." As I rode up the hill, the Head rode down. He did not speak to me, but if my pony had understood the power of a scowl, we should have been over the precipice which skirted the narrow bridle-path!

This made the situation difficult, but what really decided me in wishing to leave this exquisite country was my jail work. I was, thanks to "the snake," in charge of the jail. It was an old-fashioned place, very like the lion house at the Zoo, and every morning I would pass down the cages and ask the prisoners whether all was well. As one entered the door of the jail, the cages on the left hand were for prisoners condemned to death. During my stay there were two condemned couples. It was my duty to see them hanged, and the executions took place on a large plain outside the town. A square was formed some distance from the gallows. Three sides were lined by troops; the fourth side was for relatives and spectators. Before the execution I used to sit up all night with the doctor of the 5th Gurkhas, who was also Civil Surgeon to the station; and he, like myself, hated the business and could not sleep. There was nothing remarkable about the first couple. But the second couple interested me. One was a burly, wild-looking Pathán, and the other was a youth of singular beauty. They had been found guilty of murdering a Hindu money-lender. I asked them if I could do anything for them, and the man replied: "I killed the money-lender and would kill him one thousand times; but the boy is innocent. He is only my friend, and where I went, he went. I swear he is innocent." I impetuously said I would tell this to the authorities, but the Commissioner told me that it was useless, that all the facts had been considered, and that the Chief Court had confirmed the sentence of death. When I told the elder prisoner, he laughed and spat, and said with a sneer that he might have known that I was a broken reed. Next day I offered the pair sweetmeats, which I was told was customary, and the man said nothing, but gave a gulp. He then said: "I do not think that you are faithless, and I will make one more appeal to you. I am hated in my village, and my enemies will ask the Government to sequestrate my land, and my daughter will be landless and lost." I said I thought I could help here, and the Commissioner promised me that the Frontier penalty should not be exacted. I told the elder criminal, and he was most grateful, and so also was the youth.

When the day came I stood by them as the blacksmith knocked off the irons from their legs before they ascended the steps. They were both dignified and composed, and the elder said: "Look Sahib, there she is: remember your promise." And there, well in front of the line of the spectators, was a pretty girl of about fourteen years, who made a graceful obeisance of farewell to her father and of thanks to me.

I do not think that capital punishment has the same terror for Indians as it has for English criminals, and I believe that transportation across the "black water" to the Andaman Islands is far more terrible for the Indians. The man who murdered Lord Mayo in the Andamans had been the orderly of the Commissioner of Peshawar, much respected and liked by all classes. He killed an enemy in accordance with the Patháns rules of blood feud, but unfortunately killed him a few yards on our side of the Frontier. He was condemned to death, but the Commissioner, in spite of his entreaties, had the sentence commuted to transportation. The prisoner warned them that he would be avenged if they sent him over the "black water," and begged for death. He bided his time and then killed a Viceroy.

Soon after the execution I received an offer of an appointment in the Political Department of the Government of India, and I consulted my friends at the mess as to whether I should accept. Unfortunately none of them knew where the District of Merwára was, but they all thought that it was an advantage to be directly under the Government of India, and they knew how difficult it was to get on with the Head of the District. So in the height of the hot weather, I set off for Rajputána. The hottest hot room in a Turkish bath was mild compared with the heat of a railway carriage in those days. There was no ice, and the water in the lavatory basin would have boiled an egg. I received a kind welcome at Ajmere, the headquarters of the Commissioner of the province of Ajmere Merwára, a little oasis of British territory surrounded on all sides by Indian states. The railway ran to Merwára and on through Rajputána. I was in charge of Merwára and also had jurisdiction over about 200 miles of railway, but in order to make this legal I was gazetted as J.P. for the whole of India. Denzil Ibbetson wrote saying that he was sorry I was leaving the Frontier, but that, provided I came back to the Punjáb, he saw no harm in a short absence. He added: "It is better to rule a District than to humbug a Rája." He also said that it was folly to leave a place because one did not like one's Chief. The Chief may die or be transferred.

Merwára was a long, narrow District skirting the Aravali Hills, with Meywár on one side and Marwár on the other, full of beautiful lakes and wooded hills, and with large patches of the most beautiful of all crops, the many-coloured poppy. The people were simple and friendly. They had been regarded as a criminal tribe, but the celebrated Colonel Dixon had won them to industry, and had formed a Regiment known as the Merwára Battalion—fine, picturesque men. There was a shrine to Colonel Dixon close to my house in Beawar, the capital of Merwára, and every day I would see the Mers worship at the shrine. In the shrine, in a glass case, was a richly embroidered silk dress, which had come from Paris some forty or fifty years ago for Bibi Dixon, the Indian wife of Colonel Dixon. Near my house was another house, the Bibi Khána, where she had lived. The town of Beawar had been planned by Colonel Dixon after the splendid model of Jaipur, with very wide streets, and whenever I was not out in the District I would spend much time in the town, talking to the leading citizens. I was the only Englishman in Merwára, save two excellent missionaries, and the manager of a cotton press. I had a fairly intelligent Registrar,[1] who knew no English, and rather disliked the rural simplicity of the place, and a delightful Bengali, who never ceased to sing the praises of beautiful green Bengal and its wealth of fishes. It was my first encounter with a Bengali. He was not very clever, but he was a great gentleman, and being an exile, like myself, he rather adopted me. There was much litigation and I sat long hours in Court. One day I asked my Registrar whether the number of cases was not abnormal. "No," he said, "but your methods are abnormal. Your predecessor did not sit in Court and try cases; he would induce the parties to settle." "Yes," I said. "So do I." "But you do not send them up to the roof," he replied. The Court House adjoined my bungalow, and there was a fine stone staircase which led to the flat roof. According to my clerk, my predecessor would appear in Court at about 8 a.m., lightly dressed in pyjamas, bow to the suitors, and ask them to stand in groups, plaintiff facing defendant. He would then express his hope that when he had had his bath he would find that their disputes had been amicably settled. He would bow and retire. In about an hour he would return dressed, would bow, and ask how business was proceeding. Perhaps half of the cases would have been settled. He would again bow courteously, and say how much he wished that all would be settled when he returned from breakfast. When he next appeared the sun would be well up. More would have settled their disputes, but there was usually an obstinate remnant. To these he would say: "You cannot do justice to yourselves in this murky Court: go into the fresh air and sit on the roof," and he would add in a sharp voice: "No water must be carried on to the roof." In an hour he would usually come back to find all disputes composed, and would congratulate them on their wise decision, for, as he always said, the suitors knew more of the real facts of the case than he could ever know. So litigation rather fell off in his time; but I did not feel that I was old or experienced enough to follow the example of this quaint and, in many ways, most efficient official.

[1] *Sarishtadar:* lit. "Head of the string."

He was a Colonel, and French in name and origin. By chance his Superintendent of Police was a German, and he, too, was extremely efficient, but he ended badly. He could assume any disguise, and he and the Colonel would dress up as Dacoits,[1] and hold up wedding parties. The railway was recent, and Rajputána was full of the old fashion, of leisurely accomplishment and high-spirited jest. No one was in a hurry, and the word "efficiency" was never mentioned. Some of the older officers affected the Rájput manner of wearing their hair, the idea being to look like a tiger. I was much struck by the way some of these older officers consumed chillies.

These old officers had seen the best and the worst of the Indians in the Mutiny. They certainly knew the language and the ways of the Indians. They would speak with a kind of affectation of the *budmásh* [2] people, and Indians would speak with a kindly smile of the *budmásh* Colonel and his pranks. But he was just and was a good friend in adversity, and he was what the Indians especially appreciated, an *Admi Shinás*.[3] In other words, he understood men and could distinguish the real from the sham. The Colonel with the French name went as District Officer to Ajmere, and then retired. He taught me much. He deprecated "*trop de zèle*." Long hours of solitary life in the heat and dust of Rajputána, and the hope of promotion always deferred, had robbed him of all illusions, and he used to sing in rather a feeling manner the song of the "long, long Indian day," with the refrain, "So ends my story of Indian glory." I met others with the same story; but nearly all of them served well and fairly according to their lights, and if what they knew of Indian life had been recorded and digested, we, their successors, might have succeeded better. One good point of this lower form of the old school was their great love of talking with the Indians, and the real interest they took in the affairs of families. But they were men of

[1] According to an Indian, who told me of one of these pranks which he had witnessed, the procedure was simple. The disguised Dacoits would rush on the scene shouting "Dukker, Dukker!" and the Palanquin bearers and the wedding party would bolt.

[2] Evil livelihood [*mauvais sujet*].

[3] One who recognises faces.

leisure, often at a distance from railways and telegraph lines.

The hot weather in Rajputána was milder than it was on the Frontier, and I became comparatively free from fever. I hardly ever saw an English face, and grew used to life among the Indians. I was beginning to think their thoughts and to assimilate their ideas. The citizens of Beawar treated me with great confidence, and I did not interfere with them, and, indeed, all seemed peaceful and happy. One day some of the leading citizens suggested that it would be well if I gave an order that the scavengers and other humble "untouchables" should not be allowed to walk through the main streets, and should, under pain of penalty, shout whenever thay had to cross one of the main streets. I thought this most reasonable; but when I reached home I met my Bengali clerk, who was walking in my lovely old garden and singing in high nasal notes the beauties of Bengal. I told him, and he said: "Yes, very good indeed, but not in British territory." The City Fathers were disappointed, but our relations continued friendly. Indeed, a deputation came to see me, and after compliments, said that there was only one thing to be desired in me, and that was that I should be married, and not live alone. I told my French friend this, as an instance of the fatherly interest Beawar took in me. But he laughed and said: "They are not interested in you, but in their own women, and they fear that you may run after them." This was quite a new light to me.

Now, the life I led for some months, quite away from my own folk, grew on me. I used to listen to the horrid din of the temples, watch the little festivals and the marriage processions, hear the women, as I entered a village, sing a chorus. They carried on their heads brass jars full of water, into which I dropped a rupee. One evening I came on some men singing, and asked them to repeat the song. They refused, but after some pressure they said they would sing it in my camp—it was too improper a song to sing near the village. Then I heard of mysterious societies, who used to picnic at night in the dells of the Aravalis, of "revels and rites unholy," and of dreadful orgies[1] held in honour of the god-

[1] *Kantli Pant.*

dess Káli. I was told in a fit of confidence that in a village just out of my District a low-caste man had been killed in an affray: in reality there had been no affray, but the man had been sacrificed to Káli by the landlord of the village, who had vowed to make such a sacrifice, if he were successful in establishing a new hamlet on some waste ground. Then I heard of *Suttees*, and was shown little monuments of a very touching form of Suttee, known as *Ma-Sati*, when the mother would burn herself on the pyre of her only son. As I marched further into the District, further away from the Court and the police, the people would become more confidential, and were on the brink of telling me secrets.

One day I experienced a curious illusion. It was in the break of the rains, and I went out in the evening by myself to shoot. The ground was familiar to me, but it was all changed. There was a large lake where I had formerly walked, and on the lake was a punt with a paddle. I got in and paddled by the high bank of the lake to a little green promontory. On it, by the edge of the lake, sat a most lovely girl. I asked her what the name of the lake was, and where her village was. But she laughed and shook her head and said nothing. I paddled on, landed on the opposite bank and walked home. I was quite well, and had no fever. I could remember every detail of the place, the dress and the face of the girl, and a few days later I went back to the lake. But there was no lake and no sign of a punt, and no one had ever seen a lake or a punt in the neighbourhood. Hallucination? I do not think so. I have seen so much in India of what we in England would call the supernatural, that I have an open mind, and I think that if we lived with the Hindus, apart from the influence of our own people, we should soon find that in that land of enchantment there is indeed more than is dreamt of in our philosophy.

Our life in India, our very work more or less, rests on illusion. I had the illusion, wherever I was, that I was infallible and invulnerable in my dealings with Indians. How else could I have dealt with angry mobs, with cholera-stricken masses, and with processions of religious fanatics? It was not conceit, Heaven knows: it was not the prestige of the British Ráj, but it was the illusion which is in the very air of India. They expressed something of the idea when they called us the "Heaven-born," and the idea is really make-believe—mutual make-believe. They, the millions, made us believe that we had a divine mission. We made them believe that they were right. Unconsciously, perhaps, I may have had at the back of my mind that there was a British Battalion and a battery of Artillery at the Cantonment near Ajmere; but I never thought of this, and I do not think that many of the primitive and simple Mers had ever heard of or seen English soldiers. But they saw the head of the Queen-Empress on the rupee, and worshipped it. They had a vague conception of the Ráj, which they looked on as a power, omnipotent, all-pervading, benevolent for the most part, but capricious, a deity of many shapes and many moods; and the trouble was, that when they had become almost accustomed to a certain shape, the agent of the deity would be transferred, and wearily and anxiously they would start again to learn the nature of the new shape and the new mood. My conclusion was that the village is really happy when it is left to itself and its illusions. In Merwára, Colonel Dixon was the hallowed name and legend, and it was a pity that his long and beloved rule should have been followed by will-o'-the-wisps, always coming and going. Later I found that no Indian trusts an Englishman until he has known him for at least two years.

I received a letter from the Commissioner of Ajmere, inviting me to stay at his beautiful marble palace on the Anasagar Lake, and saying that it was bad for a man to be too long away from civilisation. So I left my little world of illusion for a time, but was happily soon on my way back, as Dacoity had suddenly become the fashion. Wedding parties moved through the passes of the Aravalis from the Marwár to the Meywár state, and the brigands attacked the processions and stripped the bride and bridegroom of their jewels. The Police Superintendent of Ajmere joined me, and for two months we made war on the brigands and lived on the pea-fowl and jungle-cocks we shot. Our larder was often low. Beef was impossible in this Hindu country, and we were too far from civilisation to hope for mutton.

But luckily the hills were full of peacocks, the hill people had no scruples, and we lived on pea-chicks for many days, eked out by bread and the vegetables which reluctant mounted police brought us daily from my garden—letters, newspapers, bread and green stuff, all in one bag and all stained by the juice of the tomato. But we were hungry, and our clever cook gave us dainty dishes and on gala nights composed quaint menu cards with the help of one of our clerks. I never saw his books of reference, but there were smiles as we read "good cheap soup." It was certainly cheap, as was all the work of this excellent and versatile artist. He could turn himself into a bellows and blow the charcoal to red heat in rain and wind. He could hold two pieces of toast between his toes, with his heel right in the fire. He could move off at midnight noiselessly, so as not to disturb the sahibs with the rattle of his pots and pans, and next morning twelve miles away we would find him hard at work making us a "good cheap" breakfast.

Far away in civilised Ajmere, our Chief, the Commissioner, was holding revels, and asked us to send him pea-chicks for his ball supper. It was easy to shoot the pea-chicks, but difficult to transport them to the railway, for the country between us and the line was occupied by villagers, to whom the peacock was sacred, and the policeman, who in the daytime had agreed to convey the birds on his riding camel, quailed when night set in and we strapped the pea-chicks to the saddle. "I shall die," he remonstrated. The chief of the police cheered him up and said: "They are merely ducks," and off he went. They were greatly appreciated at the ball. It was at this ball that the German Police Officer made his last appearance. It was a fancy-dress ball, and he dressed himself up as a police constable in the dreaded garb of blue tunic with yellow shorts, and as the guests sat at supper, he would appear on the veranda or at one of the many doors of the fine marble halls where once the Mogul Emperors lived, and shout out: "I want the Commissioner!" At last the Commissioner, who thought, as did all his guests save one, that it was a genuine constable gone mad, dashed off in pursuit, and all was confusion. No one could catch the slippery minion as he raced through the rooms, knocking down furniture, even smashing the big drum of the band, and in the grand finale he rushed from the veranda through the ball-room to the door of departure. And as he passed the threshold closely pursued by the Commissioner, his accomplice, the guest who knew, fell flat by the threshold, and the portly host tripped over him. And then all knew that the constable was the wicked German, and that the prostrate figure on the threshold was that of the bad Frenchman.

The police were of no great use for hunting the brigands in the jungle, so we raised a body of local Mers, who knew the passes and the woods. We armed them with the old Brown Bess, and they became fair marksmen. The brigands used bows and arrows, and killed two of our small force. I saw one of these just after he was killed, and it seemed to me that the arrow wound was far more cruel than the wound of a gun or a sword. By degrees we got the upper hand of the brigands, and some of them went off to join the famous leader Salji of Lulliána, a great Dacoit who set the Marwár state at defiance and mocked at the cavalry and other forces which surrounded his forest fastness. He was a fine fighter. His son was sent to the Mayo College at Ajmere. Some of these Dacoit leaders were men of good estate and high repute, who took to the road for some wrong done to them by the rulers of their States.

There was a special department of the Government of India to deal with "Thagi and Dacoity." I had business with an old informer employed by this department. He had been a real Thag. He was blind, but his information regarding the ways and the movements of Dacoits was remarkable. Thagi,[1] better known to English readers as Thuggee, had been suppressed, and some said that the profession was doomed when the Thags became careless, and strangled their victims before digging the grave, thus disobeying one of the first rules of Káli. In the

[1] The Thags were suppressed by Sir W. Sleeman under the Government of Lord William Bentinck in 1835. They moved through the country in bands, disguised as pilgrims or merchants—they strangled the unwary stranger with a handkerchief, plundered and buried him. The Thags were under the special protection of the goddess Káli. Between 1826 and 1835, 1,562 Thags were captured in British India.

place of Thagi, datura [1] poisoning became fashionable. A large well-to-do wedding party travelled by rail from the Jaipur State, on their way to the Province of Bombay. As was their leisurely custom, they broke the journey at my station to have a meal. An agreeable Bráhman also alighted at Beawar and kindly volunteered to cook the meal, to the satisfaction of the wedding party; but he put into the food a quantity of datura poison. The party proceeded by the next train, and the attractive Bráhman went with them. The poison worked, and by the time they reached Jodhpur Junction seven of the wedding party were in a hopeless condition, and the other two were practically senseless. But one, a boy, just had strength enough to tell the station-master that the Bráhman had got out of the carriage as the train slowed down, taking with him the jewels and cash of the wedding guests. Luckily there was a hospital assistant with a stomach pump on the platform, and he restored two of the party. The rest died. They caught the Bráhman in another carriage with the jewels on him, and later the two survivors identified the Bráhman as the man who had cooked their food, and also identified the jewels. The Bráhman was brought before me; the evidence was clear, but before committing him for trial by the Sessions Judge, I asked him if he had anything to say. He handed to me a paper which he wished to put in. It was a certificate from an English official in the Andaman Islands, to say that the prisoner had discharged the duties of Assistant Librarian in the convict settlement to his complete satisfaction. I advised the Bráhman not to put in this document, but he insisted that character was everything, especially a character given by a Sahib. He was a dangerous criminal, had been transported to the Andamans for datura poisoning, and was hanged for this second offence. It is touching to see the importance which the Indians attach to certificates of character given by Englishmen. Sometimes these certificates, known as "chits," [2] are written, as they should be, with care and due consideration; sometimes they are

[1] *Datura stramonium*: A handsome plant with large white flowers. The seeds madden and kill.

[2] *Chitthi* means a letter. *Chit* is a briefer note.

dashed off without thought, and sometimes they are ironical and recite the failings and other shortcomings of the proud possessor of the certificate. I have known applicants for domestic service, who have shown me letters disclosing their inefficiency and dishonesty, and always advised them to tear up these damning documents. But they would not, for a "chit" is a "chit," and there is a kind of superstition in the East against the destruction of the written word.

I was called into Ajmere to act as District Officer, and lived in the white marble palace on the side of the lake. The Commissioner had gone on leave and allowed me to occupy his beautiful residence. He asked me especially to keep a friendly eye on some young turkeys. He was a very hospitable man in a land where all were hospitable. "It snewed in his house of mete and drinke," turkeys and tinned whitebait. The Eurasians believed that the Queen lived exclusively on tinned food. This was an appanage of rank and wealth. We had never heard of ptomaine poisoning, and we consumed tinned lobsters, salmon and rabbit, and always sardines, recklessly. Suddenly the turkeys began to disappear. My head man said it was the work of a cobra. I disbelieved this, but reluctantly called in a snake charmer. He declined to be paid by results, which in itself seemed suspicious. He sat on some rocks, playing his pipes and swaying about, but the first day, charmed he never so wisely, there was no response to his piping. I had to go out very early in the morning, as there was a bad epidemic of cholera and we had to move infected crowds from one camp to another. As I went out the snake charmer was piping lustily, swaying from side to side, and when I came back for breakfast he was still making shrill music, pouring his whole soul into it. After breakfast, I and my companion, who was acting as Commissioner, used to sit on the white marble veranda jutting out over the water and shoot at bottles in the dancing waves of the lake with revolvers, and as I was shooting, in rushed a servant. "Sahib, the snake has arrived!" I went out with my revolver, and there was a fine cobra listening to the triumphant charmer. I blew the cobra's head off with a bullet, and then the charmer and my followers raised a loud wailing dirge. The charmer said: "You have ruined me and robbed me of my occupation. The snakes will all hear of this tyranny and will never come again to me." My followers all said that these were true words, and I saw then that I had done wrong. Nothing could comfort the charmer. I gave him three times his settled fee and promised him my help and support. But he went off, saying that his livelihood was closed. I felt very sorry, and never again doubted that snake charmers were genuine.

Cobras were numerous, and another smaller, but still more deadly snake, the krait, paid us visits. One evening I returned late from a cholera camp and found the house in an uproar. My friend's bearer, a charming old man, most gentle and dignified, had been bitten by a krait. My friend had killed the krait and knew that it was the real *Bungarus Cærulaeus*. He tied the old man's toe-joint with string and we put a tourniquet on his leg. I said, to comfort him, that it was a water-snake, and he shrewdly observed that if it were a harmless water-snake, it seemed unnecessary to cause him agony by the tight string on his toe. Two relatives sat by him, mourning over him, and the old man called for his account books, for he wished to make them up before he died. It was a pathetic scene. We made cuts on his toe with a pen-knife, and put hot charcoal on the wound. The old man said he could feel the cold chill creeping up his body, and they all talked of family matters, of debts owing and owed. Then there arrived the Civil Surgeon, a fair-haired giant of a man, a splendid Irishman, most skilful and devoted of surgeons. He said we had done the right thing, and amputated the toe-joint. He then turned on me and abused me furiously. It was a dark night, and as he galloped to our aid, he came on a heap of road metal, and his fine horse, of which he was proud, came down and broke its knees. The surgeon was badly bruised and some of his instruments ruined, and I was responsible, as I was President of the Municipality. However, he calmed down, and I think that the violence of his language acted as a tonic on the old bearer, for he survived, and years afterwards, when we met at Simla, he smiled and said: "*Wah, wah*, Sahib, water snakes!"

The good Irish doctor was my great supporter in the awful cholera epidemic. We used to start on our rounds at 4 a.m., before sunrise. I was never hungry at 4 a.m., but the doctor forced me every morning to eat something and to drink tea; for he held that the man who had something in him could treat epidemics with contempt. I always followed this advice, and I was later to be in worse epidemics of cholera and plague. I heard British soldiers at the Cantonment of Ajmere speak of cholera as "Corporal Forbes" (their rendering of "Cholera morbus").

There was a plague of street dogs in Ajmere, and at the cost of the Jain community we had a large cage on wheels made, into which we put the dogs. The wheeled cage was driven solemnly out six miles into the country. The dogs were enlarged and then trotted back following the conveyance to Ajmere, none the worse for their drive. So we took sterner measures. The police, with loaded sticks, would call, "Come brother!" to the city dog, and then brain him. Whereupon the Jains, who were the chief citizens, came to me and suggested that I should charter a railway van once a week and send the dogs to Jodhpur Junction. I did so, and received a most polite letter from the agent of the Jodhpur Railway, thanking me for my kind thought, but as they had plenty of dogs in Marwár, he was sending my consignment back. So we had recourse to the loaded sticks and to poison.

The Jains are very tender about life. They will not allow insects to be burned by flying into lamps, and I have often seen them filtering the lake water through a peculiar cloth into their jars, and carefully replacing the cloth in the lake lest some invisible creature should be destroyed. The Jains were great bankers, and had large transactions with all the states of Rajputána. I liked them and always looked on them as men of great probity, and of very gentle and courteous manners. But one of them, perhaps the most pleasant of all, was generally believed to have murdered a relative.

My third hot weather was approaching: the flowering

trees were glorious with colour and rich in scent, and the frogs in the lakes and marshes were in full voice. The sound of the frogs is to me more soothing than the song of birds, and the flame of the forest is a joy to see. Its colour is indeed like the "sound of a trumpet!"[1] But neither frogs nor flowers pleased me, and I suddenly made up my mind that I would resign the Service and go home. It was partly from the depression caused by malaria, and partly from a feeling others told me was a common experience in one's second or third year of India. I wrote to the Commissioner and asked him whether I should send in my resignation to him or to the Government of India. It so happened that on that very day a Secretary to the Government of India had arrived in Ajmere and was staying with the Commissioner. Crossing my letter came a letter asking me to ride with the Secretary and show him the working of what was known as the opium scales, where the precious drug was weighed, stamped and sealed for duty. Early next morning I rode to the beautiful house and found the Secretary booted and ready, and we started. As we rode along I pointed to a road and said: "That's the way to 'Pushkar Ji,' the most interesting spot in the world and the only place where there is a Temple to Bráhmah." "Could we see it and get back by 10 a.m.?" "Easily, if we ride hard, and I can tell you all about the opium scales." He noticed everything as we rode along, knew the trees, the crops, the birds, and was enthusiastic over the strange and holy lake of Pushkar, in the heart of the desert, with temples and palaces of the Indian Princes all round the margin.

No life could be taken at Pushkar, and no beef might be eaten. There was a bungalow in which I used to stay on the banks of the lake. One evening the District Officer and the Police Superintendent were sitting waiting for their dinner, when they heard loud shrieks from their servants who were on the floor below which led to the lake. As they sat intent on the cooking a huge crocodile walked in from the lake and cut off their retreat by the stairs leading

[1] There is one colour in India even more arresting and triumphant: that of the crimson Amaranth, when the crop is ripening in a Himalayan glen.

to the rooms above. The Police officer had a carbine and killed the crocodile. But this was fatal, and the Hindus swarmed like hornets and demanded the blood of the sacrilegious Police officer who had killed the sacred *mugger*.[1] The Policeman was the German, to whom I have alluded, and most fortunately his companion was the delightful Frenchman. He addressed the angry crowd and said in conclusion that he was so distressed and moved by the sight of the dead crocodile, that he could not eat and must go off at once to Ajmere. This somewhat pacified the Hindu priests. The police cleared a way, the horses were brought up, and the two officials got safely home; but the Frenchman told me that it was a near thing.

As the Secretary and I rode back to Ajmere, he said he had heard that I was resigning. He told me that early in his service he had thought of resigning, and was now thankful that he did not. He said to me: "Don't resign, but get special leave to go to Java, and compare that country with India." This suggestion rather puzzled me, and I said I would think about it. He was so charming and sympathetic, so sure that I should do well in India, that that night I wrote to the Commissioner and asked leave to cancel my letter.

The Secretary was Edward Buck, a man beloved by everyone. Later I was closely associated with him. I never knew a kinder nor more modest man. He was absolutely unselfish. He loved travel and music and sport, but was always thinking of one great thing—the development of Indian agriculture and Indian products. Lord Dufferin told me the day he left India that he regarded Sir Edward Buck[2] as the great genius of his administration. But the tragedy was that the Government starved all the useful projects of Edward Buck, and money was grudged to the scientific departments and to experimental agriculture. He never complained. He tried again and again

[1] Lit., sea-monster, but now the name of the destructive broad-snouted crocodile, more destructive than his cousin of the Ganges, the garial. Both should be avoided.

[2] In the *Observer* of Oct. 31st, 1926, I see:—"We all need a large-scale Empire-Atlas such as has never yet been compiled . . . How useful at every turn was, in its day, Sir Edward Buck's old 'Economic Atlas of India.'"

to persuade the Financial authorities, but they regarded Edward Buck as a dreamer and a visionary. He had vision, and he was one of the few who insisted on the right to think. Most of the Civil Service had no time to think, as the work gave no respite and no leisure. He had the far-away look in his eyes which thinkers often have. The kind good eyes were always seeing an India where two blades of wheat were growing instead of one. Other eyes will see this realised, but few will remember what India owes to the man whom officials regarded as a dreamer of dreams. He was indeed "a verray parfit gentle knight."

Many will remember the anecdotes of his absence of mind. Once he was travelling by train in the hot weather. The train had just started, and he proceeded to undress, wound up his watch and placed it in his waistcoat, and flung the waistcoat out of the window. A stranger in the same compartment, who had been watching him, sprang up and said: "Mad, by . . . !" But Edward Buck smiled and said: "Not mad, but rather overworked. I counted the telegraph posts and I know where the waistcoat fell." The watch was found at the place indicated. I saw one curious scene. I was talking to him in one of the two bits of flat ground in Simla, between the post office and the church, when a telegraph man came up with a telegram. Buck took it, read it, and then crushed it up and went on talking. He had a habit of chewing pencils and bits of paper. The telegraph man hung about, and when our conversation ended, and Buck was mounting his pony to ride off to his country house at Mashobra, the man asked for the telegraph receipt, which was always attached to a telegram. "Telegram," asked Buck. "What telegram? Where is the telegram?" And the man answered: "Your Honour has eaten it!"

Buck's Alpine chalet at Mashobra, known as the Retreat, now the summer residence of the Viceroy, was open house, and often he would forget how many guests were coming. But his servants never failed, and there was always plenty in that elastic Paradise. I think that Indian servants like improvisation, and I have never known them grumble when, as so often happens in the hospitable East, people drop in. They always rise to the occasion, and if you have not the necessary sardines, or the recognised drinks, someone in the Station has, and he, through the agency of his servants, contributes unknowingly to the feast. Curious things happen. I was once entertaining a doctor, an Irishman, of course, for most of the splendid Indian Medical Service, at any rate in Northern India, came from Ireland. He was a man of taste and prided himself on his port wine. There had been a disastrous flood; we lost nearly all our belongings, and the doctor had lost all his wine. I gave him port. He looked surprised, and asked me where I bought it. My man had bought it as a bargain from a Parsee shop. When the bottle was produced it was clear that it had come from the doctor's *godown*, as we called the room or the shed in which we kept our stores. The little cemetery in the Station was known as "*Mulligan Sahib ka godown*," but the Indians in giving it this name did not in any way imply that our most efficient Doctor Mulligan was unfortunate with his patients.

Edward Buck was the first and only official of the Government of India whom I had seen. To us provincials, Simla was very far, and even Mount Abu, where our little Provincial Government dwelt, was distant. But a week after the great Secretary left there came to Ajmere the brilliant camp of the Viceroy. It was the first Indian pageant I had ever seen, and I wished I had smarter clothes, a less battered helmet, and above all, I wished that Civilians wore uniform. How splendid and delightful to move in such a progress! But I thought then that the great Satrap and the young Civilian were worlds apart.

After opening the beautiful marble halls of the Mayo College, the Viceregal party went off to the loveliest place in all India, to Udaipur, the capital of the greatest of the Hindus, His Highness, the Maharána, descended from Ráma, and worshipped as a god. His manners and courtesy were certainly godlike. All the world of Rajputána flocked to the great camp at Udaipur, but I and the humorous Frenchman were left to keep house in Ajmere. He condoled with me and rather hinted that Civilians were not regarded with favour in the Political Department. At that time there were only two Civilian Political Assistants in the Department, which was recruited from officers of the Indian Army. When the Viceregal party returned to Ajmere on their way to Simla, I had to be at the Railway Station. Lord William Beresford, who was acting as Military Secretary to the Viceroy, asked me into his railway carriage. He must have been a thought-reader, for as I sat in his comfortable arm-chair, smoking, he said: "You think it is all beer and skittles, but it is not." He was a wonderful man, a V.C., and an excellent man of business; and years after I discovered that there was a marked absence of beer and skittles at the Viceregal Court. But in 1882 I was young and ignorant, and as I saw the beautiful white train glide away into the dark night, and saw the red carpet being rolled up and the lights put out, I rather wished that I was in that fairy carriage, speeding up to the Himalayas, far from the heat and the heavy smell of the coconut oil in the little lamps lit in honour of the Viceroy, Lord Ripon.

CHAPTER IV

"He shall serve among great men and appear before Princes; he will travel through strange countries."—ECCLESIASTICUS

Ordered to Mount Abu as Assistant to Agent to Governor-General for Rajputána—Political Department—The Rájputs—Pay—Servants—Their Love for English Children—On Tour with Colonel Bradford—His Life and Character—Officers of the Mutiny—Durbárs—Informal Interviews with Rájas—The Bankers of India—Maharája and Barons—Siege of Bidásar—Surrender of Barons—Meet one of them Twenty Years later—Southern Rajputána—Episodes of the Tour—Monasteries—Weddings—Indian Mentality—Illustrative Anecdotes—Difficulty of Understanding Indian Point of View—A Degenerate Rájput—Rájput Love of Horses and Dislike of Roads—Ride up and down Tower of Baron's Castle—Ceremonial—Udaipur—Its Lake and Palace—Deserted Military Cantonment in Forest—The Old Gardener—Offered by Sir Charles Aitchison Post of Under-Secretary to Government of Punjáb—Kill cold-weather Tiger and Bear in Forest of Capul Darra—Farewell Visit to Beawar.

SOON after this splendid vision of scarlet and gold I received orders to go to Mount Abu as Fourth Assistant to the Agent to Government for Rajputána, and I thus became a real member of what I think is the most interesting service in the world—the Political Department of the Government of India. Under the Agent were Residents, Political Agents, and Assistants. These officials were attached to the various states, as Representatives of the Government of India in the Foreign Department, a Department under the direct charge of the Viceroy, and practically independent of his Council. The ruling Chiefs and their ministers always distinguished between Viceroy and Governor-General in Council. They looked to the Viceroy and regarded the Governor-General and his Council as an institution for British India. In my time no member of the Governor-General's Council, not even the Commander-in-Chief could visit an Indian State without permission of the Viceroy.

I was no longer to deal with the *Ryots*,[1] but with the *Rais*,[2] with the Rájas of Rajasthán. I was fortunate in that I started in the famous home of the Princes, where the great Rájput Clans live. I visited all the States save Jaisalmir. The Chiefs varied in many respects, but there was one indefinable quality which distinguished them from all other Chiefs of India, and I can only describe this quality by saying that in all things great and small, they were always Rájputs.

In this book there will be no attempt to toy with history and ethnology. My humbler effort is to give some idea of the life of an ordinary Civilian as he passes through his service, and to recall the various types of Indians with whom he works and lives. The highest type with which I am acquainted is the Rájput of Rajputána. The dry air of the desert sands is good for man and horse, and the desert shores of the beautiful Rájput kingdoms saved that stronghold of Hinduism from the heavy hand of the Moslems. The Pax Britannica, which changed much in other countries of the Indian Continent, left the proud Rájputs untouched, left them their old castles and kingdoms, and guaranteed them by solemn treaties internal independence and immunity from external attack. I have seen the ruined buildings of old and great Hindu cities; have wondered, and tried to form some picture of the Indians of ancient times. I am in sympathy with Hindu friends, who have talked to me of the golden age of India, and I like to think that the Indians of the North, at any rate, resembled closely the fine thoroughbred men now living in Rajputána—whether they be called Kshattriyas, born from the fire of Mount Abu, or Aryans from Scandinavia or Central Asia—still always great and chivalrous gentlemen, with whom it is a privilege and an education to associate.

Abu is perched on the highest niche of the Aravalis, is very pretty and very sacred. In 1882 it was a small Station occupied by the Staff of the Agent, by some British troops, which came up for the hot weather, and others

[1] Lit., a herd at pasture, but used for anyone occupying land as farmer or cultivator.

[2] The head, chief. The expression *Rais Log* is applied to the upper classes in India.

who came up on leave. It was not, of course, as cool as the hill stations of the North, but it was heaven after the heat and glare of the plains; and I remember now with delight drinking from a cool stream on the bridle-path which led to Mount Abu up through the heavily-scented forest. The cool attracted tigers as well as visitors, and a friend of mine once saw nine tigers playing like kittens in the sweet-smelling Karunda[1] bushes not a mile from his little house.

It was very pretty and very small, and there was no room for horses, so by way of economy I advertised my two horses for sale. My Chief asked me why I was parting with my horses. He said: "I ride every morning, and you will ride with me. When a man gives up riding he ceases to be useful in India. An Englishman on foot is no good in a crowd." So I did not sell my horses, and every day of my life for twenty-one years I followed the advice of my wise Chief.

Hitherto I have not mentioned what may be of interest to young men who are going to India. I have said nothing about pay and money. Our pay was small, and I lost pay by entering the Political Department. But pay never comes into the picture of the young and unmarried, and one was better off on four hundred rupees a month in the *Mofussil*[2] than on far higher pay at Headquarters. The excellent servants of my time tempered the wind. They took all I had, but left me some pocket money. Until I married, my bearer kept my money. Looking back at my old diaries I see that my monthly average for servants was sixty-four rupees. Table servant twelve, Bearer eleven, Water-bearer eight, Sweeper six, Groom seven, another Groom six, Grass-cutter six, Washerman eight. And I should add that they were excellent and faithful servants, ready to march long distances, to sleep where they could, and to cook dinner in a rain-storm under a tree; always cheerful and content to add a few pennies to their pay, as commission or *Dustoory*.[3] They always lived hard and frugally in order to send home to their families the greater part of their pay. There is no Poor Law in

[1] *Carissa karandas.*
[2] Up country—away from the chief station (*Sudder*) where the high officials live.
[3] That which is customary.

India. There family affection ascends[1] and also descends. India has been called a land of regrets, and we all of us who have lived there regret something. I have many sad regrets, but I certainly regret those old familiar faces of the men who followed my slender fortunes: their tender sympathy in great trouble, their joy—not wholly altruistic—when promotion came, and their genuine sorrow when leave came. When I came back from leave, there, on the Apollo Bunder,[2] would be waiting the faithful servants. There was some wonderful system of intelligence, and they always knew our dates—sometimes before we did. They certainly knew when we were to be transferred from one place to another. We had an absurd notion that our silent, staid servants did not understand English, but as they waited at dinner they comprehended everything. Nothing was *sub rosa*, and the next day the whole bazaar would discuss the sayings of the Sahibs. I have known many instances of boys being met on landing by the old servants of their parents, who had left India. It happened to me when, as I thought, I had left India for good, and returned after a long interval. I was told of a young officer of the Indian Army. When he left England, his father, a retired officer, said to him: "John, if ever you are in real difficulty, shout for my old man, Habib Khan." Two years afterwards the young officer was in charge of a Company of Sepoys, who were to cross the Jhelum river by a ford. Night had come on, he did not know where the ford was, and stood perplexed by the bank of the river. Suddenly he thought of his father's advice, and proceeded to shout: "Ai, Habib Khan!" and in a few minutes from the opposite bank came a joyous response: "Coming, Johnnie Baba!" and Habib Khan came in a boat.

The love of Indian servants for English children is beautiful and wonderful. They will play patiently for hours with the *baba log*,[3] never reproaching them for their desultory, changing moods; and they have infinite capacity

[1] "My son help thy father in his age."—ECCLESIASTICUS.

[2] The ghat or stage in Bombay where voyagers land. "Apollo" is a corruption of some unknown Indian word.

[3] The child people.

for inventing new games and new incidents. Of course, like ourselves, they spoil children. My elder son, aged three, was seen by my wife playing on the veranda with a huge pair of scissors. She upbraided the tailor. He said: "The Bába Sahib cried, and I was helpless." There is no lullaby in the world which will rival that of the crooning old Indian servant. Some who were born in India never forget these childish rhymes all through their lives, and the rhymes always tell of toil and of farthings. If you meet bearers carrying a palankin along the road, if you see men doing earth-work or ramming stones into the great highway, you will hear one of these chants. They act like magic on the tired worker—something like this:

"*Um Um Bahro*
Pokila Bahro
Saidon o Paison
Um Um Bahro."

which loosely translated means:

"Put your backs into it, bearer men :
There are millions of farthings in it."

From these bearers (*kahars*) comes the great Sirdar, who rules the house, keeps the accounts, often banks his master's pay, and loans it to the other servants. Some of them, especially the grooms and the sweepers, have very strict rules of caste; they address one another in a kind of stilted courtesy, and their very titles of office are lofty. The sweeper is called *Mehtar*, or the Prince; the water-carrier is the *Bhisti*, or man of Paradise; the tailor is the *Khâlif*; and the gardener is the *Chaudri*, or Squire. Then, on marriage, there comes the white-robed *aya*, and her title, taken as so many other words are taken, from the Portuguese, signifies Governess. She usually lives up to her title and governs.

They are all good and faithful in their various ways, and perhaps if the vote were taken, the humble water-carrier would head the list, and the washerman (*Dhobi*), whose work seems to call for constant stimulants, would come last. I remember once living in a little hut in a mountain meadow nine thousand feet high. There was no room for the poor sweeper, as the other servants, liberal and kind enough to ignore etiquette in a rough camp, had to draw the line at a mere *Bungy*.[1] So every night the sweeper sat outside with my two terriers watching the camp-fire, and holding his hands to the comfortable blaze. He never grumbled. I had no separate tent for him. He understood. It was custom. He was very handsome, as the sweepers often are, and he looked a prophet as he sat gazing at the fire in the chilly night. Did he see a vision of what some of the progressive Indians are said to be seeing in the twentieth century—a very far off, strange land, where the sweeper will be sitting with his Bráhman brother?

It should always be remembered that in the dark days of the Mutiny the servants were staunch; and I have only come across one instance of treachery in all the books and letters which I have read about the bad times when the evil wind blew over India.

It was the privilege of the First Assistant to go on tour with the Agent, but he most generously arranged that I should take his place, and so I went off in early October with the Agent, Colonel Bradford.[2] We rode long marches and saw all the States. Colonel Bradford, as a young cavalry officer, had come through the Mutiny with distinction. He had lost his left arm in an encounter with a tiger. I saw the place where it happened. He had wounded a tiger and then ran along the side of the ravine, hoping to get another shot. He climbed into a very low tree and fired, but the tiger turned, and though wounded, was full of angry energy. As he came up the low tree, Colonel Bradford thought: "If I lose my right arm I must leave the service," and when the tiger sprang he deliberately offered his left arm to the infuriated beast, who clawed and bit savagely. Colonel Bradford and the tiger, then nearly spent, rolled down from the tree. The beaters had come up, and they finished the tiger. Then, in great pain, Edward Bradford walked some distance to his little tent, and a cavalryman was

[1] *Bhangi* is the common name of the caste from which men performing the lowest menial offices are drawn. They are often addicted to drink and drugs, and the name may be derived from *Bhang*, the Indian hemp, hashish.

[2] Afterwards Commissioner of Metropolitan Police.

sent off to the Headquarters of the Central India Horse, sixty miles away, to fetch a surgeon. As the man rode, he warned the villages to have fast ponies ready for the surgeon. The surgeon arrived in record time, and he saw at once that the only thing to save Bradford's life was to take the arm out at the socket, and he told the officer who was out shooting in the same camp that if he failed to hold the arm steady it would be fatal. The officer, many years after, described the scene to me. There was no chloroform in those days, and Bradford, who had never smoked, inhaled some form of tobacco while the surgeon took off the mangled arm with admirable precision. What helped to save this valuable life was the forethought of the cavalryman in ordering the villages to have relays ready for the surgeon. This system of relays, or *Dawk*, is universal in India, and great distances can be travelled at great speed if the relays are supplied at every ten, or better still, at every seven miles. On this tour with Colonel Bradford, we travelled over one hundred miles one day to Bikanir over the sand, riding *Dawk* horses posted at every seven miles, and felt practically no fatigue. It was the end of the journey at night, when we got into a camel carriage, that proved tiring.

Colonel Bradford was small and slight and always rode big horses. He would pick up the reins with his teeth, and he had a wonderful way with a horse. He was very gentle in manner, with a very pleasant voice, but dogged and determined when he had made up his mind. He had great influence with the Rájputs. They admired him in that he was a horseman and a soldier, and they recognised that he, like themselves, had the great manners that are born of respect for oneself and for others. An Indian schoolboy, describing a horse, wrote: "The horse is a noble animal, but when irritated, he will not do so." This was true of Colonel Bradford. When the limit of his endurance was reached he could be very severe, and his wrath was all the more effective in its sharp contrast with his normal gentleness. He belonged to the school of the *beau sabreur*, which flourished in the days of the Mutiny, and the young officers of that school were masters of the sword and the lance, and could do anything on a horse. Their names will always be remembered in the North of India as real *Bahádurs*. There was a curious resemblance among them: they all were gentle, modest and brave. They never said much about the Mutiny, though once Colonel Bradford took me one night to a dark grove of mango trees which adjoined an old tomb of a dancing girl where we slept, and by the light of the camp-fires and the torches pointed out to me men against whom we had fought in 1857. They were now in the service of the Rájput Chief to whose State we were paying a visit. Sometimes he would point out places where he and his cavalry had passed or fought. He told me how one evening, after an engagement with the mutineers, he was riding over the ground, which was hilly and rugged, and his men caught sight of two men of that terrible sect which ate human flesh. They were devouring the body of a trooper who had fallen in the fight. They fled up the rocks, dodging in and out of the huge boulders, but the avenging spears were after them, and no rocks could save the horrid Aghorias. He also told me that he and his brother officers led their men with light canes in their hands, and never drew swords.

I do not give an itinerary of the delightful tour through Rajputána on which I accompanied Colonel Bradford. I was always with him when he paid the Chief of the State a ceremonial visit in full *Durbár*. There was the Rája in his magnificent Rájput dress with jewelled sword and daggers: there was often the Rája's little son, a beautiful child with eyes like a fawn, gravely doing his part without shyness or self-consciousness; and then on chairs running down on both sides from the dais were the Barons of the State and the officials—the *Diwan*—the Chief Minister, and the *Bakshi Sahib*—the Commander-in-Chief. The Barons, or *Thakurs*, were usually Rájputs of the Rája's Clan, his peers in blood, though not in wealth and power, always regarding him with old-world loyalty, but still remembering that he was just *primus inter pares*. In the *Durbár*, the conversation between the Agent and the Rája was purely formal, and there would be long intervals of silence. Then trays loaded

[1] *Bahádur* is a Mongol word meaning "hero" or "champion," and when an Indian uses the word it is real praise.

with glittering offerings would be presented to the Agent, just touched by him, and promptly taken back by the Rája's people. And then came the ceremony of *Attar Pán*. The Rája would give to the Agent a leaf of betel enfolding a slice of areca nut in lime, and then would dab with a golden spoon out of a golden vessel the heavy oil of roses on the Agent's sleeve. The Heir Apparent would do the same kind office for me and the other members of the Agent's Staff. This would close the *Durbár*, and we would go back to our tents and get out of the too oderiferous uniform. But the informal interview with the Rája was quite another story, and after every interview it was my duty to record the note of the conversation. I have some of the notes still, and very quaint and intimate they seem to me now. They reveal one point, and that is that the Agent never dictated. He listened, and when asked, would make a suggestion. There would always be two, perhaps three, ways of carrying out some policy of the Rája's. Perhaps the Rája's own way would prove feasible; perhaps another way would be equally easy, and perhaps a third way would be more in keeping with the policy adopted by the Government of India. But it was for His Highness to decide. Then the welfare of the Heir Apparent might be discussed. Did His Highness propose to send him to the Mayo College for Chiefs at Ajmere? No! The Rája preferred to keep him at home. In another State there were complaints that rich Marwári merchants and bankers from Calcutta and Bombay had been robbed on their way to the Rája's capital. These complaints had reached the Agent in the form of an *arzi* or petition. "*Gumnám?*" (anonymous) asked the Rája. No! The Agent took no notice of anonymous petitions. "Ah!" said the Rája, "it must have been some of my Barons who have been 'escorting' the merchants."

I was interested especially in the Bikanir State to see great bankers from Calcutta and other important cities. They had come back to Bikanir for some family business—marriage. They had made a long and difficult journey over the desert and were treated with contempt by the State. These men were Marwáris, the Lombards of India, who had originally come from Marwár, the parent State of

Bikanir. Some of them were rich enough to have bought up Bikanir. One of them called on me and said he would give me two lakhs of rupees (over £13,000) for some charity if I would induce the Maharája of Bikanir to say "*Rám, Rám*,"[1] as he drove by in his carriage. I reported this to the Agent, and the offer was declined. I am quite sure that the proud ruler of Bikanir would have also declined, much as he desired money.

His desire for money led to trouble and broke off our pleasant tour for a time. The Maharája had fallen out with his Barons. He wished to increase their taxation; they pleaded bad harvests and desired some decrease. The dispute dragged on. Our representative at Bikanir did his best to effect a compromise, but failed, and the Barons went out and gathered to the fort of Bidásar, the stronghold of one of the leading Barons. The town was strongly entrenched, and bristled with old mortars and guns, quaint and ancient. When it was clear that there was no hope of a settlement between the Maharája and his Barons, we set off with a Brigade on December 16th, 1883. It consisted of troops of the Worcestershire Regiment, the 8th Bombay Infantry, the Merwára Battalion, one Battery of Field Artillery, the Deoli Cavalry, and some Sappers and Miners from the Bombay Army. The Brigade was commanded by a very able officer, General Gillespie. Colonel Bradford was in political charge, and I went as his Assistant. It was uncertain till we got near Bidásar what the Barons would do. Colonel Bradford feared that in their proud desperation they would resort to *Johur*, as happened in the siege of Chittor, when they burned their women and then sallied forth and were killed sword in hand. It took us ten days to reach our destination; the sand was deep and the horses could not in places drag the guns, and elephants were used. Water was scarce, and we had to carry most of our supplies. But the air was splendid. I know nothing so bracing as a winter day in Bikanir. On the night of the 26th December, Thákur Bahádur Singh of Bidásar came quietly to my tent. The Barons had sur-

[1] *Rám Rám.* The common salutation between Hindus and an invocation of the divinity.

rendered. I took him to the Agent, and he and the three other Barons were sent out of the Bikanir State for a time. The next day, at 3 p.m., we blew up the Fort of Bidásar. The charge was fired, the Sappers came running out from the little town, and after what seemed to me a long time, I saw the Fort rise almost solid, then crumble into dust, then flames and thick smoke. It was noticed that the flames did not touch nor injure a temple close by the Fort. My sympathies were divided. I saw that discipline must be maintained, and the Barons had put themselves in the wrong by an appeal to arms. As the Brigade reached the boundary of the Bikanir State, the Maharája met us with a large and brilliant following, men in chain armour, mounted on the racing camel for which Bikanir is famous. Some of the camels can travel 400 miles in four days, and are very valuable for the purposes of Dacoity. For the experienced Dacoit likes to rob at a great distance from his own home. As our troops halted on the Bikanir border, I heard two privates of the British regiment talking. "Who's that by the General?" said one, pointing to the gorgeous Chief of Bikanir. "Him? Why, he's the Rája!" "Oh!" said his comrade, "I thought he was the bloke we had come to kill!" Happily there was no killing, but I have reason to know that the Maharája was full of regrets and remorse. A Rájput Chief is shaken badly when his Barons go out, and he is ashamed for ever if he is forced to invoke the Government of India to restore order. A single Baron may become a *Bahir-watia*,[1] and no one cares. But when they all go out there is something wrong. What was wrong was set right. More than twenty years later I was with the Viceroy at Bikanir and there was a large meeting to celebrate the opening of a Nobles' Club. I sat at some distance from the platform and was talking to a group of Barons. "I suppose none of you were at Bidásar in 1883?" I asked. They looked surprised, and one fetched a richly dressed man wearing a heavy gold anklet that indicates high rank among the Barons. It was Thákur Bahádur Singh of Bidásar, happy, respected, and prosperous. This, to me, is one of the charms of life in an Indian State. What-

[1] One who leaves the road and goes into outlawry.

ever your sins and mistakes, there is always a chance of making good, and I know many instances, especially among the Rájputs, where a very wild and outrageous youth was followed by a middle-age of usefulness and honour.

It was pleasant to march away from ruined Bidásar, to get away from the wearisome sand and back to the pleasant land of Southern Rajputána, something new and of interest at every mile; always some beautiful old castle, or some new Court with pageantry much the same, but with marked and subtle differences. I liked the visits to the homes of the Barons. There was the same ceremony, but the talk was less formal and the life more real. Some of them were splendid men; good to their people, keeping up the old fashions, true to their religion and loyal to their Chief; and this in spite of the fact often present to their minds that their real profession of arms was closed to them. Nothing to fight for now with the sword, but still their honour and their dignity to defend. Even now, a damsel in distress could count on the chivalry of any real Rájput if she sent him a bracelet and called him "brother." And I always felt that in Rajputána the age of chivalry was not gone.

Riding along we would meet Brinjáras [1] hurrying with their cattle, laden with salt and grain; fine men and women, but too busy to talk on the march—six miles a day and every day. Too busy to sit down to a meal; so busy that children have been born on the marching bullocks; almost as busy as the British in India. One great grievance they had, and told me—they hated the railway. Then I would chance on some beautiful monastery, see the quiet, contemplative monks (*Sadhs*) at their refectory, watch them, in their dress of salmon pink, drawing water from the deep well in the close, all sleek and kind and cheery, wondering much at our haste and restlessness. I, too, would wonder as the Abbot sat muttering without a stop, "*Rám, Rám.*" No one took any notice of him and he seemed oblivious of the world. He was calling on his god. I always wanted to linger in these places. There was more than met the eye. The monks, and the wandering, half-naked, ash-smeared ascetics

[1] A tribe of carriers and dealers always moving; very important to the army in the time of the Deccan wars ,and highly appreciated by Sir Arthur Wellesley.

we met daily could have told me much—if not of religion or philosophy, at any rate of the places and the people that they had seen in their long pilgrimages through India. But they would rarely talk. It was a mistake to write them down as absolute parasites on the community, for they must have served some purpose in the mysterious order of Indian things. There are good and bad, but there are too many, and if the beggars and men of religion were numbered, the hordes of those who live free on India would astonish the economist. Some Indians assert that one quarter of the population eats but does not work. There are two great influences in India: the woman's influence, and the influence of those who live apart from the world. And we perforce ignore them both.

I would see on the road the barber hastening, full of importance, to the distant home, where he would find a suitable bride for his master's son, and the wayfarers all seemed to know of his delicate mission, to which they made indelicate references. I would meet old men, infirm and crippled, toiling along the road to some far-off wedding feast. I would remonstrate with them on thus overtaxing their strength, and they would always reply: "We go for the longing for the dainty food, for the rice and sugar."

At one village I came on a tragedy. A wedding guest had killed himself by eating too much of sweet food. The master of the feast said: "If only he could have waited for the salted course, all would have been well." There was no criticism; no suggestion of gluttony. It was just regrettable; it might, and probably would, happen to any of them.

Once I saw a little wedding scene. There was the small bride in her palankin, and the bridegroom, aged nine, riding on a big painted horse. The party had halted outside a village, and a few coppers were scattered as largess among the lookers-on. Up rushed a female attendant of the bride, a stout woman with a big child. She bundled the child into the palankin and then got in herself. At this the bearers of the litter raised loud protest, and then the female began. I have never, except later, in Kashmir, heard abuse to rival that of this mænad. An elderly man in the crowd told me that I should never hear the like again.

It is," he said, "the abuse of the thousand terms." The bride's party sat listening, humiliated, but quiet; and the bridegroom sat on his horse, unconcerned and yawning. At last, long before the nurse had done her thousand invectives, it was arranged that the big child should be ejected and that a spare bearer should be engaged. And off they went merrily as a wedding bell. No one blamed the nurse for her coarse allusions to the female relatives of the bearers, and no one blamed the bearers.

Some Indians are curiously inconsequent and strangely influenced by trifles, or what seem to us trifles. Their ideas are often unrelated, and in every brain there is a spacious religious compartment. This is reflected in their words and actions, and it is vain to expect that Indians will be impelled by the same motives as govern our conduct. Every day I noticed some little unexpected deed or utterance, for which I could see no logical cause or connection; but the Indians saw nothing surprising nor incongruous in these queer antics of the mind. One guest night at an Indian Cavalry mess, the hosts had called in a juggler to entertain their guests. He seemed to be of the ordinary type, and in the orthodox fashion he spat on the effigy of Atma Ram[1] before he commenced his performances. He was, however, a clumsy conjurer, and so was told to desist and depart. Then, to everyone's surprise, he stood up and began to recite from the "Faërie Queene." He was not a bad reciter, but the "lofty rhyme" of Spenser was not well received, and the entertainer left hurriedly.

The Indian will often utter an idea without any thought of its implications. One of the suggestions made by an Indian of standing to the Commission on Police was that the Government should appoint, as informers, men of high and noble family. It was a novel and brilliant idea, but it might have been distasteful to members of the Commission of high family, if they had considered the implication.

A Bengali gentleman was discussing the gangs of Patháns who used to sweep down from the Frontier year by year, to prey upon the gentle peasantry of Bengal. Ostensibly

[1] Atma Ram learnt and divulged many of the secrets of the jugglers, and was hated by them so, that they always spat on his effigy.

pedlars, these roystering blades pursued a system of payments by instalments to extreme lengths. "The Páthan," said the Bengali, "has all the ferocity of the European." I knew that he did not mean to wound my feelings as a European.

Mr. Isaacs, the hero of an excellent book of that name, told me this anecdote. He had an Arab pony of great merit and price. One day in Simla he was making a call, and he left the pony with his groom on the road. The road skirted a very high, steep precipice. When Mr. Isaacs came back there was no pony, but only the groom, with broken reins in his hand. The pony was dead, down at the foot of the precipice. Mr. Isaacs was too horrified even to speak, and the groom broke the silence by asking for an increase in his salary. Mr. Isaacs, who also was an Oriental, contained his wrath and said: "This is hardly the time to ask for promotion."

A missionary in Peshawar, whom I knew well, was once very angry. He had a *hujra*, or guest house, in his garden open to Patháns and to Afgháns from beyond the frontier. To entertain these wild guests he had a magic lantern and a galvanic battery. An Afghán of some standing came to the guest house, dined well, and as a nightcap was given a shock from the galvanic battery. He retired with courteous thanks, but soon after his man of affairs begged for a few words with the missionary. "You, sir," he said, "are wise and skilled in magic. Do you know of a lingering and painful poison which leaves no trace?" "For what purpose do you want the poison?" asked the missionary. "My master has an enemy—his brother," was the reply. "Wicked man," said the horrified host. "You and your master must leave my *hujra* at once and never come again." Next morning the Afghán had disappeared, but his agent prayed the indignant missionary to listen for a minute. "My master has a daughter whom he loved. One night, in the heat of summer, he and she were sleeping on their cots in the walled courtyard. It was dark, and his brother, who hated him, climbed the wall and felt his way to one of the cots and smote with his Afghán knife. He killed not his brother, but the girl. The bereaved father followed the murderer for months and at last caught him; but the guilty brother fell at his feet and did *melmastya*,[1] and by our code my master can no longer overtly slay him. So his only course is to kill him secretly, and we thought that you would help us. But you repulse us, and are angry: and this we cannot understand, how you, so wise, can be angry without cause."

My Munshi, who was trying to teach me Pashtu, was related to this Agent. He, too, was greatly surprised by the attitude of the reverend missionary. "We expected sympathy," he said, "but he drives us away."

One day an old ascetic and his five disciples were seated on a bridge, and the old man, who was blind, was playing a lute. There came up another Faqir, and the old man said: "Hail, brother, play us a tune." But he said: "I cannot play." "Then," retorted the old man, "you are no true Faqir." "Though I cannot play on the lute," said the new arrival, "I can show you some queer things in magic, and will do so if you and your disciples will take food with me." They consented, and the magician put arsenic into the pulse, and killed four of them. The evidence which hanged the magician was that he was seen to put a white powder into the pulse, and no one is extravagant enough to put salt into pulse.

Readers may wonder why I mention these trifling details, but they matter much in India, and those who go to the East in the Civil Service will find it both useful and interesting to notice little details of dress, food, and, above all, of physiognomy. No one can ever boast that he really knows and understands the Indians. The more one learns, the more one realises one's ignorance; but a knowledge of the little things helps to break the ice of reserve, while ignorance of some of the conventions and customs of the Indians, seemingly of no importance, may often cause serious misunderstanding and friction.

I said that among the Rájputs there was always a strong chance of making good, but I find in my notes one case which was hopeless. It was at one of the Rájput Courts.

[1] If an Afghan prostrated himself in abject submission to his enemy, the blood feud must be cancelled.

The Chief was very old-fashioned, and as he had no sons, he adopted a young Rájput of his own clan. There is not great latitude in the matter of adoption. The family tree, which is kept with scrupulous care by the Court bards, is consulted, and the heir must, as a rule, be adopted from the nearest branch, or sometimes from one of several recognised families. The youth who had been adopted was a wretched choice. His own appearance was against him, as, indeed, were appearances generally. He looked weak and vicious, and though I felt sorry for him as he sat squirming under the contemptuous glare of the splendid old Chief, I felt still more sorry for the proud Rájput as he looked at his sorry successor. He was not what an Indian who had great skill in word-making once described as a "mereling." He was very positive in his vices, and among other evil practices had been a coiner on a large scale. But Colonel Bradford was there to make the best of a bad business. He suggested that the heir apparent might study books on administration and might ride through the State and see how the people lived. Unfortunately the heir apparent said he did not care for riding. "Then," said the Agent, "you can drive." The storm broke. The old Chief boomed out a litany of contempt and malediction, of which the refrain ran:

"*Kitab Purh*
Buggi men Baith."[1]

Beast! But he used a stronger word than "beast." Nothing would stop him; he was mad with shame that a Rájput, his successor, should admit that he loved not the horse. And we came away. It was the first time that Colonel Bradford had failed. He did not, of course, always succeed, but he generally planted the good seed.

Soon after, we were at the court of the oldest ruling Prince in the world. He had succeeded to his kingdom as a boy, and was now nearly eighty—a great age for an Indian[2]—and he certainly had every right to be old-fashioned.

[1] "Read books
Sit in a buggy."

[2] The Indians are short-lived as compared with the British. "Their days are swifter than a weaver's shuttle."

The Agent spoke of the increasing use of the roads, their civilising influence and their many advantages, remarking that in the neighbouring States there were good driving roads. He spoke with feeling, for the springs of the carriage in which we had come were hopelessly broken by reason of the ruts. "Driving roads?" said the fine old Chief. "Yes, yes! a road to-day and a battery of Royal Horse Artillery to-morrow; never, never." And it was never during his rule. But in spite of difficulties of communication, it was well worth while to visit this old-world State, to be with this real king of men, just, resolute, very courteous, but taught by experience to mistrust change. So he and his warrior Barons kept to the old ways, enforced order in the State, and saw that justice was done; but under a brave show of dress, retainers and horses, there was always the carking thought that the profession of arms was gone and that they were unemployed.

There was one old Baron in another State, almost as old as the Chief, who did not like roads, and with him I formed a friendship which he called a *dilidosti*, or heart friendship. He lived in a fine castle with a massive tower of great height. With him lived his son, grandson and great-grandson, all with names signifying "lion," and the family, even in that land of brave men, was noted for its bravery. I said to my host, who had proposed a ride, that the view from the great tower must be magnificent. "Yes," he said. "You will see it when we go for our ride." Three horses came, all saddled in the Rájput fashion, and the old Baron, his son and I, mounted, but instead of riding out by the great gate of the Fort, the old man rode across the courtyard to the wide entrance of the tower. "I'll go first," he said, and to my horror he rode up a very steep ramp which ran up the inside of the tower wall to four landings. It was a common saying in India that a certain horse could do anything except climb up a wall, but these horses had the agility of cats as they bounded up the steep, stone-paved ramp without a fault. The old Baron's son kindly told me not to touch my horse's mouth. There was no wall on the inner side of the ramp, which was just wide enough for one horse, and if one of the three horses had slipped, the horse and rider must have fallen to the bottom of the tower. When we reached the summit of the tower, the view was certainly grand, and I thought I could see over the desert the quarries of the creamy marble of Makrána, and the famous Salt Lake with its opal tints, the haunt of the flamingo. It was worth seeing, but not worth that ride up the ramp. I said to the son: "I suppose we shall walk down," but he said that the custom was to ride down.

At all these castles of the Barons there was the same ceremonial as at the Palace of the Chief, and the same perfect hospitality. There was the family bard, the minstrels, sometimes even the licensed jester, though he did not wear the cap and bells, and always the dancing girls and the drummer, though they did not dance and he did not drum; and always perfect freedom and courtesy, and the most graceful manners. It was the Middle Ages in sepia.

And then to the elfin court of dreamland, to the fairest of the many homes devised by man—to Udaipur. This is the capital of the Mewár State, the home of the Sesodia Clan of the Rájputs. The Chief, His Highness the Maharána, takes his title from the capital, and not from the State; just as in Marwár, the home of the Rahtor Rájputs, the Maharája takes his title from the capital, Jodhpur. These two Chiefs, together with the Maharája of Jaipur, the Head of the Cuchwaha Rájputs, are the premier Princes of Rajputána. Officially they ranked equally at this time, but in the estimation of the Hindus, Udaipur ranks above all.

Sir Alfred Lyall was at Bombay when the great Indian Chiefs came to welcome King Edward on his arrival in India. Sir Alfred was talking to the famous Minister of Haidarabad, a Moslem—and said: "It must interest you to see the future King of England." "More than I can say," replied Sir Salar Jung. "And there is one other here to-night whom I have long wished to see, to us Indians the greatest of Indians, the Maharána of Udaipur."

Colonel Bradford and I had outstripped our followers when we reached the place some forty miles from Udaipur, where a splendid carriage and four fine horses awaited us. The Agent's luggage consisted of a helmet wrapped up in a duster; mine of a sponge and brushes, similarly enveloped; and the contrast of our dusty clothes and humble effects with the silver carriage of state made us smile. But the men of the mounted escort in chain armour saw nothing incongruous: we were on a journey and in the East everything is permitted to the traveller. So through the rather scorched hills to the lovely Lake and Palace of Udaipur. The kindest and most stately of welcomes from the Maharána, and when we went to our rooms, as if by magic everything that the most civilised man could desire, and at midnight, when our followers arrived, they found us comfortably bestowed in the "Castra nil cupientium." I wished that I might never leave this palace of enchantment. I wish I could describe it. But Udaipur, like the Táj at Agra, baffles brush and pen. The exquisite lake, with its background of dimpled, velvet hills; the white Palace mirrored in the clear water; but above all the beautiful mankind, are ever in my mind. Whenever I could get away I would row over to the island Jagnawás, with the white marble pleasure house, where our womenfolk and children found refuge in 1857, when the Maharána of that time swore that anyone who dared to violate that island should die by his hand. He had no doubts as to his duty in those difficult days, when rumour bewildered all men. He was asked by another chief of an Indian State what side he should take, and he sent back as answer a silver coin on which was stamped "*Dost-i-London*."[1] I have one of those coins still.

One could spend years in Rajputána, travelling from one fief to another, and always find beauty in scenery, buildings, and in the people. I have seen ancient, deserted cities, but it is more interesting to see ancient cities with their ancientry alive.

I came across one deserted place, a little military cantonment before the Mutiny. The forest had nearly taken it back, and I found the spot with difficulty, as my path led through dense jungle and ravines. I came at last to where the regiment had lived. The bungalows of the officers had disappeared, and the only trace of former days was the swimming-bath. I got off my horse, and sat talking by the brink

[1] Friend of London.

of the bath to my guide, when suddenly there appeared a wizened old gnome, who bowed and handed me a little bouquet of immortelles, tied so tightly, in the old fashion. He had been the gardener of the Legion which was no more. He lived two miles away in some little village; but in spite of his age he would creep back to where the garden had been. His memory was good. He told me where the bungalows had stood, and much that was interesting about his old masters. He recalled with a smile a high-spirited and beautiful girl, the young wife of a Major: how she would creep up when he was trimming the grassy bank of the swimming-pool and push him into the water. "Ah!" he said, with a sigh of affection, "she was a *badmásh*, but very kind to me." She was better known afterwards as Lola Montes.

My life with Colonel Bradford was delightful. He was a hard worker and it was a pleasure to work for him. He loved movement and enjoyed sport, and I wish that I could have stayed with him in Rajputána for ever. But in January, 1884, there came a letter from Sir Charles Aitchison, the Lieutenant-Governor of the Punjáb, offering me the post of Under-Secretary in his Government. This meant Simla in the summer, and the dazzling salary of seven hundred and sixty-six rupees a month. But I hesitated to leave Rajputána, and should not have gone had not Colonel Bradford insisted. He knew Simla. But as a compensation he promised me that I should kill a cold-weather tiger, and in the beautiful forest of Capul Darra I shot a fine tiger and a big bear. In the cold weather, tigers range a wide hunting ground, and it is in the hot weather, when the ground is too hot for their tender pads, that it is easy to find them. This beat was a sudden and unprepared affair, and the experienced Englishman who arranged the shoot warned me that the chances were that the tiger would not appear. He also warned me that, unless I felt absolutely certain of killing, I should not fire, as a wounded tiger might involve the death of several beaters. This was embarrassing, as I had had little practice with a rifle, and I sat in the fork of a tree and prayed that I might get an easy shot. How one's heart does thump, and how deceptive sounds are in a forest, when the leaves have fallen, and how like the distant bushes and grasses waving in the wind are to a moving animal! The peacock stepping over the dry leaves sounds like the stealthy tiger; the pigs come thundering by; the hyena galloping past to my right nearly drew my fire; and a crocodile which had been basking in the sun on the ledge of a rock above the clear pool to my left, splashed into the water and brought my heart to my mouth. And then, long before the beaters with their drums and hideous horns drew near, the tiger came, and gave me an easy shot, and fell just behind my tree. Scarcely a second after, a big bear came straight to my tree, and with my second barrel I wounded him badly. The poor brute tore himself, and then on top of him came another bear, and the wounded bear seized and bit him savagely. I quite lost my head and fumbled over the cartridges, and bear number two went on. The pad elephants came up, and I got on one of them and followed the wounded bear for a long way over the rocks and brushing under the boughs of trees. At last we got into the open and there was the bear dead. We skinned the tiger that night and the beaters and the villagers took away all the flesh as a charm for cattle. Someone also removed half of the tiger's whiskers, which are supposed to be efficacious when chopped up and drunk with water.

But this day's experience rather increased my disinclination to leave Rajputána, and as I was sitting at night talking to the famous shikári who had arranged the beat, while the good-natured Doctor—my old Ajmere friend—was skinning the tiger, I expressed my intention to remain with Colonel Bradford. "Don't you be a young fool," said the shikári. "Go to Simla, and don't imagine that you will get another cold-weather tiger. He is kept for Viceroys and globe-trotters, and not for the likes of you." And he explained that every tiger, brought to the table, so to speak, cost one's host £100, and a cold-weather tiger cost considerably more. And, from the guest's point of view, well worth it, every penny!

Before I went to Simla I went to Merwára to wish the people of Beawar good-bye. They gave me a kindly welcome, but everything was the same. My departure had caused no convulsion, and my successor, the last Avatar of the divine Dixon, was established in my place. They had approached him on the great problem, the banishment of the sweepers from the main streets. But though there was no change in the affairs of Merwára, I was struck by another kind of change. I had thought the people of Merwára gay in colour and light in heart as compared with the rather sombre, dour people of the Frontier. But now, when I contrasted them with the people of the Rájput States, I found them drab and listless. I had often been told by those who were older and wiser than I that real happiness was to be found in British territory, and that the lot of the peasants in the Indian States was troubled and uncertain. I thought much about this, and later on in this book shall refer to it. It is curious how the impressions made in the first years on Indian service form the real and only valuable ideas. We grow wiser and more critical as the years pass, but the early impressions remain. For instance, if I had been older and wiser I should not have paid a farewell visit to Beawar; and it is a good rule, though it may seem unfeeling, never to go back to your old haunts of office; never, even, to correspond with your old friends. For it is often most embarrassing to your successor. Seventeen years later I revisited Beawar with the Viceroy, who was inspecting the fever and plague camps of the Punjáb, Rajputána and Bombay. The cruel drought had for the time destroyed the pretty district of Merwára, the beautiful garden which had given me such delight was a dust heap, and the cool swimming-bath was dry, and the "fruitful place was a wilderness."

CHAPTER V

"Shades of the prison-house begin to close."

—WORDSWORTH

Sir Charles Aitchison, Lieutenant-Governor of the Punjáb—Simla—My Ignorance of Principles of Land Revenue—Life in Simla—Climate—Rhododendrons—Little Simla—Two Governments and Commander-in-Chief—Strong Provincial Sentiment—On Tour with Lieutenant-Governor—Unreality of such Tours—Episode of English Lady married to Moslem—My Marriage—Second Season at Simla—English Colonel and Daulat Rám—Camp at Rawal Pindi—Viceroy and Abdur Rahmán—His Methods of Governing—His Durbárs—Daulat Rám at Umballa—Illustrations of Gratitude of Indians—Jung Bahádur and his Elephants—The Bankers and Young English Officer in the Mutiny—Settlement Work in Kurnál Umballa—Moslem and Hindu Instructors—Sikh Landlords and their Methods—Extracts from my diary showing scenes of Village Life—Kurushetra, cradle of Bráhman System—Its Unhealthiness—Beautiful Country round Jagádri—Lála Bansi Lál, Banker—Loafers.

SIR CHARLES AITCHISON was Lieutenant-Governor of the Punjáb. He was one of the best men I ever knew. He had been Foreign Secretary and his notes were famous for their clearness and directness. He saved much work to his subordinates, for the note could be turned into the official letter without the alteration of a word. His well-known book on Treaties with the Indian States was familiar to me, as it was one of the text books in which I had to pass before entering the Political Department. He had great sympathy for the Indians and did all he could to improve education and to open the higher appointments in the service to competent Indians of character. He was a very just man and did not fear unpopularity. In consequence he was popular, and was certainly respected by all classes. He lived in an old tomb, and his Secretariat worked in another tomb nearer to the city of Lahore—the grave of the dancing girl, Anarkali.

In the hot weather at Simla I worked in gayer surroundings, in a house on the Mall, next door to Cowmeadow's shop. On the other side was the shop of a German who sold pianos, and near by was Peliti's, the sweet shop, the resort of young A.D.C.s and pretty girls. It is curious how places are remembered by their lesser and more intimate associations. Peliti, the chef, was more familiar than Lord Lytton—his employer: and Cowmeadow's shop was better known than the Combermere Bridge which stood opposite.

Though I was no longer working in a tomb, I felt depressed officially. One of the Secretaries, who was a true friend to me, had warned me before I left Rajputána that the work was heavy. He wrote: "The pay question is a serious one. It will cost you at least four hundred and fifty rupees a month to live at Simla at the Club. The work question is also serious. You will have to do a full eight to nine hours of desk work and occasionally more." I did not mind the long hours, but the trouble was that I was wholly ignorant of the subject with which my branch dealt. The principles of Land Revenue cannot be learnt from books and I had received no training. It was a godsend to me when cases of trade or excise or forests came my way, and the only work to which I look back with pleasure was the drawing up of rules for the Aitchison Chiefs College at Lahore. I had seen and admired the Mayo Chiefs College at Ajmere. For the rest it was making bricks without straw, and I was an unprofitable servant. It was kind of the Government to have kept me, but all the time I was longing to be back with my beloved Colonel Bradford.

Still, socially I was elated. I lived at the excellent Club and met every day the great men of India, realised the extraordinary variety of official activities, and talked with officers from every part of the Continent. I would hear what the Viceroy thought or what he had said, would be told who were the coming men, and sometimes would listen to opinions on the Ilbert Bill and on Lord Ripon's scheme for Local Self-government, corrupted by the wondering Indians into "Lokil Sluff." It was a great pity that these two measures were connected in men's minds, for the latter measure was sound but had a bad start.

I saw most sides of Simla life in 1884. Later, men

said that in Simla you could not hear your own voice for the grinding of axes. But in 1884 the grinders were few. In the course of my service I saw much of Simla society, and I think it would compare most favourably with any other town of English-speaking people of the same size. It was bright and gay. We all lived, so to speak, in glass houses. The little bungalows perched on the mountain-side wherever there was a ledge, with their winding paths under the pine trees, leading to our only road, the Mall; the one poor theatre under the Mall and in the bazaar, where some of the finest amateur actors in the world took us for a time out of India; the dances—and all danced well because they danced so often—at Benmore, owned by a German; the frequent balls at Peterhoff—the modest residence of the Viceroy—where we danced in the dining-room to the bewitching music of the Viceregal band—the lawn tennis every evening; the races at Annandale below the Ridge; the picnics at the Sipi Fair where the Viceroy's staff entertained so regally, and the constant dinner-parties—these all brought us together, and it was impossible to live apart. It was a happy life and a healthy life in every way; and it was a life of great simplicity. Everyone knew what his neighbour's salary was. It was a rare exception for anyone to have means of his own; so display and ostentation were regarded not only as bad form, but as foolish. The youngest Civilian knew that he might one day become a Lieutenant-Governor, or a member of Council, and our charming and courteous seniors always treated us as though they recognised this possibility. It was the same in the Army. The oldest Civilians and the oldest soldiers were young enough in heart to remember the days seemingly so recent when they made their shy bows to Simla, "the cherisher." It was, above all, a society of young people. In those days men always rode to a dinner or a dance in voluminous waterproofs through the torrential rain. The ladies drove in rather primitive rickshaws, and a Dyke's rickshaw from Calcutta was a rare and desirable possession.

Simla could be hot and dry before the rains came. The rains were not unpleasant, but the glorious time was the end of September, when the air was crisp and the mountains were dazzling in their new dress of fresh snow. Who can ever forget the rhododendron trees, silver with lichen, ablaze with colour of their own blooms and those of the pretty tree orchids.

The Punjáb officials lived in what was known as Little Simla. I do not think that in 1884 it had been finally decided whether the Punjáb Government should spend the summer in Simla, or should return to their old hill station—Murree. There were arguments both ways, but I think it would have been better for the Punjáb if the Government had made Murree their summer retreat. Simla was too small for two "Lart Sahibs,"[1] much less for three: and the Indians, who came rarely in those days were bewildered when, having paid their respects to the "Mulki Lart"[1] and the "Jungi Lart,"[1] they found that they must travel east and call on the "Punjáb Lart." It did not matter in Calcutta, where there was room enough for many Governments; there the Bengal officials could move without daily encounter with the Supreme Government. In Simla the two forces met daily, and though I am a great believer in the influence of personal touch, it seemed to me—perhaps the air at eight thousand feet is highly charged—that there was more friction than friendship between the two authorities. We, that is the younger men, of the Punjáb regarded the Government of India as an unnecessary and duplicating engine, trying always to turn the huge and diverse Provinces into a machine-made monotonous entity. We knew the Punjáb and its wants; we knew the Frontier, and controlled the finest section of the Indian Army, the Punjáb Frontier Force. We had our own Indian States, which were as well managed as any of the States under the Foreign Department, and we did not require the assistance nor the criticism of the Government of India. This is, I imagine, the attitude of every Provincial Government, but if they had all lived perched on the Simla Ridge, whence escape was impossible, Indian administration would not have run so smoothly as it did in the Victorian age. The distant Governments could

[1] The Indian pronunciation of *Lord*. The Viceroy was the *Mulki* Lord—Lord of the whole land: the *Jungi* Lord was the Commander-in-Chief—Lord of War. When an Indian wishes you good luck, he will say: "*Khuda ap ko lart kare*"—"May God make you a Lord."

say, "*Simla dur ast,*"[1] but Punjáb had to pass India on the Mall. There is a very strong Provincial sentiment. Every Civilian fortunately thinks that his Province is the best, and when talking to men who have been moved about from one Province to another, they will always praise the Province in which they started and stand up for its peoples and its customs. But if you pursue the subject, you will always find that they are really thinking, not of a Province, but of a District or Division of that Province. No two Districts are alike. Indeed, in the District itself there will be large communities as unlike as Yorkshire and Devonshire, Lancashire and Kent. And while we saw the mistake and the danger of the mechanism of the Supreme Government, and talked of the absurdity of forcing the various nations of the Indian Continent into a drab and homogeneous mould, we forgot that we were sinners ourselves. We were forcing the people of the Five Rivers[2] into one channel, lightly imagining that what would be thought good for the Lahore District would be equally good for Peshawar or Delhi.

One night I was riding back from a ball at Peterhoff and caught up on the Mall a very clever man, who was Chief Secretary of the Punjáb. To improve my mind, he told me that the great secret of administration was to ignore the personal factor: that in making appointments to Districts, it did not matter whether Jones or Brown or Robinson was appointed to a certain District. They were parts of a machine, and if they were not exactly alike, they must be regarded as alike and taught to consider themselves as alike. I ventured at this midnight hour to say that I had always imagined that the personal factor was of the first importance in India. Whereon he said that I should never succeed in the Secretariat. In this he was right, but in his views on the question of the personal factor he was wrong.

Simla was in every way delightful, with its clever and interesting people, always full of life and cheerfulness. There was one constant reason for cheerfulness and thankfulness, for, as we looked down on the hot dust haze which hung over the foot of the mountains, we were glad that

[1] Simla is far away.
[2] Punjáb is the land of the five rivers—*Panch-ab*.

we were not down there. But, delightful as it was, it was not India, and I was relieved when the time came to go on tour with the Lieutenant-Governor. We went to the Frontier, floated down the Indus on boats, and then marched from Bannu to Kohát and Peshawar. At this last place there was a great gathering of the people, and we had what is, I think, the best kind of entertainment for Indians—a fine show of fireworks. It was managed by an Indian from down country. John Lockwood Kipling had come up from Lahore and was living in my tent. He came to see me officially regarding some old accounts for an exhibition in Australia, to which the Punjáb had sent its art-wares. Neither he nor I cared much for accounts, and we settled the business—which had been under discussion for some years—in an hour. After dinner we were sitting watching the preliminary catherine wheels, when suddenly there was a loud explosion and the whole store of fireworks went off, much to the delight of the huge crowd. "That is India," said J. L. Kipling. "If they understood the rudiments of combination, you and I would not be here to-night."

These tours with Lieutenant-Governors and Viceroys serve many useful purposes; but everything is abnormal. For instance, when I had been in the Kohát District before, I had never seen an avenue of over a mile in length of bamboo wands surmounted by oranges. India, in *tomasha*,[1] is a very different India from the India of workaday life. But I loved the *tomasha* and I saw the oranges on the sticks with the eyes of the delighted children, who gazed with gravity on this rich and golden road.

We broke up the camp at Peshawar, went by rail to Lahore, and then set off on tour through the Districts of the Delhi Division. At one place, Sir Charles Aitchison, who was indisposed, asked me to see an Indian lady who had asked him for an interview. I was to receive her and report to him the object of her visit, but not to express any opinion. The lady came in a shut-up carriage, and her servants arranged a screen so that she might come to the veranda of my tent without being seen. She wore a dark dress, was tall and graceful, and she spoke excellent Hindustáni with

[1] Entertainment—excitement: gala: spectacle.

a pleasant refined voice. She regretted Sir Charles's illness: she had often heard of him, that he was kind and good, and after much hesitation, she determined on this, her second pilgrimage to Mecca, to ask for his advice. She was English, and had been a child in the Mutiny. Her parents were both killed, and a Moslem had carried her off to his house, had treated her with great kindness and respect, and had married her. She was now a widow, well off and happy, but she wanted advice as to whether it was her duty to inform her relatives in England that she was alive. So far as she knew, her family imagined that she had perished with her parents. "What do you think?" she suddenly asked. I could have told her, but I said my instructions were to report to Sir Charles, and I knew that his advice would be good. "But you are English, as I was, and you can tell me what you think." I asked her whether she could read English, and she said: "Of course, my kind Lord bought me English books." So I arranged that her head servant should come that evening and I would give him a sealed envelope containing Sir Charles's opinion. The opinion was that it was best not to write home.

My second season in Simla was, from the point of view of work, much the same. I was not quite so ignorant, but still knew nothing of Land Revenue. But socially everything was changed. I was married. When the news of my engagement came out, two high officials spoke to me on the question of matrimony. One, the Commander-in-Chief, highly approved. "I was younger than you and was heavily in debt when I married. I was a subaltern; my wife kept my pay and got me out of debt, and here I am Commander-in-Chief." The other, the Financial Commissioner of the Punjáb, also approved. He said: "Marry young. You will then be able to see your children growing up before you are old." One of my friends to whom I have referred, married before he came out to India, and his life was most successful. But every Civilian must judge for himself. If one has the good fortune to win a wife who does not mind "roughing it," long journeys, constant transfers; sometimes a lonely life, away from doctors, dentists and civilisation; a wife who likes India, the Indians and the adventure of Indian life; a wife of noble patience and pluck —then the sooner he marries the better. I had this good fortune. My wife had these qualities and India accentuated them.

We were married at Mount Abu in 1885. My wife's brother brought her to the Bradfords' house, and it was arranged that after the wedding we should join Sir Charles Aitchison's camp in Rawal Pindi, where the Viceroy, Lord Dufferin, was meeting the new Amir of Kabul—the great Abdur Rahmán. On the way down from Lahore to Mount Abu there were two English officers in my carriage, one rather elderly and the other young. At a station on the way down, an Indian dressed in a black alpaca gown entered our carriage and sat down opposite to me. The elderly Englishman exploded with wrath, said to his companion that the country was going to the dogs, and that he would not submit to the indignity of having a black man pushing into his carriage. The Indian, who had a very pleasant face and the whitest teeth I have ever seen, sat unmoved, and I hoped he had not comprehended the vitriolic remarks of the irritated Englishman. I noticed that he had a black bag labelled "records," and imagining that he might be a member of the Settlement Staff working in the District through which we were passing, I asked him in Hindustáni whether he was doing settlement work. He replied in perfect English that he was in the postal department. I said I was sorry he understood English. "Why?" he asked. "Because you must have heard the most improper remarks that that man in the other corner has been making." Before he could say a word, the man in the corner turned the tongue of vituperation on me. "Who was I, and what business had I to interfere?" Somewhat priggishly perhaps, I said I was a Justice of the Peace for India, and that, as he had used language calculated to cause a breach of the peace, I should call in the police at the Umballa station unless he apologised to the Indian. I gave him my name and asked him to give his name, but he went on storming. When he paused for breath, the Indian quietly said that he did not mind what the gentleman in the corner had said. "I know many Sahibs and have known many Viceroys and Commanders-in-Chief. This watch was given to me by Lord Ripon, and nearly every Sahib in Simla and in the Punjáb knows me and is my friend. Therefore, why should I care for the abuse of a person who does not know me? I beg of you to let the matter drop." It was like interfering in the quarrel of a man and his wife; but, in my inexperience, I persisted. The young officer seemed anxious to calm his companion, so I talked to him and said I meant business, and felt sure that my Chief, Sir Charles Aitchison, would support me. We were now close to Umballa, and at last the Colonel said, to my delight: "Well, I am sorry, I did not know he spoke English." All three got out at Umballa, and the Indian came back and thanked me for taking his part, and added: "If ever I can help you, you may depend on me," and gave me his card. His name was Daulat Rám. I lost the card and forgot all about the incident. I have travelled much in India, and this is the only instance I have personally known of insult and rudeness towards Indians on the railway.

The camp at Rawal Pindi was a splendid and historical event. It was marred by unusually bad weather, but we all knew that much depended on the long and daily conversations between the Viceroy and the great Amir. He certainly looked and carried himself like a strong and confident man, and as I studied his face and his gestures I thought of the great figures in history which come so suddenly and unexpectedly from the wild countries of Central Asia—rulers of men, fearless, fear-inspiring despots, men of great vision and imagination, humorous, generous, but often, according to our standards, cruel. But if we had lived in Afghanistan our standards would be different. Abdur Rahmán was the greatest Oriental of the Victorian era. He ruled his restless country with an iron hand. Crime was unknown in that land of robbers. He was a true, though not an effusive ally of the British Government, most faithful to engagement.

In the long years which followed the eventful meeting at Rawal Pindi, tales would come down by the caravans, tales told with bated breath, for the great Amir had long ears and a short way with the gossip and tale-bearer. I will mention two stories which illustrate his method. He always made punishment an object lesson, a real deterrent.

The head of the Police, the Kotwál of Kabul, was a man of amorous complexion, and the citizens of the town resented his attentions to their wives and daughters. The Amir was sitting in Durbár one cold winter day—and winter is cold in Kabul—and in a casual way addressed the Kotwál. "They tell me, my friend, that you have a hot temperament." The Kotwál, hitherto a great favourite, laughingly deprecated the suggestion. "Take him up to the top of yonder hill and tie him to a stake and pour cold water on him. That will cool the Kotwál." And in the evening the water froze and the Kotwál died in ice.

These durbárs lasted for many hours. In spite of the Amir's quips, and the stories of his life in exile and his sage remarks on the world and its ways, the courtiers who attended the Court—and none dared to be absent—found that sitting in silence became tedious, so they invented a language of the eyelids. So expert were they in these signals that one of them could signal verses from Hafiz in this fashion. Sometimes the Court would be enlivened by the arrival of some envoy from afar, by some petitioner, for all had access to the great Amir. Sometimes a rich present would come to placate the power of Kabul. One such present gratified Abdur Rahmán. It was a tray covered by beautiful coins of gold called mohurs.[1] The Amir bade a page hand it round for the inspection of his Court. One of the courtiers dexterously slipped a coin into the long boot of his right leg, and the tray passed round and was replaced at the foot of the throne, and the conversation, or rather monologue, dragged on for another hour. Then the Amir said that as a young man he was famous for the beauty of his legs; but of course now that he had become more sedentary there were perhaps others among those present who had more shapely legs. The courtiers with one voice said that this was impossible. "We will see," said the Amir, and he called to a page and told him to draw off the long black boot of his right leg, and then to take off the boots of the courtiers. When the page came to the unwise courtier, he put out his

[1] A beautiful gold coin worth fifteen rupees; much used by Indian callers as a ceremonial present, which is touched and remitted. Mohurs, and Chiks worth four rupees (Sequins) were convenient terms for bets.

left leg and the boot was taken off. When all were unbooted, the Amir displayed his right leg and all praised its beauty. But he said that this might be flattery, and the Cazi[1] was called in to act as judge. He glanced at the two rows of outstretched legs and at once decided that the leg of the ruler of the God-granted country was not only the most shapely of the legs in the hall, but was without doubt the most beautiful leg in the world. A murmur of approval followed. But the Amir said: "Stay; one of the legs is a left leg—take off the boot from the right leg and give it a shake." And out fell the gold coin. "Send for the executioner and off with his right leg!" And the executioner, with the hot oil which is used for amputations, came and in the presence of them all the leg was taken off at the knee.

Before the great assembly at Rawal Pindi broke up there came alarming news from Panjdeh, and all of us thought that the day had come, and that the Russian scare would take concrete form. Soldiers hurried away from the camp and everyone hastened back to their duties. I was bound for Simla and had telegraphed to Umballa for a conveyance to carry my wife and myself to Simla—a long distance by road. We arrived at Umballa on a sultry night. The station was crowded. At last I saw a clerk of the Postal Department and asked him where I should find my *dák ghári*[2] for which I had telegraphed. He said that all the conveyances were taken and that I could not get up to Simla for another ten days. "Is there an hotel here?" "Yes, but it is full." I was in despair, when a man dressed in a black alpaca gown came up and asked if he could help me. I told him my desperate plight. "Ah," he said, "that is all right. I was going up in my inspection carriage with the party of the Commander-in-Chief, but he will excuse me, and your party will find the journey very comfortable." This friend in need was Daulat Rám, the head of the postal and posting service from Umballa to Simla. In the flurry and press of the crowd I had not recognised

[1] An exponent of Mahomedan Law.

[2] *Dák* means transport by relays of men or horses, and is now used for post or mail. *Ghári* is a cart or carriage. *Brum Ghári* is the brougham; *Fitton Ghári* is the phaeton.

him as the man who had intruded on the Colonel's peace. But he had recognised me.

I have only told this story because it bears out a conclusion which I have formed regarding the gratitude of Indians. I have often heard men say that the Indians are not grateful and that in their language there is no equivalent of the expression "thank you." It is true, perhaps, that the ordinary Indian is not grateful for anything done for him in the daily routine of official work. I have known many cases of Englishmen sacrificing themselves, and giving their lives to save Indians in time of famine, cholera and plague. And, indeed, every member of the Indian Civil Service was ready in emergencies to risk his life for the Indians committed to his charge. This fact increased the prestige of the Service, but it did not always win personal gratitude for the individual. It was part of his official duty. The Indians counted on his devotion, applauded it, and soon forgot it when the calamity had passed. It is the unpaid courtesies which appeal to them. I remember an old Civilian, who had worked hard and had done his duty officially. He was retiring on pension, and on such an occasion there is a crowd of friends, British and Indian, to say farewell at the railway station, with bouquets and necklaces of sweet-smelling flowers. But when this official left, the platform was empty, and he exclaimed: "After thirty-five years' faithful service only a missionary and a *box-wallah!*"[1] He had done his duty officially, but probably he had done nothing for the Indians in a private capacity. If an Englishman goes out of his way to help an Indian, or any member of that Indian's family, my experience is that there is very real gratitude.

I can give many instances of this, but two will be sufficient. The great Minister of Nepal, Jung Bahádur, was going to an important assembly in Calcutta, and was anxious that his famous string of elephants, of which he was very proud, should reach the capital in good condition. But on the long march from Nepal the elephants grew thin, and the official in charge was in great alarm. At one of the halting places this man heard the praises of a famous

[1] Pedlar or packman.

sportsman, a planter, and rode out to see him. He told him that his place, indeed his life, depended on a good supply of sugar cane for the elephants. The planter at once responded and sent in loads of sugar cane to the elephants, and did more, for he sent supplies to the stages ahead. So the elephants arrived sleek and well in Calcutta, and Jung Bahádur was pleased. He was told of the generous planter who had given the sugar cane. Some six months later the planter received an invitation from Jung Bahádur to join one of his famous beats for tigers in the Nepal country. He went, and Jung Bahádur gave him a permit to shoot every year, and supplied elephants and tents. He also, in his gratitude, gave the planter valuable concessions for timber. "For," said Jung Bahádur, "this Englishman did more than he was asked."[1]

In the Mutiny a great firm of Indian bankers had promised to deliver thirty lakhs of rupees on a certain date, and the silver was sent off in good time. But the convoy fell in with the mutineers who were hastening to Agra, and the silver was taken. Before the rebels reached Agra a young officer of Indian cavalry caught them up, and the mutineers fled, leaving the treasure. The young officer's orders were to proceed with his troopers to a place at some distance: he was moving off, when one of the bankers' men told him of the destination of the treasure, and added that

[1] I heard much of Jung Bahádur's daring and prowess. The late Sir Dighton Probyn, who knew him well, once told me this story. Jung Bahádur visited England before the Mutiny, fell deeply in love with an enchantress and begged her to give up London and go with him to Nepal. She went as far as Paris, and when they parted, Jung Bahádur gave her a ring and promised that he would fulfil any behest she might send with the ring. Time passed and the Mutiny was at its worst and many feared that England would founder in the black waves. Much depended on Nepal—would she side with the Mutineers or with us? In London someone remembered the devotion of Jung Bahádur, and an Equerry from Buckingham Palace was sent to ask the beautiful Aspasia to use her influence with Jung Bahádur. But she had her pride: "If the Queen wishes anything of me, the Queen herself must ask for it." So she was commanded to the Palace, and the message went, carried by swift packet-boat to the East. The Mutineers received no help from Nepal, but perished in thousands in the malarious swamps of the Terai, where they were driven after the long agony of Lucknow. Jung Bahádur kept them off the high ground of the hills, and our cavalry along the Frontier prevented them from seeking the healthy air of the plains of India.

Sir Power Palmer, who was then a young cavalry officer, told me later, when he was Commander-in-Chief, of the ague-stricken spectres he had seen as he patrolled the boundary. It would have been merciful to have killed them, but Cawnpore was in men's minds.

unless it arrived in three days the firm would be dishonoured for the first time in history. The young officer was moved by the story, and by hard marches and by a considerable detour managed to deliver the thirty lakhs on the very day. Thus the honour of the bankers was saved. Time passed and the officer heard nothing of the bankers; but years afterwards, when the officer was married in England, a magnificent wedding present arrived. The children of the officer grew up and were married. How the bankers gained their information as to the events no one knows, but there has never been a marriage in this family without a splendid gift from India.

In my own case, for over eighteen years I travelled from Umballa to Simla in great comfort and always could count on a conveyance, and Daulat Rám was always there to greet me. He was a brilliant organiser, and when a Commission on Transportation came from America, they said that Daulat Rám's system was the most admirable scheme of road transport which they had seen in any country. He was always quiet and modest. I never heard him give orders, but his Staff, drivers and stable-men, tough and sometimes turbulent, were devoted to the seemingly gentle "Lála Sahib." I asked him, when I saw him for the last time as I was leaving India, the secret of his success, and he replied: "Pardon my rudeness, but the reason of my success is that I ran my own show and had no Sahib over me." He was my firm friend till he died, and his family are my friends. His grandson was with me in England in 1923, and, following the road I took in 1879, he goes out as a Punjáb Civilian.

Towards the end of the Simla season of 1885, my good friend, the Revenue Secretary, suggested that I should go away for six months and work with a Settlement Officer. This was a great chance, but it had its drawbacks. I was told that it would be impossible to take my wife, as I should have to travel light. But she saw the importance of my learning my work, so leaving her with the family of our friends, the Ilberts, I started off on reduced pay and in reduced spirits, for six months' camping. Listening to the jangling bar of the *Tonga*[1] yoke as I sped down the dusty

[1] A two-wheeled cart drawn by two ponies.

road to the plains, I wondered whether I had not been foolish in declining the offer of Sir Edward Buck to go home in charge of the Indian exhibits for the Colinderies Exhibition.

The "Settlement" of a District is the most important and the most educative work which can fall to a Civilian. He has to survey the land; study the various soils; the crops; the conditions and resources of the peasants; the land tenure; the communications and the markets. He has also to ascertain the characters and methods of the village headmen, and the village accountants; and generally he has to learn, and learn thoroughly, all that concerns the agriculture and the well-being of the villages. Finally, he has to "settle" for periods of twenty or thirty years the land revenue which each village is to pay to the State, and has to decide in each village the actual fields which belong to the individual peasant, and the amount of the village revenue for which that individual is responsible. It is a work which never ceases day and night. All day the Settlement Officer rides from village to village inspecting and checking the survey and the entries in the field register, making notes on the appearance of the crops, the people and the cattle, talking to the cultivators and watching them at their work; sitting by the wells and judging their capacity for irrigation; and, at night, after long talks at the village *chaupál*, writing up notes in his tent. This work may last from three to five years, but the *Bandobast*[1] *Sahib* goes on, never tiring and always interested. He naturally becomes fond of the people, because he knows that their happiness for twenty or thirty years will depend on his valuation. It is therefore essential that his proposals should be supported by painfully-won knowledge, and by practical, almost expert, reasoning. He has to convince three authorities, known as the Settlement Commissioner, the Financial Commissioner, and the Provincial Government. While the quiet Settlement Officer is plodding along, the Government of India wants money

[1] *Bandobast* signifies arrangement, scheme or programme. No higher praise than to tell a man that he has made a *Pucka Bandobast:* no greater blame than to say that the *Bandobast* is *Cutcha*. In India, everything is *Pucka* or *Cutcha*. Houses and roads are *Pucka* or *Cutcha*, according as they are made of burnt brick or stone, or of sun-dried bricks, according as they are macadamised or of earth. *Pucka* means "ripe" or "mature": it also means "thorough." *Cutcha* means "unripe," "half-baked."

for some new scheme of administrative advance, and the Provincial Government wants more money for education or police. Everyone wants money, and the man who finds the money is the peasant, that splendid, patient man, that "ryot" who never riots, unless the village money-lender drives him too hard. So the good Settlement Officer must hold the balance between the Government, who say "give," and his friends, the peasants, who point to the poor crops and say they are ruined. It is a curious fact that just a year or so before the Settlement Officer arrives in the district, the crops have a mysterious way of falling off.

The Settlement area of Kurnal-Umballa was full of memories of the Sikh wars and of the Mutiny. I went to Kurnal to receive instructions, and called on an old lady, the oldest resident. I saw many empty bungalows, but very few people, and remarked to her that the white population seemed small. "Yes," she said, "they are mostly in the cemetery."

There is a sadness in these deserted habitations of our countrymen: from the first they were apart from the genius of the neighbourhood, and now, in their desolation, they are shunned as haunted houses. Sometimes I would come across in waste and distant places the untimely tomb of some gallant officer who had fallen fighting, but I never felt that this forlorn spot was British soil for ever; indeed I always wished that the pyre rather than the grave had been our portion when the end came. The hot winds, the deluge of the rains and the resistless fig tree soon deal with these vain sepulchres. But even sadder was the sight of a moated and castellated hall, where once a soldier diplomat held high state, now desolate and "full of doleful creatures." One night, driven by a pitiless rain and cold, I set my bed in such a hall, but the great bats and the black swarm of musk-rats prevented sleep.

For six months I worked away. My chief was a very kind and helpful master, and after a time he entrusted to me the work of assessment in the circle where I was camping. This made me feel the great responsibility of mv worked and though my valuations would be very soldier diplomat and checked by my Chief, I had learnt swarm entrusted by this time to know that it is the first pen that counts. As Sir Charles Aitchison often told me: "The young Assistant, if he knows his work, has more power than the Lieutenant-Governor." And this is true in most parts of the world.

It would only weary my readers if I described my daily work. I was taught my business by two excellent Indians of great experience. One was a fine, generous Moslem, who rode good horses and was always called by the people Shah Sahib. There was much of the Mogul in him, and later on I induced him to follow me to Kashmir. The other was a very astute Hindu. Some defect in his eyes gave him a sinister look, but he was better at the work than even the Shah Sahib. He was unpopular, but he got good work out of his subordinates, and was always accurate and never in arrears. We became good friends and had long talks. One day, to my surprise, he flashed out at me: "You have made us a nation of weavers." I asked why. "Because you have forbidden us to carry arms."

In the circle assigned to me there were one hundred villages, occupied by Rájputs who had been converted to Islam, with Sikh overlords. It was curious to notice in the *Chaupál*[1] in the evening the Sikh sitting on the bedstead and the Rájput squatting on the ground. Some of the Sikh landlords were very cruel. There was a custom by which the landlord took half the standing crop, and also decided when the crop should be cut. To injure his tenants, and to prevent them from establishing occupancy rights, one of the landlords had for no reason declined to cut ripe crops, which were ruined by birds and vermin, and eventually began to sprout, and as I rode by I saw many acres of good crops spoiled in this way. Next day, and for days after, I came across other instances of his gross tyranny, and I reported him and had his name removed from the list of those who had the privilege of attending the durbárs held by the Lieutenant-Governor.

In April the sun grows very hot, and in the poor tent which was assigned to me the smell of the warm roof was overpowering. I was sitting in my tent one evening

[1] A little open square in the village where the people gather in the evening to talk and smoke.

at sunset, when my orderly announced the arrival of the tyrannous Sikh, who had hitherto avoided me. He knew—for nothing is hidden from the Indians—that I had reported him. I was therefore surprised at his visit, and pleased, as I thought I might persuade him to be kinder to his tenants. I rose, gave him my own chair and sat on my bed. After compliments, I asked him what he thought of the crops and the weather. He said: "I am too ill to think of crops." I expressed my heart-felt regrets. "I have come," he said, "because I hear you have a famous remedy (*Dáru*) sent out from England. It passed my residence." Then I saw. A kind relative had sent me a small cask of whisky. It ought to have gone to Simla, but it came to a station about thirty miles from camp. It had arrived leaking, and the station-master had sent me a peremptory letter complaining of the smell of my cask and demanding its instant removal. So I sent my camel man to bring out my cask, and the smell of it as it passed through the villages excited the longing of the Sikh. I told my servant to bring some of the "remedy" in an enamelled tin jug, and I poured out a glass of the whisky into another enamelled tin mug. I asked him whether I should add soda-water, but he shook his head and said good medicine was better without water. He drank the spirit off at one gulp. I again approached the subject of crops, but he said nothing, and pushed the mug towards me. "I feel better," he said, "far better, but not completely well," and I poured out the rest—in all it was more than a pint. He again drank it off, and again I tossed the ball of conversation; but he sat silent. When after a decent interval I said I had letters to write and suggested that he might be going, "Go!" he said, "I'm not drunk yet." So I called for his man of affairs, and he went off in great displeasure.

These Sikh landlords drank hard, and had none of the charm of the Rájputs of Rajputána. I used to call on them in order to induce them to be fair to their tenants. I take the following extracts from my diary:

"Visit Shamsir Singh of ——. A long room opening on a court: rather dark: English carpet: four or five oil lamps, and a globe with an old candle. Some rather gaudy oleographs: a table with oranges: hard-boiled eggs and a cake. Tea very sweet; one metal cup; one brass lotah;[1] a glass; a sugar basin, and my own cup, which had been borrowed from my tent. The old uncle, Lal Singh, a typical Sikh, dressed in an old-fashioned silk coat with gold braid. I apologised to him for having twice called at his castle at an early hour, when I found him with nothire on but his bed-quilt. Shamsir Singh was dressed in an English grey tail-coat. His brother and his son completed the party. The writer of the family at my request read out the history of the house, compiled by Shamsir Singh. Among other facts the history states that Lal Singh's share of the grant from Government was resumed for murder. The old man never winced, but stretched out his legs and looked around at the comfortless and incongruous room in which he was born just seventy years ago. After a very interesting conversation, we all go out to the village Chaupál and sit round a good bonfire. Shamsir Singh evidently treats the villagers well, as they crowd to the fire and talk independently enough. I ask my stock question: 'What do you talk about when you gather here of an evening?' 'We talk of one another's fields, of the harvest and of the day when we have to pay the Land Revenue.' Then I ask them what are the most unpopular departments of Government. 'The local revenue authority, and next the police,' and they tell me details. Then we talk of the great army which has recently passed through the District on its way to Delhi. They had not thought much about the Army, nor why it was going to Delhi, but they had thought deeply on a remark made by one of the messengers[2] of the local Revenue office: 'If you do not furnish the supplies, the Army will loot your villages.' The amount of damage done to our good name by these underlings on five rupees a month is incalculable. Then I call for a story, and Rugbir Singh, a Hindu Rájput, tells in verse, learned by him from

[1] A small brass pot used by Hindus for drinking and sometimes for cooking.

[2] *Chuprasi.* A man on low pay attached to every office and official in India. He carries on his sash or coat a badge (*chupras*) indicating his office. In my experience he has done infinite harm to our reputation. Ali Baba is moderate when he says: "The Chuprassi paints his master in colours drawn from his own black heart. Every lie he tells, every insinuation he throws out, every demand he makes, is endorsed with his master's name. He is the arch-slanderer of our name in India."

a Bráhman, the story of Rama's march to Ceylon. The wicked uncle is much amused. He likes poetry, and used to spend days with Mahomed Shah, a celebrated ascetic, listening to the songs which minstrels sang at his abode. So fond was he, a Sikh, of this pious Moslem, that he offered to dig a well and plant a garden around his cell. But the ascetic said: 'If you make a garden of my waste retreat I will go off to the jungle.' The old man told me that he had a house at Thanesar. I said, 'Do you go there to worship and bathe?' 'No,' said he, 'I go there to shoot.' 'Yes, and to bathe too,' said his nephew, who wanted to keep up appearances before the villagers. 'No,' said the old Sikh, 'I go there to shoot.'"

One day Uncle Lal Singh told me how, in the days of "derring do," his father galloped about this country throwing his turban into one village and his whip into another to establish his claim by conquest.

Turning over a page I come to another entry in my diary: "Get up at dawn. Head Surveyor asks permission to read a poem before we start. It is cold, but I have to listen. It is in praise of me. Much sickness in village. News of death of Gholam Ghaus; died of a cough. Up to the last kept calling for his horse, as he wanted to join us. A quiet sensible man: had travelled to Haidarabad in the South. The wonders he had seen in Bombay had made him prematurely old. We met the barber, who is off to give news of the death. See religious house of Mahadeo at ——: very popular and beneficent. At another shrine talk to a jolly friar. I ask him when he is going for a ten years' spell of the jungle, and he roars with laughter. Meet a gloomy peasant—his gram[1] crop ruined by the sand in the air: his wheat destroyed by rust, rats and locusts. I remark that in spite of this it looks a good crop. 'Yes,' says the Hindu moneylender, 'I notice a fine lot of grass.' The Sikh landlord presents me with a 'Dali,'[2] consisting of one bottle of brandy, two tins of jam and a bottle of lemonade, which

[1] A pulse used for horse food. *Cicer arietinum*. Gram-fed mutton was a luxury, and the epithet "gram-fed" came to be applied to the great and privileged, e.g., Gram-fed Secretariat.

[2] Basket or tray in which gifts of fruit or vegetables are made to visitors. Every day the gardener brings his *Dali* of vegetables to the veranda.

I return with thanks. Somewhat embarrassing to the oil presser to be visited by me and about fifty visitors. The buffalo, blindfolded, goes on turning the mill, the oil-presser feigns ignorance as to the relative virtues of linseed, rape and taramira, and says that the Headman knows more about oil than he does. The Headman agrees. Meet the wicked uncle, Lal Singh. His horse rears and the old man is thrown. He is up again in a second and remounts the young colt. He has a perfect seat. His nephews show no concern. They tell me of a neighbour, one Jasmir Singh. He owns an elephant, and the elephant was attached for a debt. So Jasmir Singh sends the elephant into Patiala territory. Another Sikh who had become surety for Jasmir Singh hurries off in pursuit, but when he and his friends find the elephant the Mahout [1] refuses to drive the elephant back. So the brave Sikh says that man can die but once, and in spite of the jeers and warnings of the Mahout he gets on the elephant and drives him home. The whole countryside is amazed, and I hear mention of it frequently. Jasmir Singh is always in debt, and his one asset, the elephant, has been attached three times.

"In one village a Jat bride is leaving her home in a palankin, weeping and wailing according to custom. Her bearers trudge away with her over the fields. The bridegroom's relatives sit smoking the stirrup pipe. No one takes the slightest interest in bride or bridegroom.

"Find Dewa Singh, the Headman of a village on his back. He over-ate at a wedding and fell off the roof of the house and broke his thigh. I advise him to be carried to Umballa to be treated in the Dispensary. He acquiesces, but my companion says that this is only politeness and nothing would induce any of them to go near Umballa."

A part of the country in which I worked was most unhealthy. It was known as the Kurushetra, and its chief town was the sacred Thanesar. It has a double claim to distinction, as it was not only the theatre of the Great War described in the Sanskrit, the Mahábhárata, but was also the cradle of the Bráhman system. The people all seemed

[1] Driver of an elephant. A dangerous calling when a male elephant goes mad (*Mast*).

to suffer from spleen. In one place, Nawad, they told me that no man lived to be forty. The people attributed their bad health to the oily scum of the water of the Markanda river. One village, which had two hundred houses thirty years ago, now has only thirty-one houses. Pehowa was another very sacred town in this horrible region. I met a body of Kashmir officials who were carrying the bones not consumed on the pyre of the late Maharája of Kashmir. These bones, known as *Phul*, are taken to Pehowa and Thanesar, and finally to Hurdwár, and at each place the Bráhman priests received one lakh of rupees. The remains were carried on a richly caparisoned elephant, followed by four cavalrymen all smoking hookahs. In front some twelve infantrymen shambled along, preceded by a raucous brass band who were playing "Cheer, boys, cheer!" But a less cheerful company I have never seen. When I arrived at Pehowa the Bráhmans were quarrelling over the division of the money, and the Head of them had gone off in pursuit of the Kashmir deputation. I never saw a more repulsive group than the Bráhmans of Pehowa and Thanesar. The former ate meat and spent the offerings of the pious on liquor and other luxuries.

The higher country of Kaital was a pleasant change from this diseased and priest-ridden swamp. But if the rains failed there was great suffering. Right away from the villages I came across an American missionary and his wife. He told me that the Palwa grass of this tract was equal to the best blue Kentucky. The missionary did a big business in cattle.

The most delightful part of my charge was the country round Jagádri. The most interesting man in this town was Lála Bansi Lál, a great banker and merchant. He was a handsome old man of fine presence, and had a large household, and most of the best land in the neighbourhood either belonged to him or was mortgaged to him. The people said that he was a hard man, but they all respected and indeed liked him, for he was very charitable to the pilgrims on their way to the sacred source of Mother Ganges. I often visited his Sadhabirt (a hostel for the religious), where Bansi Lál gave shelter and food to the pilgrims. They begged their oil and vegetables from the bazaar. There was also a well-kept Serai for travellers, which was managed by the bread-sellers of the town. They charged a small sum for food and shelter. It was pleasant to see the people so happy and so appreciative of their good quarters, and I learnt much from my visits to these huge inns; but it was not pleasant to find sleeping in a corner room an Englishman, a well-educated man of good family, who had gone down hill. The Indians liked him for his kindness and simplicity. He was fond of books, drink and sport. He used to sleep by day and drink at night. I found that it was impossible to help him. I came across other cases of a like nature.

Sometimes these derelict men were interesting, and I never felt for the poor loafer the hatred which old John Company had for the interloper. I have seen the loafer as a troublesome and limpet-like guest in a Dák Bungalow, running up a bill and terrifying the hypnotised Khansáman; as an unwelcome visitor to my camp far away from any railway, indignant and abusive when offered food without drink, and a pass to Bombay instead of a gift of money. I have met him at railway junctions, uncertain and seeking my advice as to the city or the Rája he should next exploit; have admired him as a temporary and wholly inefficient servant of some ostentatious Indian magnate who preferred a white coachman to safety. There was always the inevitable end—fiery country spirits and a bad smash, and then to pastures new. The kindly villagers would find him food and shelter, indeed, do anything if he would only move on to the next parish as quickly as possible.

The loafer could at times tell stories of the life of the bazaar and the views of the villagers which were new and startling. He had no pride and the people seemed to throw aside their reserve when talking to the white vagrant in shabby clothes. Sometimes he would settle for good in a village, and I was told of a German who had established himself as Headman of a village between Delhi and Meerut, who sheltered and saved two English women in the Mutiny. Then there was Shepherd—General Shepherdhoff—late of the Imperial Russian Bodyguard, an expert swordsman. In 1902 this versatile Slav, who had been in jail for five years for river Dacoity in Bengal, was convicted of fraud and was sentenced to six months' imprisonment. Just before this, swordsman though he was, in trying to slice a potato, on which his Indian servant lightly rested his foot, the General blundered and unfortunately cut off the man's heel.

When I was in Peshawar two quaint loafers came in from over the Border, and I took their statement. One was a deserter from the Army, and the other a sailor who had left his ship in Calcutta. The sailor played the fiddle and the soldier danced. They passed from village to village and found their way to the Frontier. They went up the Kurram valley and eventually reached Kabul unhurt, because the Afgháns regarded them as mad and so their lives were sacred. The Amir Abdur Rahmán heard of their arrival in his capital and they were commanded to give a performance. The sailor described the reception by the great Amir. "His Majesty took a fancy to us at once and sent us food and good blankets and had us to the Palace the next day. 'I like your looks' he said, 'and to-morrow I'll send you a Mullah, and he will make you into good Mahomedans.' But we said: 'No, we are pucka Christians and it is no use sending the reverend gent to us.' On this the Amir got angry and called us names, and that very day sent us off down the road to Peshawar."

They were a feckless, hopeless folk, and India is a bad place for the unemployed European. I never knew a loafer who made good. Stowaways sometimes won through. I met one who became an importer of Australian horses. One of his horses won the Viceroy's cup, and in honour of the event Lord William Beresford drove the whilom stowaway home from the races. As they were passing the Ochterlony Monument in the great Park of Calcutta, he said: "That monument looks different to-day, different to what it looked when I used to sleep by it at night and live on bananas in the bazaar." "How did you pay for the bananas?" asked Lord William. "Pay? Bless you, I never paid. I used to bite the end off a banana and then ask the price, and when the fruit-seller said, "One pice, sahib," I would hand it back. But the fruit-seller would always say: "Keep it, sahib."

Sometimes I heard of mysterious Europeans in remote places. In 1905 the English Police Officer at Hurdwar told me that there was a white woman living with the Jogis in the caverns of sacred Jumnotri, thirteen thousand feet above sea level.

Officials shun the loafer, and he, for good reasons, avoids the official: he has no wish for deportation. India suits him: he hates the strenuous life of the West. He is often a philosopher, a cynic, but he knows much that is hidden from us. He has his own point of view, and my well educated acquaintance in the Serai dispelled some of my general ideas regarding the Indians.

CHAPTER VI

"Towered cities please us then,
And the busy hum of men."
—MILTON

Serious Illness of my Wife—Kindness of Neighbours—Offer of New Appointment—Work in Punjáb Secretariat—Under-Secretary to Government of India—Lord Dufferin's fine Council—Submit Cases to Viceroy—Concession Hunters—Charm of Lord Dufferin—Lady Dufferin's Fund for Women of India—Rudyard Kipling's poem "The Song of the Women"—What "the Purdah Cloaked"—Civil Servants Overburdened with Work—District Officer between the Devil and the Deep Sea—Interviews Abridged—Value of Silence—Calcutta; its Splendid Hospitality—Tours to Madras and Burma—Christmas at the Lighthouse—Lord Dufferin Goes—Lord Lansdowne Comes—Accept Offer of Settlement Work in Kashmir—Respective Merits of Life in the Districts and in Secretariat—Charm of Simla.

TOWARDS the end of my six months of Settlement work I was recalled to Simla by an alarming telegram telling me that my wife was seriously ill, and I went through the worst time of my life. I shall never forget the skill and devotion of the two Civil Surgeons of Simla, nor the wonderful and exceeding kindness of our friends. The Civil Surgeons of India belonged to the splendid Indian Medical Service, and in times of sickness and distress it was a comfort to know that there was always in reach not only a highly skilled doctor, but also a real friend, who understood our work and trials, and was, in the highest sense, sympathetic. As for the kindness of the English in India when trouble comes, it was a revelation to me to learn what women will do when they fight with death. Many, whom we only just knew by sight, offered to sit up at night, and some, only known to us by name, sent jellies and soups of their own making. In the 'eighties, nurses were almost unknown even in the larger towns, and the few who followed that noble calling were untrained. But for self-sacrificing devotion and delicate understanding, the English woman in India was hard to beat, and I owe my wife's recovery to two dear ladies who never flagged nor failed. And later, when real nurses came to India, I have known many cases where the typhoid-stricken boy, fresh from England, was saved from death by a complete stranger, who would take him from his poor little bungalow to her cooler residence, and win him back to life. There is no place in the world like India for real friendship, and the greatest friendship usually springs from some great trouble, when the barriers of reserve are broken down, and behind the brusque manner and the cold aloofness, one finds a wealth of goodness and kindness. Just as the poor are kind to the poor, so in India the white exiles cannot do enough for one another. Much has been written of the *Memsahib*;[1] but when the great account is made up, her sweet charity in sickness and in sorrow will outbalance the little faults and the foibles to which men, as well as women, in India must plead guilty. For it is a land not merely of regrets, but of trials. Climate, separation, long voyages and short purses would try the temper of angels. Looking back over long years, and with the critical and sometimes censorious mind which comes as one grows old, I have nothing but admiration for the Memsahib, and pride that England produces such brave and patient women still as brave and steadfast as they were in the Mutiny.

One day, as I walked along the Mall in sad mood, I met a stranger who hailed me. He was the Postmaster-General of India, and he offered me the appointment of Postmaster-General of Madras. He said I should be my own master down there, and pointed out the many advantages of the post. It sounded to me delightful, and I asked his permission to consult my chief, Sir Charles Aitchison. I wrote to him for advice, and he said he would talk to me when I reached Lahore. I went down and stayed at Government House. In the morning, at breakfast, Sir Charles said he would speak to me that evening after lawn tennis. And then he spoke. "It is the temptation of the Devil. Your wife is ill. The high pay is an attraction in your

[1] A corruption of Madam *Sahib*.

present circumstances; but I advise you to refuse it, because it takes you out of the ordinary line. It is good work, no doubt, but it is not your work." And he added this maxim: "Never ask for a post, and never refuse a post. If you ask for a post and fail in it, Government will never forgive you. If you fail in a post which Government offers to you, that is their blunder, and they will forgive you." I went away disappointed, but Sir Charles was right, as in my experience he always was. All the same he was advising me to break his own rule.

My six months' work under the Settlement Officer made all the difference to me, and I now understood the meaning of Land Revenue. But I never felt that I was of much assistance to the office and was always conscious of the overwhelming knowledge and experience of the Revenue Secretary. He was a tremendous worker and made a worship of his work. Once he handed me two reports to review and said: "Work entirely on percentages." The reports bristled with statistics. An excellent European clerk came into my room, and I asked him whether he was used to taking out percentages. He smiled and said: "I do little else." And when I told him I was not used to this particular exercise, he said that he was not pressed that morning and would gladly help me; and in a very short time he brought me the figures. I wrote the two reviews before the evening, and the next day the Secretary came into my room, evidently very pleased, and he showed me Sir Charles's "complimentary remarks." "I don't know how you did the reviews so quickly," he said, "it must have taken you some time to work out the percentages." I explained that the excellent clerk had done this. "But," he said, "I expected you to do this yourself." I then gave him my views. "The clerk was practically my clerk; the work of taking out percentages was a clerk's work and not the work of an Under-Secretary; and if I had spent hours on these figures I should have been in no way wiser, and the reviews would have been delayed a day." But he was disappointed in me. He believed that downright dogged drudgery was the only training for a young man. Under him I worked long office hours, and took home heavy tin boxes laden with files, but in spite of it all I did not learn much. And during the whole of my time in the Punjáb Secretariat I rarely saw an Indian. Sometimes the Representatives of the Indian States of the Punjáb would pay me ceremonial visits, and as I grew to know them would unbend and tell me of the time when Ranjit Singh ruled the Punjáb. These men were of the old school, with very courtly manners, and most reticent on the subject of their respective States. None of them spoke English, but one of them evidently saw points in our language and would introduce a few English words. When I was discussing with them the rules of the Chiefs' College at Lahore, the question of punishment came up, and I rather advocated the English method of corporal punishment. Whereon the Representative of the Patiala State said: "*Shayad*[1] more in keeping with-his-dignity *hoga*,"[2] if a light fine were inflicted on his Chief, who was then a minor.

I did not care for the work in Simla and longed to be back in Rajputána. Colonel Bradford offered me the post of guardian of the young Maharája of Jodhpur, but he did not advise me to accept the offer. Then came the offer of an Under-Secretaryship in the Government of India. Sir Charles Aitchison wrote me a charming letter, and I was overjoyed. It was a great advancement, but the chief attraction to me was that I was to be Under-Secretary to Sir Edward Buck, who was Secretary to the Government of India in the Department of Land Revenue and Agriculture. I have an old photograph before me as I write of Lord Dufferin's Council and Secretaries in 1888. In my opinion it was the best team of Indian administrators ever brought together, and Lord Dufferin was a consummate Whip. Sir Charles Aitchison, who had retired from the Service when his term of office in the Punjáb expired, had been brought back from England by Lord Dufferin to control the two Departments—the Home Department and the Department of Revenue and Agriculture. Sir Frederick Roberts was Commander-in-Chief, and Sir George Chesney controlled the Military Department. They were both great men, statesmen soldiers, who had been through the

[1] Perhaps. [2] It will be.

Mutiny and knew India, and understood the Indian Army. It would be presumptuous of me to express an opinion as to the efficiency of the Army, but from what I heard and saw and have subsequently read, I feel certain that, for the money, these two devoted soldiers gave to India a magnificent force, and I am very certain that the Indian troops were proud of themselves and their Chief, and that they were happy and contented. I was present at the dinner Sir Frederick Roberts gave when the old Punjáb Frontier Force passed to his command. We do not always welcome change in India, and there was a special sentiment attaching to this famous fighting Force. But all accepted the change without a word of criticism, for all knew that it was an advantage to come under the direct command and the skilled administration of Roberts and Chesney. There are two books which I advise all who go to India to read, one is Lord Roberts's "Forty-one Years in India," and the other is Chesney's "Indian Polity."

My immediate Chief, Sir Edward Buck, was the only Secretary who was permitted to make long and frequent tours, and in his absence I presented official papers to the Member of Council who controlled the Department of Revenue and Agriculture. If the Member considered the case of sufficient importance, he would mark it for the Viceroy and the Secretary would submit it when he made his weekly visit to see His Excellency. The first time I went in the place of the Secretary I was ignorant of the functions of the Viceroy's Private Secretary, and went straight to Lord Dufferin's room, escorted by an A.D.C. and followed by my *Chuprasis* carrying heavy dispatch-boxes containing seventeen cases. I thought that Lord Dufferin was somewhat surprised at the week's output, but he sat patiently and affixed a blue chalk "D" on each case as I satisfied him that the suggestions of the Department followed precedents. It took some time, and at the end he made some encouraging remarks, and dismissed me. When I got downstairs, the A.D.C. told me that the Private Secretary wished to see me. "What have you been doing?" he asked. "Submitting cases to the Viceroy," I replied. "Yes," he said; "but in future you must see me first, and I can tell you which cases you should submit, and which cases I can dispose of with the Viceroy. We shall never get through the work otherwise, and by your long sitting you have kept back two other Secretaries."

I soon learned the value of a Viceroy's time and found that there were other Departments as important as my own. To the Viceroy, the Foreign Department was of peculiar importance: to the Government of India, the Finance Department was of chief account. Next to the Viceroy, the Financial Member of the Council was the most powerful man in India, for he could nip in the bud our fairest and most promising plants, and as a rule he was deaf to our plea that our schemes would bring large profits to the Exchequer. His horizon was always gloomy with the clouds of famine and war, and he clung to the proposition, in which we all acquiesced, that light taxation was the first requisite of the Indian administration. So it was a cheap Government, and frills such as education and science were discouraged. Railways and irrigation were lawful, but even there the pace should be slow, and, though both were highly profitable and urgently needed, the borrowing of money should be on a scale which would not affect India's credit in London. Meanwhile, there was a wealth of minerals and vegetable products lying unused, and my Department dealt with these products. We brought out a magnificent dictionary of economic products, a work which, like "The Swiss Family Robinson," almost makes one's mouth water. Such riches only waiting for the fairy wand of enterprise!

But I think we were too safe and old-fashioned for the men of enterprise. I had two cases which taught me something of the ways and difficulties of the concession-hunter in India. The first was a very pleasant man, who came out to buy the ruby mines of Burma for some big capitalists in London. Everyone liked him, as he was gay and charming. But I saw him more often and saw him in his moods of depression, when he thought that the concession would be given to one of his rivals. He would make my blood run cold by telling me that unless the case were decided in his favour within a week, he would be forced to commit suicide. It was a relief to me after these heart-moving interviews to see him the next night at a ball, the gayest and the brightest in the room. He secured the concession. We had no means of knowing what the real value of the ruby mines was, but they had a fabulous reputation, and the pigeon-blood ruby of Burma ranked high among gems. We gave them to the highest bidder. Lord Dufferin told me that we had given them away, but subsequent events showed that we had exacted a full rent, which was afterwards reduced by half. But the British public was carried away by the glamour of the name. There was a reminiscence of the mines of Golconda and a great rush to buy shares, which went up the first day from one to one hundred.

The other hunter for a concession was of a very different complexion. He looked and dressed like a funeral mute, and gave me infinite trouble. In spite of his appearance he was reputed to be very wealthy, and we understood that he would work the concession with his own money until he had proved the existence of paying oil. When after a month's negotiation I insisted on this understanding, he was furious, told me that I did not understand the meaning of concessions, and left Simla in anger. He said that we were antediluvian in our methods. He was a geological expert, and probably was right. India was certainly no place for the European concession hunter.

It was always a red-letter day for me when I took work to Lord Dufferin. It may be thought that I too easily describe the men under whom I served as charming. But Lord Dufferin was more than charming—he had the charm. His voice, his gesture, his power of making each think that his one object was to have a good talk with him, his interest and sympathy, and his delightful humour, won all our hearts. He would tell me of his experiences in Russia, and draw comparisons between the manufacture of the intelligentsia there and the rapid production of failed B.A.s[1] in the Indian Universities. In these far off-days the Indian National Congress was holding its meetings almost unnoticed; but

[1] Daily letters would arrive from applicants for employment. The writers styled themselves as a "poor familiar man," i.e., a man with a family; and as a "failed B.A.," i.e., a man who had failed to take a degree.

the quick eye of Lord Dufferin noticed the activities of what he called a microscopical minority.

While Lord Dufferin was governing India, Lady Dufferin was hard at work at her noble scheme for bringing medical relief to the women of India. She brought women doctors from England, and started schools of medicine for Indian women, and, thanks to her gentle influence and perseverance, the scheme prospered. She did me the great honour of making me Honorary Secretary of the Fund. There was a Council—all men—and Lady Dufferin presided. I have known many Councils and many Committees, and am convinced that the ideal Council is a body of men presided over by a woman. I have never seen the experiment, but it is possible that a Council of women with a man as President would be equally successful. This was the first attempt on a grand scale to do something for the women of India. It required great tact and patience, and called for constant energy, and Lady Dufferin certainly won many enthusiastic supporters in the Provinces. We learnt some dreadful facts about the sufferings of women, due to ignorance, old tyrant custom and superstition. And we also heard much about the terrible mortality of the little children of India. When Lady Dufferin was leaving India, the women of a place not far from Calcutta sent her a farewell message, touching in its simple gratitude. I forwarded this to Rudyard Kipling and he wrote "The Song of the Women." I obtained his permission to reprint this in the Annual Report of Lady Dufferin's Fund. It expresses in exquisite words the facts as Lady Dufferin found them. I quote some of the song. Some day it will "find a path through the sad heart" of India:

"By light that passed with none to stay the failing,
By love's sad harvest gathered ere the spring
When love in ignorance wept unavailing
O'er young buds dead before the blossoming,
By all the Purdah cloaked, the cool moon viewed
In past grim years, declare our gratitude.
By hands uplifted to the gods that heard not,
By gifts that found no favour in their sight,
By faces bent above the babe that stirred not,
By nameless horrors of the stifling night."

Many of us guessed what the *Purdah*[1] cloaked, but the Government was ever for non-interference in religion and in customs. They did intervene to prevent *Sati*, and have done their best to stamp out female infanticide. But it would have been better for the soul of India if in those spacious times of power they had used their power to point out the potential evils[2] of too early mating and the cruelty of girl widowhood. But Government in India had little time for questions of the soul.

About this time an English M.P., known as the Member for India, visited Calcutta, and I had some talks with him. He believed in the Indian Congress. I suggested to him that it would be better to approach the great problem by the path of social rather than political reform. But he scouted the idea and took no interest in Lady Dufferin's efforts. I did my best to enlist his sympathy in the cause of Indian women. I pursued him on land and on sea (for I travelled home with him) with the argument that India could never grow and prosper unless the women were healthy and free to look out on the daylight and see the world around them. And I told him that Indians in their various water-tight compartments, countries, divisions and groups could never acquire a political status in the world while their women remained blinded and bound by old customs and superstitions. It seemed obvious to me, but it was not obvious to the "Member for India," nor has it been to his successors in that difficult and ambiguous post. To make matters more complicated, the Indian boy was being crammed with English text books, while the Indian girl remained in dark ignorance. As a fine old Sikh, the Rája of Nábha, said to me: "We educate our sons, teach them English and Western ideas, and then marry them to girls who have had no education. The result will be a breed of mules."

Very wise was the beautiful and venerable Hari Singh,

[1] *Purdah* means a curtain to screen women from the sight of men. A woman who observes the rules of seclusion is known as a *Purdah-nishin*, one who sits behind a curtain. I was always told that the *Purdah* system was introduced into India by the Moslems. But it was soon adopted by the Hindus. It is strange that a custom, necessary perhaps to the nomad Arabs in their tent life, should have so profoundly influenced Hindu civilisation.

[2] I have purposely refrained from reading "Mother India" which deals with this difficult subject.

Rája of Nábha, a State in the Punjáb, and I learnt much from him when I was his guest in 1903. He talked of religion, philosophy, of horses and men. Old as he was, his pleasure was to ride unbroken colts of his own breeding, and he was like a picture on a horse. He had been selected as one of the Rájas to attend King Edward's coronation in London, but the British doctors said that the voyage would kill him. He fought against their decision, but at last submitted. He said to me: "For a Rája there are two duties. To go to battle for the King Emperor, and to travel over the seas to do him obeisance. I have failed in both, but there is this to console me in my grief. I might have reached Aden, Suez, even Marseilles, alive, but if I had died at Dover it would have cast a gloom over the Coronation."

As I drove with him through his capital, I noticed that he had smiles and courteous bows for the children, but rather stiff salutes for the men. At one of his daily Durbárs which I attended, he was discussing an official of his State who had failed in his duties. He said: "When a horse stumbles, I get rid of him; when an official loses his memory and gets *chakars*[1] in his head, get rid of him."

There may have been men in the Civil Service who thought of what was coming, of the ends to which we were working, but I never heard discussions on the subject of the future of the Indian peoples. Still men had thought on this subject in the early days of British rule. Elphinston[2] in his leisure time tried to see clearly for himself how Western education and a free Press could be compatible with our system of administration, and he seems to have been in favour of our "retaining the Government and military power, but gradually relinquishing our share in the civil administration, except that degree of control which is necessary to give the whole an impulse and direction." But in Elphinston's time there was leisure to think. In the times of which I write, every English official, whether in the Secretariat or in the Districts, was over-burdened with work. Their

[1] *Chakar*—a wheel or circle. The word is used for the quoit or iron ring the Sikhs wear round their turbans.

[2] "Life of Mountstuart Elphinston," Vol. ii, pp. 180 and 186.

mission was clear: it was to secure the welfare of the millions, to prevent corruption and tyranny, to prevent and to fight famine, plague and pestilence, and to ensure that every Indian should have the free right to enjoy unmolested the rites and the rules of his religion, his caste and his tribe. While the English District Officer gave impulse and the Secretariat gave direction, the real administration was in the hands of the Indian officials. These Indians as a rule did their duty, but with rare exceptions all Indians, when they have lost their first youth, are apt to take official life easily. They become philosophical and sedentary. The pleasant siesta is prolonged, and they sigh as they see the crowd of importunate suitors, "Cui bono?" The *Chuprasi*, who has taken toll from each one of those suitors, knows the answer: it is all to *his* good!

Now, the District Officer not only has to give impulse to his philosophical Staff, but he has also to prevent the course of justice being blocked by religious, racial, or caste prejudices. He can hardly forget this, for never a day passes without hearing from a suitor, whose case must be sent to some Indian official, the impassioned appeal, "*Khuda ke waste ham ko kale admi ke pas mat bhejho*," which means, "For God's sake don't send me to a black man." It was sad to hear this, and I always hoped that with education and more enlightenment the hatred and the distrust which Indians have for "the others" would disappear. But experience convinces me that in the East education will never make the Moslem love the Hindu, nor make a man decide against a man of his own caste. So between the Devil—the Secretariat, asking for more information—and the deep sea—the people of a vast region shouting for justice—the District Officer had not much leisure to think on the tendencies of India: while the Secretariat had no time to look up from their office desks. We all of us became more and more abounding in a wealth of statistics and reports, but perforce abridged the old-fashioned interview with Indian callers. These interviews took time, no doubt, but were not a great strain on one's intellect, for the Indian visitor was quite happy to sit in silence. All he wanted was that his neighbours should know that he had sat a certain time with the

Sahib. There was a Lieutenant-Governor of the Punjáb, very able and deservedly popular. An Indian friend of mine paid him a visit and was delighted by the kindliness of his reception. He had remained for an hour in the great man's tent. I asked him what they talked about, and he said: "The Lord Sahib, with the greatest kindness, kept smiling and remained silent." I was once interpreting for a Viceroy, who had a long and vigorous conversation with a great Indian Chief. When the interview was over, the Viceroy was good enough to say that I had never done better, and that of all the many interviews he had given this was the best. "It might, however, have been better." "How?" he asked. "If you had both remained silent." He scoffed at my foolish suggestion, but he was wrong.[1] In the Great War I went with Sir Pertáb Singh to call on Sir Douglas Haig. He was, as usual, very busy, but he received us at once, smiled and went on writing. Not a word passed. Sir Pertáb sat happy, purring like an old tiger, and after about half an hour we left. It was a silent communion. Sir Pertáb said, after a long pause, "Douglas Egg Sahib, he soldier, me soldier, he knowing me not talking." Sometimes words are "as slaves spreading carpets of gold," but more often English vivacity and eloquence did harm. How beautiful is the happy word, rare and resistless as lovely eyes. So hard to find the one word, but when we chance on it we are rewarded by the Indian's gasp and ejaculation, "*Sat Bachan*" (true word). He does not like many words, but he responds to the right and comely word.

Calcutta in 1886 was beautiful and fascinating: so green by contrast with the camel-coloured plains of the Punjáb, and the sandy tracts of Rajputána, and, to me, so spacious and magnificent. As an artist travelling through India said to me: "You have taken your Rotten Row and plumped it down by your Thames." The glorious park known as the Maidan, skirted by the great river with its four-masted sailing ships, and bounded by the palaces of Chowringhee, and the noble residence of the Viceroy, remains in my memory as one of the most beautiful nooks in our vast Empire, a worthy ornament of the great city which comes next to

[1] "Silence more musical than any song."—ROSSETTI.

London. It is full of haunting memories, where the historian of our race may find inspiration, and our countrymen feel a glow of worthy pride. All should see the Táj in Agra—but should also see the Memorial Hall in Calcutta. I am told that the veteran Sikhs who guard this shrine of the great Queen will not go on duty at night in that inner hall where the great statues stand unless they go in pairs. For the statues "talk strange talk." All Calcutta to the diligent seeker is rich in strange and romantic happenings. It was a lucky chance which brought Charnock, in 1690, to the mud flats of the Ganges delta.[1] Calcutta was a place of great hospitality, and the Hill pheasants, as the Simla folk were called, met with great kindness at the hands of the merchants, the Bench and the Bar. This unfailing kindness was all the more praiseworthy, as our four months' residence in Calcutta had an unsettling influence, and certainly raised the level of rents. But in those happy, far-off days, rents were still within bounds, and servants and horses were almost cheap.

During my time in the Secretariat I was sent off on two tours. One took me to Bombay and Madras: the other to Upper Burma just after its annexation. I was much struck by the beauty of Madras. Rain had fallen and the colour of the red roads and the blue sea delighted me. Madras is the old British India, ample room, and dignified spaces, but a climate where ample room is a necessity, and haste and hurry are unwise.

Burma was a new world to me, unlike any of the countries I had seen in India. Of course I missed much by my ignorance of the language, but the colours, and the dainty people, spoke a language which all could understand. Next to the Táj at Agra I think that the Golden Pagoda in Rangoon is the most arresting of man's many efforts in expression. The building stands high, and dazzles with its blaze of gold. The people, too, who come there to worship—the women in their exquisite dress of many-coloured silks—are in harmony with the beauty and

[1] Calcutta (population 1,263,292) is the second in size of the Cities of our Empire: like Bombay (pop. 1,172,953), Madras, Rangoon and Karachi, it sprang from the haphazard swarms which settled around the modest warehouses which the British built at the trade outlets.

splendour of the glorious Shwe Dagon. Near by are some pretty lakes, and the women as they walked on the green verge looked like a garden of tulips. I visited Burma three times and always spent as many hours as I could spare at the Golden Pagoda. An Indian crowd is remarkable and admirable, but the Burmans do not crowd. They are there in their thousands, but they never jostle, and the lovely silk dresses are never crushed. The market-place was full of interest. The pretty women dressed in their best, preside over the stalls, gracefully waving in their tiny fingers large white cheroots, and seemingly indifferent whether their customers purchase or pass by. One such goddess I saw. She sat aloft on her pyramid of wares while below an old Indian groom was trying to beat her down as to the price of some tobacco. But she sat gazing at the smoke curling up from the cheroots, took no notice, and the old man shuffled off. They all smoke in Burma, and a man said to me that he would not be surprised to meet a cow smoking. The women in Burma all hope to be men in the next transmigration, and I heard of a Missionary lady near Prome who was much liked by the Burmans, but the reason why they took her medicines so readily was not that they believed in her skill as a doctor, but because they were certain that by virtue of the laws of Karma she would become a man in the next world. The religion of Burma seemed to me happy, graceful and easy. It was Buddhism at its best. An English friend, who knew the language and religion of Burma, and had spent a year in a Buddhist Monastery, once heard an old man praying to Buddha to tell him the winner in the 36-animal lottery,[1] and promising that, if he won, he would become a monk. My friend remarked that money would be useless to him if he became a monk. The crafty old man replied in a whisper, "Oh, I shall only become a monk for a week, but Buddha does not know this."

I did not like the houses of teak wood, as they did not keep out the heat. Nor did I like to see Chinese carpenters and Chinese traders everywhere. They were annexing Burma, marrying the Burmese girls and getting hold of all

[1] In Burma they use the names of animals instead of numbers in their lotteries.

the paying business. I had come to Burma to see the vast tracks of unoccupied land through which the new railway to Mandalay passed, as it was thought that this waste region might prove an outlet for some of the congested Districts of India. But, in a sense, the immigration had begun, for everywhere I saw Indian police and Indian plate-layers. The Burman loves his leisure and dislikes work. As the first train ran through to Mandalay, I noticed on the platform of a small station three women weeping, and I asked an interpreter to inquire the cause of their distress. They said: "We weep because our husbands are dead and will never see this wonderful railway." There was a great assemblage for the opening of the railway, with luncheon in a huge tent well warmed by the sun. Even at the end of February, Mandalay could be very hot—and it was certainly the dustiest place I have ever seen, more dusty even than Lahore. We were given warm champagne, and very warm hunks of turkey and ham, and as I listened to a long statistical speech about the railway, I decided that I would go out for fresh air. But just then up got Sir George White, V.C., who commanded the army in Burma, and as I hung on the words of this racy and charming speaker, I felt no further need for fresh air, and I realised, for the first time in my life, the power and charm of oratory.

There was a strange sense of impermanence in Mandalay. The embers of the war in Upper Burma were not dead, and nearly every night there was a huge conflagration, which had to be extinguished by the troops.

One other little expedition I made from Calcutta. My Chief, Sir Charles Aitchison, was ill, and the doctors advised sea air. A steamship was placed at his disposal, and I was asked to accompany him. We passed down the river, and on the dangerous shoal, the James and Mary,[1] I saw the masts of four steamers wrecked on its shifting sands. We anchored at the Sandheads. There is a large lighthouse about half a mile inland. So I went to see it. I took with me all the newspapers we had, amongst them a bulky weekly, the *Hereford Times*. I approached the light-

[1] The *Royal James and Mary* was shipwrecked on this sandbank in 1694. Careful and daily survey has made the Hooghly river as safe as the Suez Canal.

house by a high causeway which ran through the mangrove swamps. As I passed, a huge drove of wild pig swept over the causeway and splashed into the mangroves: and that was the only life I saw in this most melancholy place. It was Christmas Eve, and I noticed as I drew near the lighthouse that the flagstaff was bedecked with green branches. A wild-looking Englishman came out of the lighthouse, and I asked him if I might see the lamps. I added, pointing to the flagstaff, "I am glad you keep Christmas." "Christmas," he said with a snarl, "that hideous mockery! No, that was done by the other man." I then offered him the newspapers and he noticed the *Hereford Times*. "Ah," he said, "I knew Worcester and Hereford, and used to go to the Festivals." I told him of the pigs and asked him whether he ever shot them for the pot. "No." I asked him if he ever saw anybody here. "No, but I see a good many bodies here—bodies of wrecked men, and that is why I do not shoot pigs, for the pigs eat the men." I asked him if he walked for exercise. "No," he said, "this is my exercise," and he pointed to a coffin which lay inside the entrance of the lighthouse. "When I want fresh air I make the Lascars carry me round in that." I rather hurried through my inspection of the lighthouse, for the keeper depressed me. As I left him the "other man" came up and greeted me—a stout, pleasant-looking mariner. I asked him to walk some of the way back to my ship. He told me of his mate's aloofness. "There was nothing for it. I am sorry, as it makes it a bit lonesome, but the trouble is, he is a gentleman." When I returned to Calcutta I found out the "gentleman's" record. Born to a good property in Worcestershire, squandered on the turf, he was shipped off to Australia with a few hundred pounds, speedily lost at the Melbourne races: then a berth on a steamship trading to India, which he soon lost. Lastly, work in the lighthouse service. He would live hard and quietly for a year, and then take a holiday. His holiday was to travel as far as he could in India, first-class, and frequenting the best hotels.

Life in India is always full of change. Every five years, a new Viceroy, new members of Council: sometimes a new direction: but the old Secretariat goes on with its safe and established policy. A new Viceroy raises hope in the minds of Indians who may have stumbled badly, or may have failed to obtain some boon for which they and their forebears have worked for generations. There is nothing like the patience and persistence of an Indian with a purpose. I was acting as Secretary when Lord Dufferin retired, and Lord Lansdowne succeeded him as Viceroy. It is a great and moving occasion, full of regrets, of doubts, and of anticipation. I watched the two great pro-consuls, both so successful, and so deservedly popular in India, and I thought that the parting guest was the one to be congratulated. He had come safely through, and could make over an India without a cloud on the horizon. But the wisest know that there are many horizons in the vast continent of many countries.

About this time I was informally told that there were three appointments which might be offered to me: the Under-Secretaryship in the Foreign Department; the post of First Assistant to the Resident in Haidarabad, the great Indian State of the Deccan; and the work of Settlement Officer in Kashmir. The official who decided these appointments considered that the first two were the best. But I had always looked on Kashmir as the land of my Indian dreams. Friends warned me that behind the clouds of the mountains which hid the beautiful valley from the world I should be out of sight and out of mind. But though I was ignorant of the conditions of the country, the lure of the very name, Kashmir, compelled me.

As my object in writing this book is to give young Englishmen an idea of the life, the work and the chances of an ordinary Indian Civilian, I must at this stage say something of the respective merits of the life in the Districts and the life in the Secretariat. The former is the freer, and fuller of interest and excitement; and though the hot weather—in the Punjáb, at any rate—makes life a burden, the camping in the cold weather is a glorious existence. The crisp air and the bright, pleasant sunshine; the drowsy music of the Persian wheels as the little cups come up brimming from the wells; the wholesome smell of the unleavened bread and the pulse in the little pipkin; the shy gaze of the pretty children, and the kind welcome of the villagers, with their simple wants and their little troubles often so easily remedied. And then those blessed winter rains, pattering on the tent, and lulling to further sleep in the dark morning, and the sound from the village of the peasants singing, and even laughing as they slip on the greasy mud of the narrow lanes. As I listened to the singing, I realised what rain for the wheat and the pulse meant to the villagers. It is rare to hear a laugh in India, and even the little children give up laughter when they are old enough to go out with the cattle and help in the fields. They become thoughtful, and the shades of the prison house fall on them all too early. There is too little of "sunburnt mirth," too few "plump infant laughers."

And then, in the midst of this idyllic peace, which almost passes our understanding, like a bombshell there comes some great crime, or act of violence, which often baffles, and always makes one realise that in the quiet backwaters there is passion and romance. Hardly a day passes without some adventure; and to the man who does not mind occasional solitude, and likes the Indians, life in the District is full of interest and enjoyment. Every District Officer has queer stories to tell. I know so many, that it is difficult to know which to select. A friend of mine, Head of a District in the Punjáb, one of those quiet matter-of-fact men to whom adventures rarely come, told me that a Headman of a large village filed a criminal suit against a man in a neighbouring village, alleging that he had violated the Headman's daughter and had fled. A warrant was issued, and the police and trackers got on his trail and followed him over the jungle country down to Rajputána. Everywhere the offender left traces. They tracked him to Ajmere, but there he disappeared, and the case was given up as hopeless. About six months later my friend was riding through his District, and saw a boy of six or seven years crying by the roadside. He pulled up, and the boy said he was tired, too tired to walk back to his village. So my friend picked him up and trotted off towards the village. The boy talked away happily, and incidentally said that he was the brother of the Headman's daughter. "Ah," said my friend, "I am sorry you did not catch that scoundrel." "Oh," said the boy, "we caught him right enough and killed him and buried him in a field." The police again went into the case. It was a village romance; the father and eldest brother of the girl had come on the young couple, and, in order to save the family honour, had killed the lover. The brother then went off across country to Rajputána, leaving a hot scent. At Ajmere he took the train and quietly rejoined his family, and life went on as usual. The body of the lover was found in the field.

These people, who seem so simple, are artists in the fabrication of evidence, and they stick at nothing when the family honour is involved, or where the possession of land is concerned. "*Zar*, *Zan*, *Zamin*," gold, women, and land. If these three could be eliminated, then the Indian village, when the well-distributed rains come, and the hateful *chuprasi* comes not, is truly a garden of Eden.

Life in the Secretariat also has its charms. To those who have the rare gift of administration there are greater opportunities in India than in any part of the world. But the current work is so heavy that it is only the very exceptional men who can use these opportunities. In my opinion one of the great merits of life in the Secretariat is the social environment of a place like Simla. Lord Dufferin one day told me of the various Capitals in which he had lived and worked: and he said that nowhere had he found a more delightful society than in Simla. Of course it was official; but there was such variety. One might meet at dinner, experts on Thagi and Dacoity; on Forestry; on salt mines and salt lakes, and the ways of the smugglers of salt; on exploration, and the heroism of Indians, who carried their lives in their hands for years together beyond the Frontiers, and the intrigues beyond and the intrigues within; on opium, its use and rarely its abuse—one might meet experts on every subject under the sun, and throughout their talk there always ran the thread of Indian character. In England there is a prejudice against talking "shop," but I never tired of listening at Simla. Perhaps it was becau against young. But I look back on Simla society as on throughout wittiest and most refined community I have the known.

The men knew and liked their work: the soldiers were picked officers of a large and very efficient Army; while the women—and here, again, my views may be mellowed and blurred by the golden haze of memory—many of the women were beautiful and fascinating, and most were understanding. And the pathos of the retrospect! These splendid men working like slaves, their wives encouraging them, telling them that it was the greatest of England's missions and endeavours, well worth the exile, the separation from children, and the certainty of the scrap-heap at an age when many are at their best—what must they feel in this strange new world, when they are told that they were all wrong and sinners against the new-world Rousseau and his law of self-determination. They may take this comfort, that they were loyally carrying out the work prescribed by authority, and that the millions in British India, who revered the name of the Queen Empress, were never more prosperous and more contented than they were in the good days of Queen Victoria's last Viceroys.

CHAPTER VII

"If there be a heaven on earth,
It is this, it is this, it is this."
(Translation[1] of Persian verse on wall of the Diwan-i-Khas, Delhi, which runs:
"*Agar firdaus bar ruy i zamin ast*
Hamin ast u hamin ast, u hamin ast.")

Kashmir—Its Sale to Guláb Singh, Chief of the Dogras—Has Belonged to Many Masters—The Way of Guláb Singh—His Successors—Maharája Pratáb Singh Succeeds to a Bankrupt Kingdom—Determines to have a Settlement—This Unpopular with Privileged Classes—I am Boycotted—I Appeal to Cæsar—Sympathetic, but Boycott continues—Incident of Colonel Natha Singh—Insist on his Dismissal—Boycott removed—Spies and Rumours—Kashmiri Methods—Bráhman Opposition—Approval of the Great Mullah—Story of Gaganger and Beautiful Girl—Colonel Natha in New Guise—Rishi Bat remembers me at the Last—India the Land of Regrets—Indian Women—A Letter from a Hindu Wife to her Husband.

WHEN I was setting out for the long journey to Kashmir, Lord William Beresford, who never said a foolish thing, gave me cryptic advice: "Don't accept a cook from the Kashmir State." And other friends in Simla also gave me hints that I should find myself not wholly welcome to the State authorities. One old friend, who knew something of Kashmir, said: "If you are going up for a loaf, well and good; but if you are dreaming of getting anything done, look out for trouble." But in spite of these forebodings, I was full of hope. At any rate, I was going to Kashmir.

The State of Jammu, Kashmir and its dependencies, covers a large area, as large as Great Britain. The ruling family is Rájput, the Mian Rájputs or, as they called themselves after their slogan, the "Jey Deo Rájputs" of the Dogra country—the land of the two lakes, the cradle of

[1] "And, oh, if there is an Elysium of earth
It is this, it is this."—(MOORE, *Lalla Rookh*.)

the Dogra nation. A fine race, active fighting men, often poor, and always proud, as men of hilly countries are wont to be. It was the fame of their fighting prowess that chiefly induced the East India Company to sell to the able Chief of the Dogras—the Maharája Guláb Singh—the delectable valley of Kashmir, annexed by the British after the first Sikh war (1845). The Dogra power on the flank of the Sikh forces was justly considered a valuable asset. When the second Sikh war (1848–49) coloured the map of the Punjáb red, some regretted the sale of Kashmir to the Dogra Chief. But in my opinion, based on some knowledge of the possibilities of Kashmir, it was fortunate that we sold it. Now, as in the days of the Sikh kingdom of the Punjáb, the Dogra nation may prove a determining factor if there be trouble in the Punjáb: just as the great power of Nepal may some day play a great part in the destinies of the fat fertile Indian Provinces which lie adjacent to her frontier. For the Dogras of Jammu and the Gurkhas of Nepal have not been enervated by long years of the skin-deep civilisation of British India, both have strong views on discipline and authority, and the barriers which hold in these fighting peoples would be down in a moment if British forces were withdrawn from India; or if what is known as the British Ráj[1] showed real weakness. The forces of Kashmir and of Nepal are stronger relatively than they were last century, and they have this great strength, that they are national and homogeneous.

Kashmir has belonged to many masters. The great Mogul Emperors loved and appreciated the charm of the valley, and when Jehangir was dying and was asked if he wanted anything, he replied: "Only Kashmir." His lovely pleasure gardens are still a joy for ever, and the silver-bark plane trees, the glory of Kashmir, came in with the Moguls. About the middle of the eighteenth century the valley passed into the hands of the rulers of Kabul, and the times of the "Shaháni Duráni" are still remembered with a shudder. At the beginning of the nineteenth century Kashmir was taken by the Sikhs. They were not easy or benign masters, but they were better than the rapacious wolves from Kabul.

[1] Rule.

Then in 1846, after the first Sikh war, Kashmir and all the hilly and mountainous country situated eastward of the river Indus, and westward of the river Rávi, was sold to Maharája Guláb Singh of Jammu, a great man and a strong ruler. After his purchase he looked ruefully at the map of his new estate and remarked that one-third was mountain, one-third water, and the rest was alienated to leading families. He set to work. He took care that the revenue of the country reached the Treasury, and he cut down unnecessary expenditure. He repressed crime with a stern hand, and his grim object lessons in punishment are not forgotten. During the six years I passed in the villages of Kashmir, I cannot remember a single crime of importance; and during my residence there were no police save in the capital and the few small towns.

One of Guláb Singh's object lessons was told me by an eye-witness. The Maharája was making one of his annual tours through the country when his cavalcade came to a river, over which a bridge was being constructed by convict labour. Guláb Singh watched the work with interest and especially noticed the skill and energy of one man. He sent for him and praised his efforts. The man, emboldened by Guláb Singh's appreciation, said he had a favour to ask: "Could he be released?" "What was your offence?" asked the Maharája. "Only a little matter," said the convict. The official in charge of the convicts explained that the offence was the murder of a little girl for the sake of her jewels. "Oh," said the Maharája, "bring a pen and ink." The convict was stripped and laid on the ground, and the Maharája took the pen and drew a line down and then across his trunk. Then a sawyer was ordered to saw the man in four pieces. "One piece shall be sent North, one South, one East, and one West," said the Maharája, who was mounting his screaming stallion, with its red pillow-like saddle and the golden stirrups. "For I want my people to know that I do not regard the murder of a girl for the sake of her ornaments as a little matter." This form of crime was very common in India, where personal property frequently takes the form of gold and silver ornaments on children. It was unknown in Kashmir in my time.

If Guláb Singh could have seen his estate fifty years after, he would have admitted that he had not made a bad bargain, for in 1900 there was no State in India more prosperous. Some say that the purchase money paid for Kashmir was recouped in a few years, and under good management the fertile soil of Kashmir and its splendid forests of deodár can yield a large revenue. Guláb Singh died in the year of the Mutiny and was succeeded by his son, Ranbir Singh, a man of noble presence and good intentions. But he was not master in his own house, and the clever Bráhmans of Srinagar, the capital of Kashmir, took advantage of his mild, courteous nature, and plundered the villagers. In 1877–79 there was a terrible famine in the valley of Kashmir. It was due to misrule, and the tragedy saddened the latter part of Ranbir Singh's life. I remember meeting him and his three sons at the Durbár held in Lahore in 1881. I think that he was one of the handsomest men I ever saw, and his youngest son, Rája Amar Singh, at that time was indeed a thing of beauty. Maharája Ranbir Singh died in 1885, and I have mentioned in a previous chapter that I met his remains near Pehowa. One morning, when I was crossing the first of the seven bridges of Srinagar which spanned the Jhelum river (Hydaspes), an old man pointed to a large fish in the river and told me that Ranbir Singh had transmigrated into a Mahaseer.[1] This bridge, known as the Miran Kadal, was close to the palace where Ranbir Singh had lived, and no one was allowed to fish between the Miran and the Háwa Kadal —the second bridge.

Ranbir Singh was succeeded by his eldest son, Pratáb Singh. He was my good and constant friend from 1889, and after I left India we maintained a regular correspondence. He was a man of the most kindly nature, very shrewd, old-fashioned in some ways, and intensely devoted to his religion. He succeeded to an administration which had become a by-word, and had none to help him to restore order and system. The Bráhmans, known as Kashmiri Pandits, had seized all power and authority, and the Moslem cultivators

[1] A species of *Barbus* thought by some to show more sport for its size than a salmon.

were forced to work to keep the idle Bráhmans in comfort. In 1889 the Kashmir State was bankrupt. The rich land was left uncultivated, and the Army was employed in forcing the villagers to plough and sow, and worse still, the soldiers came at harvest time; and when the share of the State had been seized and these men of war had helped themselves, there was very little grain to tide the unfortunate peasants over the cruel winter, when the snow lies deep and the temperature falls below zero. There is an old saying in the Kashmiri language, which I often heard in 1889:

"*Batta Batta*
Tah piyáda patta."

"We are crying for food and the tax collector is after us." Meanwhile in the capital the Pandits and the officials lived at their ease. Whatever happened they must have cheap rice and cheap fuel. So conditions became impossible, and the Maharája determined to carry out a Land Revenue Settlement of his country, and I was offered the post of Settlement Officer by Lord Lansdowne. But when I arrived in the beautiful valley, I noticed that my welcome was chilly, for, though the Maharája wished for a settlement, the officials, to a man, had made up their minds that there should be no settlement which might interfere with their perquisites. So they warned the villagers that the Settlement was not intended seriously, that I, the Settlement Officer, would soon be sent back to India, and that any villager who talked with me would incur official displeasure. I found survey parties recruited from the Punjáb, but they were in a despondent mood, for one of their Superintendents had been seized and was now in prison, and it was rumoured that before long all the Staff of my department would be in jail. Another drawback to an otherwise interesting task was that the State had not paid our salaries for three months. For a month and a half I splashed about in the rice fields, checking the survey, and visited every village in the Sind Valley, but not a Kashmiri would speak to me. I told the villagers and their Headmen that they would suffer, for without their help I could not fairly assess their fields. All I could ascertain was the crops and the method of irrigation.

Some six months before I reached Kashmir, the Maharája had been temporarily deposed by the Government of India and a State Council was appointed, of which the Rája Amar Singh was President, handsome, able and accomplished. To him I wrote constantly, pleading for the release of my Superintendent, and asking for the pay of myself and my Staff. But I got no satisfaction. Twice I rode into Srinagar. The first time the Treasury official offered to pay me in Singhára nut—the water chestnut, which is ground into flour and eaten. The second time they tendered me oil seed in payment. But I indignantly declined and insisted on being paid in "double rupees," as they called the Indian rupee. Kashmir had its own mint, and issued two kinds[1] of rupee, both debased.

I was desperate and ashamed and remembered the warnings of my Simla friends. So I determined to appeal to Cæsar, despite his deposition. I rode in from camp, but when I reached the Palace they told me that the Maharája had gone to the boat-races on the beautiful Dal lake. I thought of Nero fiddling, and I thought of my survey parties starving or probably looting the villages—for in Kashmir, as in other parts of the world, the villagers and the lowly have to pay for bad administration. I found my light boat on the canal which led into the lake, and, reckless and dishevelled after a long hot ride, pursued the Maharája. Ah, that lake, the most exquisite corner of the world! the very mirror of fair Kashmir. In its clear waters you can see the great mountains, the forests, the snows framed in vast circles of water lilies, pink and white; in autumn the lovely lake is crimson and gold with colours reflected from the noble planes and the lofty poplars.

I was paddled over the deep clear water of the lake by strong men, who rhythmically swung their heart-shaped paddles and invoked "Dastgir" and the other saints of Kashmir. I do not remember what or whom I invoked, but as I drew near the gentle green slopes of the garden of breezes, sheltered by giant planes with silver bark, and

[1] Known as *Chilki*, and *Khám*. The former was a pretty coin bearing the letters I.H.S. Some thought that these letters indicated that the mint master inclined to Christianity. They really stood for the words *Jammu Hari Singh*.

heard the strains of "Paloma" played by the State band, and saw the colour and the crowds on the house-boats, I, in my Kashmiri homespun, would gladly have sought another port. For it was the day of the boat races, and my men, skilled and ambitious, and ignorant of my misgivings, rushed my light *shikára*[1] high up on the grassy bank into the very presence. There, in the beautiful garden of breezes,[2] stood His Highness the Maharája of Jammu and Kashmir, in the midst of his court, and all along the bank were the English visitors who throng to Kashmir in the summer season—such pretty dresses and such real live men. For the wise real men in India avoid Simla and the Hill Stations and make straight for the Happy Valley. Clumsily I got out of my boat, and as my business was to appeal to the Maharája, and as for my purpose he was still Maharája, I made my bow to him. I had not seen him since 1881, but for the next five years I was destined to see him often. It does not matter now why the Maharája was deposed, for he was reinstated during my sojourn in the State, and no Chief stood higher both in the estimation of the Hindus and the Government of India than Pratáb Singh.

It so happened that in spite of my workaday dress and unceremonious arrival, I came on the Maharája at the right minute. As a deposed chief he had no wish to be at this festival, and he was bored and irritated. He was feeling friendless and desperate and so was I. He courteously welcomed me and asked me from what village I had come. He knew the village and knew more about it than I did in spite of my survey. He then said that he was entirely cut off from all State business, and though deeply interested in my work and anxious for my success, could not in any way co-operate with me. If only I could give his own language, his queer idioms and phrases, how different would be this record! But Pratáb Singh cannot be translated. He talked on, and I quickly realised that he knew all about my movements, and much about the men who were working with me. He and his two brothers had spies in my camp, who wrote daily an account of my doings—this I discovered

[1] The *shikára* is the lightest of the flat-bottomed craft of Kashmir.
[2] The *Násim Bágh.*

some time later—and he knew all that I knew and much more.

After an hour's talk or so, as I had to ride back more than thirty miles, I ventured to say that I had come with a request. "Ah," said he, "you must go to my brother, he is Maharája." "I have been to him," I replied, "and he says you are Maharája. Will you give orders to the Treasury to pay me in British rupees, and will you release my Superintendent from jail?" "Yes," he said, "I will; but your Superintendent is a rascal, and if you were wise you would let him die in jail." The Maharája was right. For three years I supported that Superintendent, but he was found out, and he died in jail. However, his release at this juncture cheered up my doubtful surveyors, and when the money arrived they looked more favourably on me. For six long years they plodded through the rice fields, cut through the jungle and made fine and fairly accurate maps, and the endless statistics on which I imagined that I should base the land revenue of Kashmir.

I paddled away, invigorated by that dear garden of breezes. But though the surveyors were happy and more confident, the villagers continued to shun me. I said to them as they worked in the fields: "You had better talk to me, otherwise when I fix your revenue I shall make awkward mistakes." But I might as well have talked to the village shrine or to the iris-covered graveyards. About a month later I was riding up the Sind valley to the lovely mountain meadow known as Sonamarg, where my family were living in the warm summer months. The State provided me with cavalrymen who carried my letters, and at one place, where I changed horses, a cavalryman said to me: "There is something going on in the village which you might like to see." As even the cavalrymen had been told not to talk to me, I was grateful and went into the village. There, in front of a fine house with steps in front of it, was a large and excited crowd of peasants. As I walked into their midst and inquired what was happening, a man put his head through the press and showed a whisker half torn off his face and bleeding. "Who did that?" I asked. "Colonel Natha," said the crowd. At that moment a fine looking Dogra officer came out of the house and stood on the steps, looking proudly and contemptuously at the crowd and at me. "Are you Colonel Natha?" I asked. "Yes," said he, "and who are you?" "Like you," I replied, "a servant of the Kashmir State. Did you tear that man's whisker off?" "Yes," said he, "and they won't go to Gilgit unless we use violence. The Kashmiris worship violence."[1] "Well," said I, "if you remain a servant of the State, I shall not continue to serve the State." He replied: "You had better collect transport for Gilgit yourself, I am sick of the work." I kept my temper and walked back to where my fresh horse stood, and rode on to Sonamarg. I was disgusted with the sight of the bleeding whisker, and greatly perturbed to find that the order had gone forth to collect transport for Gilgit. It meant taking away hundreds of cultivators from their crops at the most critical time. It meant sending these poor people over two hundred miles in a difficult mountainous country, across high passes of everlasting snow. It meant death for hundreds and frost-bite for the rest. It meant that those who were left behind had to pay huge sums to officials for exemption. And it meant that the State was deliberately trying to ruin my work by calling for forced labour from the very valley in which I was working.

However, I did nothing that night, but in the morning my headman informed me that three villages, men and women, had bivouacked on the open mountain that night, and that other villages were on their way up. Sonamarg is just on the border of Little Thibet, and there was a telegraph line which ran from Kashmir to Leh. So I telegraphed to the Prime Minister, telling him of my encounter with Colonel Natha, and requesting that he should be dismissed from the State service. I also wrote, giving a full account of the matter. A telegram came back saying that the order to collect transport in the Sind valley had been cancelled. I gratefully acknowledged this concession, but said that Colonel Natha must be dismissed, or I should resign my appointment under the State. Some days passed and I sent

[1] *Zulm-Parast*, worshippers of tyranny. A word in the mouth of every Hindu in Kashmir, when explaining some high-handed action. If the villagers did worship tyranny, full opportunities were given to their cult.

in my letter of resignation. Then came a letter saying that Natha—he was a cousin of the Maharája—had been dismissed. I asked that his dismissal should be notified in the *State Gazette*, the only paper which ever was seen in the villages. There was great demur to this, but I prevailed. Knowing my Kashmiri by this time, I determined to make sure and went down to the capital the day before the *Gazette* was printed. I called at the office and asked permission to see the proof of the *Gazette*. There was no mention of Natha, and the publisher said he had received no instructions. To remove any doubt, I telegraphed to the Prime Minister a proposed draft, notifying Natha's removal, and that day came the reluctant consent. That ended all my real troubles in Kashmir. When I went back to the villages, the very children talked to me, and the sudden change from grim silence to glad loquacity was astonishing and even embarrassing. Under the planes and the walnuts, on the green banks over the grey-green stream, they would talk for hours and I would listen. Or, better still, as the nights grew colder, they would sit in a circle round the campfire of cedar wood, taking snuff in birch-bark packets, and telling me curious stories.

It is difficult to describe the relief I felt. It was bad to be shunned by the people of the valley, it was depressing to know that my own staff thought I would fail, and it was irritating to hear that the English visitors to Kashmir regarded me as a lunatic for leaving Simla for an enterprise so full of humiliation and so impossible of success. Every hour almost had brought to my camp some new rumour, which, like all other rumours in Kashmir, had its origin in the *Háwa Kadal*[1]—the Bridge of Air. The Kashmiris are called "Háwabin," "those who see the air," and they loved and lived on rumour. To them nothing seems real or permanent, and the very idea of settlement was strange. Every morning my best of head-clerks, Keshu Ram, and my loyal and devoted chief orderly, Satár Bat, a patriot in the best sense, and an enthusiastic believer in his Kashmiri

[1] *Kadal* is the Kashmiri word for bridge, built of deodár logs, cantilevered at a certain height. The second of the seven bridges which spanned the Jhelum river as it passed through Srinagar was the *Háwa Kadal*, the haunt of gossips and the hot-bed of propaganda.

fellows, greeted me with sad and anxious looks. The spies in my camp, known as "well-wishers," had sent in some damning report regarding my mistakes, and the rumour-makers on the *Háwa Kadal* had convinced the city people that I should soon be recalled from my unwanted and upsetting activities. In the evenings there was always a crowd of petitioners, and I would sit under a plane tree for two hours listening to the recital of many wrongs. Men would appear stark naked, smeared over with grey mud; sometimes with a brick suspended from the neck by a wisp of straw, symbolical of poverty. One day a man met me, carrying in his arms a dead child, dead some time, and unburied, for the hostile headman of his village had grudged him the ground for a grave. One petitioner had followed me for over a week, and I had told him repeatedly that his affair was outside my province. He again appeared, and I ordered him to be removed. "Stop!" he remonstrated, brandishing his petition paper, "this is not a petition, it is a poem." He read it, and the crowd listened with approval. The poem recited his grievances, and one line, I remember, said that thanks to the "Band-o-bast Sahib," the "jackal, the sheep and the cabbage could lie down together in peace."

One day I noticed an elderly pandit in the crowd. He was standing on his head, but this did not seem to surprise the other petitioners. I told one of my orderlies to bring the agile pandit forward, and asked him the reason of his unseemly attitude. He said that: "Thanks to my settlement, his affairs had become so topsy-turvy that he did not know whether he was standing on his head or his heels." It was a fair hit, and I laughed, and all the crowd laughed, none louder than the elderly pandit. Indeed, from the point of view of the pandits and the city people, I was a most upsetting influence for the first few years of my operations. My object was to encourage the peasants to cultivate their fine land, and to restore the land revenues of Kashmir. The object of the pandits was simply to take the best of the land and to force the Moslem cultivators to work for nothing. The wicked system of forced labour had ruined the country, and as I settled in each division of the valley the revenue that the villagers were to pay, in cash, and not as heretofore in kind, not to middlemen pandits, but to the State, I set free the villagers from the crushing exactions which were enforced by the privileged classes under the tyrannous system known as *Begár*.

No wonder that the city disapproved of me, and that the *fermier* pandits, who lost their power and perquisites, disliked me. When I started my work, everything was taxed. Fruit trees, birch-bark, violets, hides, silk, saffron, hemp, tobacco, water-nuts and paper were treated as State monopolies and farmed out to the pandits. The right to legalise marriages was farmed out, and the office of the grave-digger was taxed. Prostitutes were taxed, and everything save air and water was brought under taxation. Meanwhile agriculture, the only stable source of revenue, languished, and the treasury was empty. The land revenue was, as a rule, extorted from the villagers by violent methods. I once caught a revenue officer using the thumb-screw on an unfortunate peasant who had paid his land revenue in full, but declined to pay an equal amount as a bribe to the officer. But the revenue thus collected did not reach the State treasury. Fully a half was intercepted by the officials, and this was debited against the helpless cultivator as arrears of revenue.

But though I was determined to put an end to the corruption of the officials, and to the monstrous privileges of the pandits, I had a certain sympathy for them, and I did my utmost to raise the position and pay of the officials, and to secure for the pandits abundant and fairly cheap rice and cheap fuel. Thus by degrees the relations between us became friendly, and indeed pleasant. Nowhere in the East have I met any body of men so clever and so courteous as the Kashmiri pandits: but they had no mercy on the Moslems. Perhaps they remembered the cruel times of the Emperor Aurungzebe, and the brutality of the Patháns, and their treatment of the villagers was the repayment of old scores of savage persecution. They have long memories in the East, and education and progress seem powerless to remove or lessen these old enmities. It must have infuriated the pandits to see the emancipation of the Moslem cultivators carried out by a beef-eating[1] foreigner—to the ruin of old vested interests, and, as they wrongly imagined, in opposition to the real wishes of the ruling family.

The final approval of my work in the villages was peculiar. In my daily rides up and down the Sind valley, I used to hear the people speak with bated breath of the Mullah.[2] They regarded him as divine. Whatever he prophesied came true, and he was more powerful in Kashmir than the Maharája or the Governor. I became interested in this religious man, who seemed to be ubiquitous, and one day asked Satár Bat whether I could visit the Mullah in a cave on the mountain-side, hidden away by forests. But Satár Bat was very positive. "Often," he said, "the Maharája has wished to consult the Mullah, but the saintly man had declined the honour and had driven off the Maharája's messengers with insult and curses. He is a very terrible man, and none of us would dare to guide you to his cave." Later on I was encamped on a high bank of a river, far away from the Sind valley, and when I rose in the morning I heard a hum of voices on the opposite bank, and saw a great crowd of peasants, and presently Satár Bat came to me in great excitement and gasped out: "The Mullah has come! It is a great matter and a great honour!"

I saw the Mullah step with great dignity into the ferry boat: I saw the boatman prostrate himself, as had the crowd bowed down as he passed along. He was a man of about fifty, clad in white, and when we met by my tent I noticed that, though his face was austere and ascetic, his eyes had a twinkle in them. We sat down for some time in absolute silence, and without any order on my part everyone went to a respectful distance. Then he spoke in good clear Hindustáni. He had heard from his people of my work, and though I and my officials through our ignorance had made many mistakes, and though at first he had thought we should fail, he now had some hope that we should succeed. He had been told of my collision with Colonel Natha, and that I had vowed that if he remained in the State service I would

[1] In Kashmir, kine killing is a very serious crime, once punished by death. In my time men were imprisoned for life for the offence. Our only meat was mutton.
[2] A learned man, a teacher, a doctor of the law.

resign. He was pleased that I had kept my vow, and it was for this that he and his people trusted me. "But," he added, "you must be careful. Careful of the hate of the city and the officials, and careful not to free my people too quickly. They are under the curse and are well called the worshippers of oppression. For if they become absolutely free and careless of their rulers, they will be lazy and improvident. And one other matter—you have taken on yourself affairs that do not belong to you." Here I spoke for the first time. I said: "In my work, everything which affects the well-being of a village is my affair." "Is it?" said he. "Is divorce your affair? I thought it was mine. I heard of the young couple at Gaganger; was that your business or mine?" "Yours," I replied.

And this is the story of Gaganger. One evening I sat with my wife and our small son by the banks of the river which divides Kashmir from Little Thibet, and as we sat there an old woman appeared leading her daughter —a brown-eyed goddess dressed in russet grey—the fairest beauty we ever saw in Kashmir, and Kashmir is famous for the beauty of the women. She had eyes "like the fishpools in Heshbon." The old woman had a favour to ask: "Would I kindly divorce her daughter?" "Why?" "Because her husband beats her. Twice she has fled from Gaganger, and rather than go back she will commit suicide." "But I have nothing to do with divorce." "Oh, Sahib," she said, "you have to do with everything in this valley. My daughter's husband has gone to cut wood, and to-night, when he returns over the bridge, my two sons will seize him and bring him to your camp." Two hours later the husband appeared, escorted by the girl's brothers. He was as ugly as the girl was lovely. I asked him whether he beat his wife. "Yes," he said, "I beat her because she won't cook my food." "I cannot allow a scandal of this kind in the valley," said I, "and for your own happiness you had better divorce your wife and marry someone who will cook your food." "Yes," he said, "but I love her." I told him to withdraw, and asked the two brothers whether the matter could not be settled. "It could be settled for twenty rupees. He promised our sister twenty rupees (£1 6s. 8d.) for new clothes, and he has never kept his word, and this is the sole cause of the trouble." I then called for the girl and her mother, and the mother said that all would be happy if the husband would pay the money, and the girl's face lit up with joy. So I summoned the husband, taxed him with his mean breach of faith, and ordered him to pay twenty rupees to his wife. He had only one rupee and a half, and the wood he had carried from over the river might be worth another half a rupee. So I bought the wood and Keshu Rám advanced the balance, and they all went away in smiles.

Every year afterwards there came to me at Srinagar two rather inferior apples from Gaganger, a distance of ninety miles. This was the *Dali* of remembrance, and the only *Dali* I would accept from the Kashmiris.

"It was your business," I said to the Mullah, "but was I wrong?" "Yes," he said, "you were wrong, just as I should be wrong if I told you what land revenue you should take from Gaganger."

He told me much of interest about the customs of the people, but he uttered no word of scandal or criticism of officials. He spoke to me as he spoke to an erring disciple, but I knew that he wished me well. When he left he wished me good fortune. I never met him again, but he used to send me messages of good will.

I have mentioned Colonel Natha. In the winter I used to move my survey parties to the plains, where the State territory marches with the Punjáb. There again at first I was met by a strict boycott, and work was very difficult and life rather depressing. One day, as I was riding along, three well-mounted Dogra Rájputs galloped towards me, and at first I thought they would ride me down. But they reined up just in front of me and the leader said: "Don't you remember me, Natha, and the man with the whisker? Your camp has gone on to one of my villages and I have come out to meet you." I rode along with him, rather puzzled. He was a delightful companion, and I asked him to come to my tent when I had bathed and had my breakfast. He came, and I said: "I think it is very good of you to meet me in this courteous and friendly way. For I did you an injury." "Injury?" he said. "What injury?" "Why, I insisted on your dismissal from the service of the State." He laughed loudly. "It was no injury. I wanted to be back in my own country and in my own villages. I hate Kashmir and all its people." From that day Natha and I became fast friends. I was on very close terms with one of the crack regiments of the Bengal Cavalry, and the officer commanding especially wanted Dogra Rájputs of good family. Natha himself was a large landowner, but he had many poor relatives, to whom service in the Indian Army in the higher ranks was at once an honour and a godsend, for the Rájputs, for all their brave appearance, are often very poor, and I was able to find work for many of Colonel Natha's *bhai band*.[1]

In all classes I have found most attractive characters, and when one remembers that the English in India are birds of passage, not long in one place, it is surprising that the people should make friends with us at all. It is often said that they soon forget us, but that is not altogether my experience. I had three men, leading villagers in the Sind valley, who always accompanied me when I was in camp. Two were Moslems and the third a pandit, Rishi Bat by name. These three men knew every inch of the country, knew the soils and the irrigation, and could, if they could have been trusted to be impartial, have valued correctly the assets of each village. I learnt all and more, far more, of the Sind valley from these three men than I learnt from my own surveyors, and as I moved on to the other villages and divisions of Kashmir, I found other similar companions, who were recognised by the countryside as men of knowledge. But when I was in a real difficulty I was always glad to have the advice of my original friends of the Sind valley. I gave them no rewards: sometimes I killed a sheep, gave rice and sugar and snuff, and we had a feast. But when the end came and I left Kashmir, I do not think that any of my voluntary advisers were disappointed when they received nothing but my written thanks.

Last year I heard from the English official who is carrying on my old work. He wrote: "Do you remember Rishi

[1] Brethren, relatives, members of the same caste. When an Indian obtains an appointment, it is his bounden duty to find work for his *bhai band* in the same office or department. Nepotism is not regarded as wrong, but as virtuous and natural.

Bat, a Zemindar? He died a little while ago, and when he was dying someone asked him if he wanted anything, and he said: Yes, he had one wish, and that was to have seen Lawrence Sahib once again." Remember Rishi Bat, the tall wiry pandit, with a disabled eye which gave the idea of a merry wink! Rishi Bat, always cheerful and patient, ready to ride any distance, careless of weather, rain and snow, never grumbling if there was no food, quite content to be out at night if only he had his beloved *Kángar*[1] and a pinch of snuff, and always resourceful and always wise! They are a people worth one's best efforts, and despite the changes which have come over India, I still hold that an Indian career is the finest field in the British Empire, full of interest, opportunities, and when retirement comes, full of regrets. "The land of regrets," as a writer called India, is a true tribute to its charm and allurement. What do I regret most? That I never had the pleasure of meeting the women of India and of understanding their life. I knew enough from my six years' experience of Kashmir, experience of the camp and of the Court, to realise that they wield the real influence. Zorobabel was right when he maintained that the power of women was greater than that of wine or of kings. "Who is it then that ruleth them or hath the lordship over them? Are they not women?"

We are apt to form our opinion from statistics, and to conclude that as there are few girls in the schools the women of India are illiterate, and we reason from English analogy and think that because women are secluded in India they are necessarily ignorant of the world and of the life outside. Physical seclusion does not always imply mental aloofness nor languid lack of interest, and it is possible that the purdah system may quicken the imaginative faculty and stimulate the desire for information and knowledge. Tod, writing one hundred years ago, says that in Rajputána "there are few of the lowest Chieftains whose daughters are not instructed both to read and write": and though it is foolish to assume that what is true of Rajputána is true of

[1] The *Kángar* is a small earthenware bowl of a quaint shape, held in a frame of wickerwork. In the winter, and even in the summer, when rains chill the air, hot embers are put into the *Kángar* and it is slipped under the voluminous gown which all Kashmiris wear.

the many other countries of India, it should be remembered that the Hindus look to Rajputána as the hearth of fashion and manners. We are so ignorant of the women of India that it may be that many thousands who would never go to a school have nevertheless received some education in their own homes. If it were not for purdah, these literate women might have helped to educate the children of India, for there will be no real education in India till the Dame-school comes.

I am certain that in those countries of India where I have lived, the women's influence is great and inspiring, and if it be true that men make the laws and women make the manners, then all credit should be given to the women. There is nothing in the whole world which is more admirable than the manners of the Indian, high or low; nothing finer than his quiet dignity and his honest self-respect. I could give instances of Indian women who have proved themselves as great regents, even military commanders, but I will conclude this chapter by a letter from an Indian lady in the middle rank of life to her husband far away over the dread dividing seas. I knew him, and I wish with all my heart that I had been privileged to know her and thousands like her. Every day for twenty years I was near them. They could see me from their latticed windows, but I could never speak to them, nor share their thoughts. Every day I could talk to their husbands on every subject under the sun save one, and that probably to them the most beautiful and inspiring of subjects.

This crippling convention has cut us off from the real India, and we have never come near her heart and mind and soul. But some day the Fairy Prince will come and wake the sleeping beauty of the East to full life and fine endeavour.

This is the Rajputni's letter written in Hindi:—

"*My dear, when your letter comes, my heart is made happy. I write to you every week, but sometimes your letters to me are delayed. Why should I be annoyed with you? I am your servant, and you are my all! . . . Every morning when I wake I do homage to your picture; and my picture, is it not imprisoned in your heart? Why, then, are you distressed in mind?*

Often do I see you in my dreams, but never in a state which would cause me anxiety. Question your heart. Does it not tell you that at all times I am with you in spirit? Who is there in this world, besides yourself, to whom I would give a thought? What does it matter how or where one lives, in a mansion or in a wilderness, so long as the heart is true? I am steadfast in my faith always. There are but two conditions in this life, peace and trouble. When you were with me all was peace; in your absence all is trouble. God alone knows when I shall see and do homage to you again and thus be freed from trouble. . . . Your letters reach me on Wednesday. When a letter comes, I am happy till the following Tuesday. When a letter does not come I am sunk in despondency for a week, asking myself, 'what can it be that has deprived me of a letter from my Lord this week?' And I never fail to write weekly to you. I could not forget you, for you are to me what the broad deep sea is to the fish. . . . Why do you praise me so much? I am not worthy of praise. Nor could I become estranged from you, for then should I make a hell of this house. No, no; in no circumstances can I be separated from you. You are my lord and master, you alone can fathom the depths of my heart and understand its desires. For me there is not your equal in this world. Therefore, trust me and believe that no thought of mine is hidden from you. You ask me to write more in detail. The reason why I do not do so is because I do not wish to weary you. Occupy yourself with the duty the performance of which will give satisfaction to God, and now indeed is the time, above all others, when you can work so as to please God. . . . I have no need for money, it is your presence that I desire. You are my joy. What is money to me? . . . Do not worry yourself about anything. Do your duty and your work with all your heart."

My other regret is that I did not see more of the ascetics, the astrologers and others who lived in another world—the eldorado outside our ken. I had some chances, but the world was too much with me, and my work had to be finished. This reflection, however, calls for a separate chapter.

CHAPTER VIII

"Now these things are so."—HERODOTUS

Charm of Kashmir—Only Man is Vile—Unfair Criticism of Kashmiris—Subterfuge Their One Armour—Their Weakness and Their Strength—Astute yet Superstitious—Black Magic—Shrine Worship—Fatal Result of Superstition—The Power of the Curse—Story of Faqir's Curse—Another Coincidence—My Friend's Fraudulent Servant—His Fate—Delight of Life and Work in Kashmir—Fights and Anxieties—Lack of Privacy—Actors and Poets—Nature Turns against us—Earthquake—Cholera—Flood—Offer of Work at Home—Decide to Accept—Retrospect—Not a bad thing to Work under Indians—Sir David Barr the Ideal Political Officer.

THERE is a beautiful old lady, with whom I love to talk, who tells me of her father, Charles Dickens, and in my antediluvian, Victorian way, I confess that Charles Dickens means very much to me. This beautiful and most clever old lady always asks me: "Would you live your life again?" and I tell her: "Every moment of it!" And as for my six years in Kashmir, I would live those years fifty times over.

It is difficult for me to write about Kashmir, for I have already written a large book on the subject, and just as one scorns to take ideas and advice from one's own family, so still less can I condescend to quote from "The Valley of Kashmir." But to live six splendid years in that valley, unspoiled by railways and roads, innocent of factories and coal, and long streets and concrete houses, sleeping in boats or in tents always pitched on green turf under the shade of plane or walnut trees, and always within sound of running, singing water—that is a life to live over again. Such a climate, with the sun at its best! The Capital is well named the City of the Sun, for summer or winter the sun smiles and sparkles in Kashmir. The air is no mere compound of gas, but a blend of dance and laughter, smiling even in drear December when the temperature is below zero: is blue, like the sapphires from Zánskár, but I never knew whether the blue came from the sky or from the rivers and lakes, or from the iris, which is the flower of the valley. And from each of the countless valleys which pass on the waters of the encircling snow range to the fabulous Hydaspes, there is the view of the naked majesty of Nanga Parbat, and the sheen of jagged Haramak, which seemed to be always to the north. The Easterns have known the magic of Kashmir for centuries. The Moguls knew it, but Kashmir, like Corinth, was not approachable by everyone, and, though twice I have heard august consent given to the making of a railway, the tutelary divinities of this happy valley have intervened. Since I last saw Kashmir, roads have been made, and motor cars now run. But I doubt if even a railway could rob the valley of its strange and unique charm. I have said all I can say of its colour, its flowers and its fruits, and in the days when I first visited Kashmir, the only jarring note the censorious critic could hazard was that the people were *Kashmiris.* So they are, in spite of centuries of repression and wanton cruelty. They always said to me that they had been under the curse (*Páp*), and they always gave me the impression that they were just recovering from some great fright. But they were really a very fine people, a people who had never had a chance. Physically they were splendid, in spite of the effeminate dress[1] which foreign tyrants had imposed on them: while the women are famous for their beauty and their charm. As cultivators, as artisans, and as artists they are unrivalled in the East, and for brains the Kashmiri Pandit[2] is hard to beat, as all India knows well.

But the critic—and he drew his ideas from the ruling classes in Kashmir—said that the people were lying, treacherous and immoral. When I began my six years' task in

[1] Once a Kashmiri came to my camp. He was naked and had been cruelly beaten by an uncle, who had driven him from his home. I gave him an old suit of homespun, and said that as he was now dressed like an Englishman, he should go home and assert his rights. He did so with considerable thoroughness, for the next day the battered uncle was carried into my camp on a litter.

[2] In Kashmir the Bráhman is always called Pandit, and he carries the name with him when he migrates to India. They are to be found in many of the provinces of British India, and in the Indian States in the higher ranks of officialdom. In Burton's "Anatomy of Melancholy" the Indian Brachmanni are classed with the British Druids, the Aethiopian Gymnosophists, and the Magi of the Persians.

the valley, I shared these ideas, and for the first six months much that I saw confirmed me in the opinions of the critics, who had only known the *hánjis*, the boatmen of Kashmir. They had not lived, as I had, for six years in the villages: and I say after careful examination that the Kashmiris are perhaps as great a people as any in the East. They are not noble, as the Rájputs, independent as the Patháns, nor virile as the people of the Punjáb. But they will beat all three as cultivators, as artisans, or as wits. And in domestic life, the Kashmiri villager is the equal of any peasant of India. When I first met them they were hopeless. Their one weapon against the tyranny and corruption of the officials and the privileged Pandits was subterfuge, and as I was somewhat in the official line myself, they lied to me with "all the polyglot facility of a Levantine Jew." But day by day, moving from village to village, listening to all, and watching the eyes of the elder men as the younger ones told their Arcadian stories, I realised that the lies were a formula, or mere recital, a kind of common form recognised by the countryside for centuries, and due to me, the griffin of the valley. By degrees, after following my camp for weeks, they would grow weary, smile, and tell the truth. After the second year, when work became heavy, time grew scarce, and land became valuable, those quick-witted people saw that direct statement and simple truth brought results. But to the end, as I sat under the chequered shade of the plane trees, deciding claims for land, I did not watch the faces of the voluble parties to the suit, but rather searched the eyes of the old men in the white dress, who formed for me a circle round the litigants. Their eyes told the truth.

I have given my testimony regarding the Kashmiris in "The Valley of Kashmir." It was the fashion to say hard words of them, but none, English or Indian, who berated the Kashmiris, knew anything about the villages, and it was only fair that I should say what I could; and six years continuous camping in the valley gave me opportunities for forming an opinion.

They were in truth a very hopeless people, but as they gained confidence they threw off their indolence, and I saw large tracts of country which had been left waste turned by their skilful toil into fat belts of fertile fields. I saw, also, the growth of self-respect and of manliness, and am confident that under a just government they will win a good name.

Like most dwellers of mountain valleys where nature is sudden and awful in thunder, earthquake, avalanche and flood, the Kashmiris were full of superstition. One cannot live in daily sight of Nanga Parbat, that mighty snow promontory 26,620 feet in height, without a sense of its serene sublimity and of man's littleness. The Kashmiris always gave me the impression that they stood in awe of their surroundings, and they certainly did not believe in the permanence of anything. To use an Oriental figure, they felt like an elephant when there is a *Dal Dal* (quicksand). When misfortune came, they would sigh and say that it was due to the curse; but they distinguished between the troubles caused by nature and by man. In times of cholera, earthquake and flood, they were silent and resigned. But when despoiled by a too rapacious official, they would rend their garments and cast dust on their heads, and bay the sky with their lamentations. In their own phrase, they would make London hear. When I asked them where this London was, they would explain that it lay beyond Sukkur-Bukkur on the Indus, the Ultima Thule of their valley minds.

My work in Kashmir was based on facts and figures concerning the land and people of the valley, and I gathered around me Moslem and Hindu landowners, who not only knew the facts, but had the most surprising genius for appraising the real value of other men's land. They supported their valuation by most logical and convincing arguments, and during my twenty-one years in India I have never met the equal of these Kashmiri sages. For five years I met them daily, rode with them—they on their little valley ponies which carried them, their bedding and their beloved Kángar—and at night sat with them till late by the camp-fire, passing round the snuff in little packets of birch bark. These surprising men, so astute and so ambitious, often so conceited—one told me in private that he was "Airavata among elephants, a monarch among men"—would sit by the camp-fire and tell in grave and earnest fashion of the Nágs of Kashmir, the snake deities who haunt the numerous and exquisite springs of the valley. Sometimes, as I started off in the early mornings on my ride round the villages, I would be joined by one of my sages, and when we were alone he would tell me in the most matter-of-fact tones that as he was coming to join me he was stopped on the path by one of the snake gods, who warned him of what might happen in the day. I never smiled at this or showed incredulity, as this would have broken the spell. For it charmed me to find these very business-like men, so concentrated and absorbed by land affairs, had yet another existence—and perhaps a better existence—in a region of divination, magic and sweet springs, where the snake god held sway. "It was easy," they said, "to tell the snake god, if I should ever meet him, for his eyelids never moved and his body cast no shadow." Sometimes there would be hints of witchcraft and black magic, and tales were told me with bated breath of the practice of driving pins into dolls; and whenever some great person died of a lingering illness, there would always be suggestions of the black art. Dr. Buhler[1] says that in former days both the Kashmiri Sáktas and Saivas were famous for their proficiency in the black art, and the famous chronicle of Kashmir, the Rájatarangini, mentions that several Kings were killed by means of sorcery (*abhichára*). He adds: "Now it is said that only a few Abhichárikas exist and that these carefully hide their art, as the Maharája is much opposed to them and punished them. . . . It may be that witchcraft is now not much practised in Kashmir, but the belief in its efficiency in Yoginis who celebrate their foul rites on the desert mountain sides, and in *Bhuts*, is perhaps stronger and more universal in Kashmir than in India proper. The Kashmiri Pandits gave me the impression that they were a *gens religiosissima*." I had the same impression regarding the villagers, at heart Hindus, in spite of their forcible conversion to Islam.

When I found that these wise, solid men believed in an occult world, I was able to realise the hold that the sacred shrines of the saints of Kashmir had on the people, and to understand the power of the ascetics—there were

[1] "Tour in search of Sanscrit MSS," 1875.

good and bad ascetics. I saw them nearly every day, saw them almost in regiments when they came up from all parts of India to visit the sacred cave of Amarnath up in the mountains, so difficult of access and so dangerous for old folk and the very young. But the greater the danger, the greater the merit, and when I suggested to the Maharája that a path should be made to the cave, he pointed out that much of the merit would disappear if the way were made smooth. I was not thinking of Karma,[1] but of cholera, for the pilgrims to Amarnath were too often the carriers of what used to be the most terrible of all the visitations of the fair valley.

Sometimes the superstitions and the quaint imaginings of the people came home to me. I had an orderly, most honest and steadfast, in whom I trusted much. Every year I gave him a month's leave. One September he returned from leave and told me that all was well with his family and his fields. Two days later he asked for more leave, which I could not give, as another of my orderlies had just gone for his month's holiday. "Then," said he, "I wish to resign." I expressed my surprise. He had been in my service for four years and our relations had always been friendly. But he persisted. I took him aside and asked him the real reason of his wish to leave me. He then told me that the English doctor, an old friend of mine who lived at the bottom of the cliff on which my log-house was perched, waited for him in the dusk and sprang out as he passed on his way from me to his quarters in the mountain meadows below. 'Why does he spring out on you?" I asked. He replied: "The Doctor Sahib wants my head for *Mumai*." I had heard of *Mumai*, which is to be obtained by boiling a human head, and is supposed to be a powerful charm or remedy for disease. "I will speak to the Doctor," said I, "and remonstrate with him for interfering with my staff.' In terror he begged me to say nothing. I asked him whether the Doctor ever pounced upon him in broad daylight, and, as it appeared that he always waited for the dusk, I offered

[1] "The Karma—all that total of a soul
Which is the things it did, the thoughts it had,
The self it wove—with woof of viewless time."
—(*The Light of Asia*)

to let him off duty each day an hour before sundown. To this he agreed, and for two days all went well. But on the third day he did not appear, and on the fourth day, as he was still absent, I sent my chief orderly to inquire. He had disappeared. I sent a horseman to his village, and he brought the news that he had not been seen by his family since he returned from his leave. I then informed the police, and I searched for days to find my excellent and loyal follower; but no trace was ever discovered, though we explored some caves and examined some of the deep pools of the mountain torrents.

I have alluded to the curse, which was general. But there were special curses, and I have been told how these curses always achieved their fell purpose. I myself knew a man well, in strong health, who fell into a pining sickness under the curse put on him by a mendicant. One famous curse interested me, and, as I took some pains to verify the dates and the facts, it is perhaps well to record the story of the Faqir's curse. He was a Moslem—"one poor in the sight of God"—and he set himself down in one of the most desolate places I have ever seen, not a tree to shade from the intense heat, just baked earth and boulders by the bank of a mighty river. But the Faqir delighted to plant trees and bushes, which he watered with his small *lotah*,[1] making many thousands of journeys to and from the river. The trees thrived, and the Faqir's garden was much admired by the pious who visited the holy man. By ill luck the Government thought fit to send an Indian Cavalry regiment to this inhospitable spot, and three of the officers, one of them the Doctor of the regiment, saw that the Faqir's *Bágh*[2] was the only green spot in this arid misery. They approached the Faqir and offered to buy his grove. But he had established himself, and his disciples, who came from great distances, some even from Kabul and some from Sind, knew the place, and it would be upsetting to move. So as persuasion failed, the officers said they must have the grove, and set to work to build a hut within the Faqir's demesne. As the hut drew near completion, and the three

[1] The brass pot in which drinking water is carried.
[2] *Bágh* means a garden, but is more often a grove or orchard.

officers were giving orders regarding the finishing touches to the work, the Faqir appeared. "Hear my curse," said he. "Within a month of your first sleeping in this house, one of you will be dead; within three months another will die; and within a year the third will die. And within two years this hut of yours and my grove will be gone."

A month after they took up their abode in the hut, one of the officers went off to course ravine deer with hawks and hounds. He was a fine rider and was well mounted, but, crossing one of the sudden nullahs, his horse pecked and the rider's neck was broken. The other two had forgotten the Faqir's curse, and in India death comes often and swiftly and is the common lot. Three months later, to the exact day, one of the other two officers went to a large military Cantonment to play polo. He, too, was a natural horseman and kept good ponies. All went well until he mounted his second pony. The pony seemed suddenly as mad as a moth, bolted down the polo ground full speed, and killed himself and his rider against the hard, whitewashed brick wall of a building. The sad news reached the Doctor, the last survivor of the three dwellers in the grove. He remembered the curse and grew anxious and introspective. The hot weather had arrived, and it was difficult to sleep in the heat of a night of Punjáb hot weather. All had gone on leave who could escape this blast-furnace heat. More and more introspective, he asked the Colonel for leave, but leave is not given in the hot weather. Then he asked for a transfer to another regiment. This was still worse received. But when the Colonel realised that there was something basic, he appealed to the authorities, and the Doctor was transferred very far down country beyond the Punjáb, and, one would think, out of the jurisdiction of the reproachful Faqir. Just a year after these light-hearted officers had settled into their hut in the bosky grove, the Doctor was at a regatta on the broad, still river, very sacred to the Hindus, where probably the word of the Moslem Faqir did not run. There was a race for ladies' pairs, and as the Doctor was light, he was chosen as coxswain. The two boats paddled down to the start. Then there was some confusion, and the Doctor, who had twisted the tiller ropes round his wrists, was suddenly in the water and under the boat. He was drowned, and a year later, also to the very day, on mountains very far away, there was a landslip, which stemmed the torrent and made a vast lake. Then, at the time when rivers rise and when men in the Punjáb seek for shade, the mighty river burst the dam and poured down on the Punjáb and, incidentally, swept away the Faqir's grove and the Sahibs' hut.

Of course this is coincidence, and coincidences are remembered, but when events do not coincide they are not remembered. But it seems to me that I, as a lover, almost a collector of coincidences, have found more in India than I have in England. A great friend of mine—indeed, he was a friend of all—saved up his pay for three years in order to go home in the cold weather, to hunt in England. As we all did, he made over his pay to his excellent Bearer,[1] and when he arrived in Bombay on his way home, he asked his Bearer for notes sufficient to pay the return passage to England. He would take the balance of his savings the next morning. But in this he was wrong, for when the morning came, the Bearer was gone and the savings with him. My unhappy friend sailed, and was indebted to acquaintances for the "pegs" and other luxuries which he consumed on the voyage. On reaching London, he reported his plight to the ever-sympathetic India Office, and prayed that his leave might be curtailed in order that he might go back to India to save money for a season's hunting three years hence. As he was a valuable officer, the India Office consented. My friend, thus stranded, went off to see an old hospital friend in practice at Norwich, and as he walked across the square outside the station, he saw his perfidious Bearer selling tracts. He accosted him and asked for his savings. "All gone, Sahib. Satan came into my head. I thought you would search Bombay, so I took a passage to England. I have lost the money, and now I am a 'beggar man.'" My friend had a regard for his Bearer—we all have a regard for them—and he said: "Would you like to go back to India? If so, I will send you to King & Co., and next week we

[1] A domestic servant who has charge of his master's clothes, household furniture and (often) of his ready money.

will leave London." "And afterwards the Police in India?" asked the Bearer. My friend paused, and then compounded a felony, but the pause was fatal. He then wrote in pencil a note to King & Co. to take care of the Bearer, and gave him £2 for his expenses and bade him adieu and went on to his Norwich host. They dined and talked of old hospital days, and my friend asked about a man whom he had liked and admired. "Oh, he is doing very well in Edinburgh and would be delighted to see you." My friend had his bashful doubts, but a telegram was sent, and next day came an early telegram begging my friend to go North. He went, and after a delightful evening, the Scotch friend told him that he had a splendid theatre in the hospital, which he would show him the next morning. When they entered the theatre, my friend saw his Bearer dead on the table. Obviously a coincidence.

Kashmir was my paradise, for the work was a constant pleasure. But in a way it unfitted me for the life outside paradise, and though I have had the happiest chances and the most delightful experiences since I left the happy valley, I always compare my life now with my life then, and nothing has rivalled Kashmir. When the Kashmiris weave their lovely carpets they always leave one thing undone, for their religion teaches them that nothing done by man must be perfect. I finished my work in the valley, but there was a tract of beautiful country not belonging to the State which I had promised to "settle," and when the end came I left this unsettled. And now year by year I have a vivid dream that the boat is ready and that all my plans are made. I have chosen my best men for this last piece of work, have sent on my tents and supplies, and am going to make no mistake this time, and the map and the settlement of the land shall be perfect. But I always wake before my boatmen shout "*Yo pir*"[1] and make the boat tremble with the strong stroke of the heart-shaped paddles, and I know that if the boat ever does start, it is "finis," or as the Moslems write on their tombs, "*Khatm*."

I imagine that all men regard their own work as the

[1] The boatmen of Kashmir when they start paddling invoke their Saints, and one of the commonest cries is "*Yo pir*," "Oh Saint," from stroke, to which the rest of the paddlers respond "*Dastgir*," the name of the greatest Saint.

best, but perhaps those are the happiest who work for their own people. But I grew to regard the Kashmiris as my own people, and in my opinion there is no work in the world like that of a Settlement officer in India. He is always fighting for the people against the Government, who want more revenue: against the Forest Officer, who wants more forest and cares little for cultivation: against the money-lenders, who want more land: and against the privileged classes, who want something for nothing. It would be dull work without fighting, and in Kashmir I had to fight during the whole of my six years. Still, I must do justice to my opponents. Though they did not hesitate to fabricate evidence, to intimidate and molest the villagers, they were good losers, and often reminded me of the genial English burglar who, taken unawares, says to the police: "It's a fair cop, guv'ner!" It was all a game, and some of my best friends in Kashmir were men who at first had done their utmost to upset my work. Fortunately for me I had time to get level with them, and it was easy to be patient and wait in such a climate and in such a paradise as Kashmir. It is not so easy in India, when the hot weather sets in. But even in Kashmir there were anxious times. There were always anxieties arising from intrigues in the City, and for the first few years the rumour-makers of the *Háwa Kadal* saturated my camp with stories of my impending dismissal. Officials whom I was forced to remove for corruption, torture, and other delinquencies of oriental complexion, had relatives at Court, and I was warned by well-wishers that I was skating on thin ice. But in the long run I found that it was wisest and fairest to strike at the tall poppies. It was lonely work, for the English visitors to the Valley were on pleasure bent, and were not interested in the administration of Kashmir. To them I was a nuisance, for the boatmen and the City folk always told them that I was responsible for the rise in prices and for the scarcity of transport. Before I came to Kashmir any villager could be seized and forced to carry loads for twopence a day. But I wanted the villager to look after his fields, so that he might pay the land revenue which I said he must pay. If he did not or could not pay this revenue, I was discredited.

As regards prices, they were nominal in 1889. But public works such as road and waterworks, and the payment of the officials in cash instead of in grain, brought the silver of the State hoards into circulation. In 1889 I could buy eighty fresh eggs and fifteen quarts of good milk for sixteen pence, and a suit of homespun for six shillings and eightpence. As money circulated, these articles realised real money prices. The rise was very small while I was in Kashmir: but as the rise took place during the Settlement, the Pandits of the City blamed me, and influenced the minds of the visitors. Still as I was always out in camp the murmuring of the visitors did not perturb me.

Though lonely so far as the English were concerned, I was far from lonely from the Kashmiri point of view. Indeed, from early morning to bed-time I was never allowed to be alone. Often when taking my bath I would see a hand gliding inside the hanging fall of the tent, with a petition in the hand, and for six long years there was no privacy. But it was all so full of interest, humanity and good humour that I never tired of their importunity. Such actors and story-tellers, and such children! When I caught them out in an obvious lie, they would make a clucking sound with their tongue, and the whole crowd would laugh, the inexact man laughing the loudest. Sometimes I would come across the *Bhaggat Log*, the wandering actors of Kashmir, and would "cote them by the way" and bespeak a performance, for these clever mimes taught me much of the ways of the officials and the wiles of the peasantry. They had wardrobes of great value, and some of the companies were famous. The only songs which I really enjoyed in India were the songs of the Kashmiri *Bhaggats*. They were in great request at weddings and harvest time, and on the whole they made a fair living.

I doubt whether the poets (*shâir*) of the Valley were equally fortunate, and most of them, to whose shrill voices I have listened, seemed miserably poor and very thankful for my small largess, given not because I liked their Kashmiri verse, but because I honoured their calling. Some seemed almost insane, and one who often came to my Camp was, although a Moslem, an excessive drinker. He had been a tutor to a high official, and he justified his propensity for strong spirit by quotations from the Persian poets. One day, when I was not in the mood for his verse, I declined to give him whisky; whereon he reviled me in the fiercest terms, said that the iron age of the Hindus had indeed arrived, and left my camp in tears. I have some of his poetry still. It must have sounded better as he recited it than it reads now: but it does recall Kashmir days and the hard times of the villagers until "Sir Lawrence came from London and arranged the Settlement," which is the refrain to each stanza. Poor poets of Kashmir. They had to flatter their chance patrons. As I listened to them under the beautiful planes, the villagers seated on the sunlit sward down by the clear stream from the mountain snows, I thought of Alexander. I did not "affect to nod," but did nod, as the poet droned on.

The real and great anxieties came not from man; but came when Nature, ordinarily so kind to the happy valley, turned against us. The earthquake I experienced was slight: but it is always demoralising, and the people remembered the earthquake which some fourteen years before killed nearly 3,500 persons. Twenty years before I went to Kashmir there was a terrible famine, and, though there were no trustworthy statistics, it was generally believed that only two-fifths of the population of the valley survived. Everywhere I found justification for the Kashmiri proverb "*Drág tsalih ta dág tsalih na*," "the famine goes but its stains remain." The famine left its ugly mark not only on the fertile valley, but also on the minds of the people, for they are clever enough to know that with good administration a real famine should be impossible in Kashmir. In 1889 the population was still too small for the proper cultivation of the rich soil of the Valley, despite the fertility of the women, who, on an average, gave birth to ten to fourteen children. But, as my Kashmiri friends used to tell me, "God takes his share," and when cholera comes, as it came in 1892, the share is large—it was over 18,000. I was in camp and in the city all through the height of the epidemic, and saw the ravages and demoralisation caused by this dread disease. Defoe, in his "Plague of London," did not hesitate to depict the failure of the strong English character in an awful pestilence, and it is not to be wondered at if the less stable Orientals become unhinged in a visitation such as that of 1892. All business was stopped, and the only shops which remained open were those of the sellers of white cloth for winding-sheets. Men would not lend money, and in the villages the people would sit all day long in the graveyards absolutely silent. In the city the people would go out at dawn to the gardens and parks in the suburbs, returning at night to hear that more of their relatives and friends had perished. The long lines of biers borne to the graveyards, resembled an endless regiment on the march, while on the river a long procession of boats floated down to the burning ghats, and living passengers in other boats passed by them with averted faces. Men telling me how they had lost all the members of their family would break into hysterical laughter, and I have never seen such utter despair and helplessness as I saw in 1892.

The last of my anxieties was the great flood of 1893. Fifty-two hours of warm rain brought down the snow from the mountains; brought down bears, panthers and pythons, drowned men and cattle; and covered with its cruel waters the finest crop of rice and maize I had ever seen Mercifully the flood reached its climax in the daytime, and the people were prepared. Six of the seven city bridges were swept away. I reached Srinagar by boat and entered my house by boat. By good fortune I had just built a new office of two storeys, an uncommon feature in Srinagar, and my maps and records were saved by being taken to the upper floor. I found my precious records intact, but also found two ponies who had climbed the stairs and had taken possession of the veranda. Good luck for me, but bad for the Pandits, since if my office had been destroyed, as my house was, four years' work would have been lost. I spent days in a boat looking for landmarks. As far as the great Wular lake the country was like a still sea beneath which grand crops of maize and rice lay rotting. Houses and fine ricks of wheat, barley and rape-seed were carried off, and the country presented a pitiable sight. Directly the rain had ceased, on July 20th, a bright hot sunshine followed, and this had the effect of rotting all crops standing in water.

Rice, as an aquatic plant, has a greater power of resistance than maize, but the floods below Srinagar were so persistent that only a very little of the rice submerged survived. The smell of the rotting maize and rice was very pungent, and the villages were for the most part deserted, as the cultivators had fled with their cattle to the uplands. Here and there on the *karewa*[1] cliffs cattle were collected, and the people were bivouacking in the open air. Up from Shadipur to the Sind Valley great damage had been done by the floods, and in the delta of the Sind the fields were strewn with timber and, still worse, with deep white sand, which destroyed the rice for the year and rendered the fields unfertile for some years to come. Men were dancing and weeping in their ruined fields, and in all directions there was wailing and despair. Marvellous tales were told of the efficacy of the flags of saints which had been set up to arrest the floods, and the people believe that the rice fields of Talumula and the bridge of Sambul were saved by the presence of these flags, which were taken from the shrines as a last resort.

Fire is bad, but in some ways a flood is worse, for it brings sickness and much muddy misery. As our home was ruined by the flood, we lived in a house-boat which I had built, and my son was attacked by typhoid fever. When the fever was at its height, there came a letter from England offering me very attractive work at home. My survey of the Valley was finished in September, 1894, and I felt that any appointment in India would seem tame and without savour after the independence and the variety of my life in Kashmir. I decided to accept the work at home, provided I found that after a trial I could cope with it. It was a great wrench to leave Kashmir and to leave India, but there is a passage in the Sikh scriptures which says that the pastures across the river are always the best. In India one often longs for the pleasant pastures of England; in England one yearns for the colour, romance and the aromatic breezes of the coral strand. Prudential voices came to me quoting that most cowardly of proverbs "The rolling stone gathers no moss;" but I determined to roll, and I went on rolling, gathering no moss, but gathering experiences and happiness.

[1] Plateau.

One other reflection before I leave beautiful Kashmir and see for the last time the Garden of Breezes on the exquisite Dal Lake. It is not a bad thing to serve under Indians. For six years I was under the orders of the State Council of Kashmir, which was composed of distinguished Indians. They never thwarted me, but were always helpful and always encouraging. They knew their business, and were, in their own lines, experts. But in their relations with the Maharája, the President of the Council, they never presumed on their expert knowledge, for they realised that he knew more about Kashmir and its people than they could ever know. There was a Moslem member of the Council who on occasions would speak of the other Hindu members as "his krupt cleegs" (his corrupt colleagues). But this was said in fits of temper, for they were not corrupt. There was among the Hindu members one whom I had known many years before, who had a curious idea. He bought a male infant, and kept him in a dark room till he attained majority, for a child who never sees the sun may in the darkness learn the secret of the philosopher's stone. I liked this member least of all my masters, but he was a very wise and able official. Thus, when I read of the rooted objections of young Englishmen to serve under Indians, I sometimes smile and recall with gratitude the happy six years I spent in Kashmir under a State Council. It was Indian, but it was efficient, honest and fair, and it was always loyal to its Chief. The method of government, which I watched closely for six anxious years, was possible in an Indian State: but it would have been impossible in a Provincial Government of the European bureaucratic type.

I must add one other tribute to this State Council. During my six years' residence in Kashmir, the Council held firmly the balance between the Hindus and Moslems, and there was not a single incident of what is now known in India as communal clash. I recall, too, that in Kashmir during the last two years of my Settlement, the representative of the Government of India was that best of all Political Officers, Colonel David Barr, the ideal officer, who never interfered until he was called upon: yet so attractive, sympathetic and human was he that all, whether Indian or English, came to him with their troubles, and never came in vain. It was a wrench to leave Kashmir, but to part with David Barr, so full of wit, wisdom and experience was an added pang. He left Kashmir before me. He was anxious to go back to Central India, in which he had spent most of his life. He was obviously the man to fill the office of Agent to the Governor-General for Central India, but he was too modest to ask for the post. I suggested that he should telegraph to Simla: "Please see psalm 132." He did so, and the Lord, as the Viceroy was often called, remembered David.

CHAPTER IX

What have they wrung from the silence? Hath even a whisper come
Of the secret, whence or whither? Alas for the gods are dumb.

—Sir Alfred Lyall.

Reluctance to Write on Religious Subjects—Ignorance of theological Literature—Unequipped by Study or Temperament—Hinduism in Three Northern Countries of India—Hinduism the Indigenous and National Religion—Based on One Idea, Reverence for the Bráhman—Unmoved by Mogul Conquest—Unshaken by John Company—Bráhmanism Described—Men Desert, but they Come Back—The Indispensable Bráhman—No Signs of Weakening—The Home and the Bráhman Director too Strong—Power of Caste—Reincarnation—Some Good Results of Bráhman System—Scope for Worship—Life of Hindus not so Dull as we Imagine—Fairs, Feasts and Visits of Homage to Religious Men—The Faqir—His Detachment from the World—Contemplation—Unwise to Ignore the Bráhman and the Faqir—The Astrologers—*Fama* and Hypnotism.

UNFORTUNATELY I am doubly disqualified from writing a chapter on religion in India. In the first place, no one unless he be a great Sanskrit scholar should venture to discuss the religion of the Hindus; in the second place anyone who writes of another religion should know something of his own. I have always regarded religion as a strange, sacred and personal affair, not to be discussed with the passer-by, and have rather shrunk from the stranger who might have had a message.

I have browsed on every kind of literature, but never ventured into the field which might have proved the most fascinating of all. I have no knowledge of the great library of theology, and "Line upon Line," the Prayer Book, the Bible and "The Pilgrim's Progress" are my only equipment. But I have listened entranced to great preachers in our glorious cathedrals, and have been carried by humble but inspired men in some quiet parish church through "golden vistas" into heaven. In spite of my ignorance of theological literature, I have always realised that the greatest of all influences is that of "an interpreter, one among a thousand," and have often thought that there were such men in India—that India which we, the British officials, never knew.

I have contemplated the faithful at the hour of prayer in some exquisite mosque, and realised in the rhythmical prostrations what things might be wrought by prayer. I have gazed uneasily at the Hindus worshipping in the dim, mephitic temples, smelling of oil, blood and acrid flowers. I have watched them deafened and distracted by the din of drum, conch and gong, making their offerings to the grim idols of their thirsty gods, all absorbed in a world closed and barred to me. I would ask the pale-eyed priests and the people what it all meant, but they would shake their heads and pass on.

Every day as I moved through the country there would be the ascetic at the cross-roads, the monks in the monasteries, the keepers of the shrines; under every fig tree a naked, ash-smeared religious man, mute signposts to the wayfarers, looking for the path, the one and only way. They stared through and beyond me and never demanded alms, for their bowls were well filled by the poor country folk, who gave of their best to these men who had renounced the world.

Sometimes I would come across evidence of the *odium theologicum*, mostly among the Moslems. I would hear mutterings of the antipathy between the Moslems and the Hindus, but I cannot remember any hatred or conflict between the countless sects of Hinduism, though at times I heard of disputes regarding the division of the offertory.

The various sects bore on their foreheads the distinguishing mark of their peculiar creed, but this seemed to me the only difference. Here again I am not a trained observer, for as a boy I loved the fireworks of the fifth of November but never understood the simulated hatred of Guy Fawkes. I once watched a man in a thin frock coat with a long upper lip and acidulated aspect, chalking on a wall the words "No Popery." It thrilled the others, but had no appeal for me. There must have been something lacking in me. Even now, as I write this book,[1] a prelate has told us that certain beliefs

[1] 1927.

to which I have always clung, "are not far from those of the cultured Hindu idolator," but even this fails to arouse me.

Thus unequipped by temperament or by study for the attempt to compare religions, I shall only describe my own impressions in those countries of India where frontiers meet —in Rajputána, in the Punjáb, and in Kashmir. I write without prejudice, as I saw very little in Hinduism in the North of India which repelled me, while I noticed much which was admirable and wholesome.

I speak of Hinduism, because in the Punjáb and in Kashmir as Settlement Officer, the only Moslems I saw were converts from Hinduism. Theirs was a tepid form of Islám, and I noticed the difference between men of the same tribe; the converts to Islám seemed in all respects inferior to those who had retained the old faith. They were less industrious, less frugal, and I think less trustworthy than their Hindu fellow-tribesmen. They had lost more than they had gained by their conversion to Islám.

When I was in Kashmir an Arab preacher visited me. His object was to put life into the languid observances of the Moslems of the Valley. I introduced him to the leading men of the country, but after a long tour through the villages he returned, baffled and dejected. He told me that he had found no true believers—in their hearts the Kashmiris of the Valley were as Hindu as were the Bráhmans of the Capital.

I had already seen the real believers on the Frontier and knew the splendid spirit of the fine fighting men who are grouped as "Punjábi Mahomedans." I realise that with them Islám is a great and living force, but, in writing of India, it is well to remember that Hinduism is the indigenous, I might almost say the national, religion. It controls 216 millions, while Islám holds 68 millions of the people.

I found some differences in Rajputána and in Kashmir. In the former country, the regular orders of the ascetics were more in evidence than they were in Kashmir. Vishnu was the popular god; Krishna, the beloved hero. In Kashmir, Siva was the chief object of worship, and it seemed to me that the cult of Vishnu was the happier and the brighter of the two. Perhaps this was imagination on my part. I had listened to the legends of Krishna and of the other joyous deities associated with Vishnu the "Preserver," and had attributed the fine bearing and the noble conduct of the Rájputs to their worship of him. Similarly I saw in the Kashmir worship of Siva the "Destroyer," "who rules for ever in death and love," a more gloomy and more cruel outlook, but, here again, I may have been influenced by the stories which cluster round the name of Káli, the dread consort of the Destroyer, and may have connected the harsh and oppressive treatment of the Moslems of Kashmir with the peculiar tenets of the followers of Siva, "*Le Dieu des exterminations*," that droughty[1] god, whose temples should be surrounded by water.

But after a time I came to the belief that the compelling influence which holds the millions of India in unbreakable bonds is not to be found in the adherence to any special god; in the fear of malign deities; in the dread of ghosts of the unhappy men, dead without male issue, cut off by violence; nor in the belief in the myriads of wayward spirits and strange superstitions which move the minds of India. It is to be found rather in one sentiment, one great force, which runs through Hinduism—the strong and abiding reverence for the Bráhman.

I have never heard the name of the god Bráhma mentioned. I have only seen one temple erected to him. But I would meet a Bráhman in every village, and the live and active Bráhman, without whom nothing in Hindu life, however trivial,[2] can be done, is the director and the arbiter of Hindu society. Bráhma[3] created the world, and the Bráhmans carry on his work.

Bráhmanism is a tremendous force, and I doubt whether, in all history, there has ever been a system so powerful, so coherent, and so elastic. It has well been described as a "way of life in itself." It cannot be described by the terms hierarchy or sacerdotalism, for Bráhmanism directs action and controls conduct—functions which call for no sacred

[1] "*Il ne faut pas se dissumuler qu'il se peut que les Dieux aient encore soif, comme cela eur arrive souvent.*"—Anatole France.

[2] This is admirably described in that mine of marvellous knowledge, Ibbetson's "Census Report of the Punjáb," *para* 202.

[3] "Only great Brahm endured: the gods but live."—*The Light of Asia.*

sanction, and have no concern with priests. It is all-embracing and knows no difference between things sacred and profane. Without the Bráhman, no Hindu can be born, married, or die; and woe to the harvest if the Bráhman's fee has not been paid at sowing and at reaping. Long before the Christian era the profession of the priest had become hereditary, and his power had increased,[1] and Bráhmanism had become the greatest and most dominant of the castes. The Bráhmans established themselves as the arbiters of the caste system, aggrandising their own power and social position by keeping the other classes in their proper and lower places.

Later, foreign conquerors from the north-west swooped down on India, but their business was to beat down the men who ruled and fought, and they ignored the real power in the land—the persuasive and persistent Bráhman. Unmoved by the imperial splendour of the Mogul, unshaken by the business grip of John Company and the subsequent triumphs of the British engineers over space and drought, he can afford to watch with quiet indifference political experiments, exotic and of foreign inspiration. All these are for him so many smoke clouds, behind which he quietly works and consolidates.

Though Rajputána was the country least affected by the conquerors of India and though the King class survived, Bráhmanism is still respected, the temples are well endowed,[2] the religious houses are rich, their inmates sleek, and all the castes of Rajputána vie with one another in feeding the Bráhmans. Sometimes the proud Rájput is more interested in the annals of his own family than he is in the great story of Ráma, and pays greater reverence to the bard than to the Bráhman priest.

[1] "Imperial Gazetteer of India, 1908," Vol. ii. p. 228. "In the Rig-Veda the sacrifice was merely a means of influencing the will of the gods in favour of the offerer; in the Yajur-Veda it has not only become the centre of thought and desire, but its power is now so great that it compels the gods to do the will of the priests. Religion is now a kind of mechanical sacerdotalism, in which a crowd of priests conduct a vast and complicated system of external ceremonies to the smallest details of which the greatest weight is attached. Simultaneously with the elaboration of the ritual went on the growth and consolidation of the caste system, which, securing to the Bráhmans social as well as religious supremacy, has held India enthralled for more than 2,500 years."

[2] Tod's "Rajasthan." Chap. XIX. "There is scarcely a State in Rajputána in which one-fifth of the soil is not assigned for the support of the temples, their ministers, the secular Bráhmans, Bards, and genealogists."

Government and the system of Bráhmanism sometimes clash, just as every day the practice of life clashes with the teachings of Hinduism. I have seen monkeys destroying valuable crops, while the Hindu cultivators looked on helpless, imploring me to shoot the sacred marauders. When I refused, they probably included my name in their imprecations on the despoilers.

Bráhmanism is a wonderful system, so gentle and easy, so clutching and ineluctable, such a simple scheme for the control of mankind. Sometimes I think of it as a huge octopus which grasps all India in its soft tentacles; sometimes as a Tartar horde moving slowly through the land, over hills and through dark forests. It marches in good order, disciplined by master minds, by men as nameless and unseen as is the God Bráhma. From dim recesses of the Indian world, "from creeks and inlets," recruits pour in to join the army. They come of their own accord, there is no need to send out sergeants. They come, not for the sake of new gods, since they bring their old gods into the camp. They come, these wild, barbarous, dark-skinned children of the forest, just for social advancement, for recognition as members of the system of India. Bráhmanism is the only wear; on its flag there is the legend "izzat,"[1] and it is good to be respectable—to get into society—it costs little at first—just the food of the Bráhmans.

As the recruits flock in, deserters leave the ranks, but without protest, malediction or punishment. In India there are many men of ideas and vision; they see new paths and they strike out with a host of followers. But the patient Bráhman smiles. He has great hereditary qualities, amongst them the quality of waiting. He has seen mass desertions. He has seen many an inspired teacher trudging away to the delectable mountains. He knows that in good time they will all come back, that they cannot do without their Bráhman—not even the Sikhs, the Jains, not even the Buddhists.

There are Western thinkers who hold that Bráhmanism, like other systems, will decay; that new ideas will undermine

[1] *Izzat* is as dear to an Indian as life. It means honour, repute, and the world's esteem.

the pagan structure; and that British education will lift the mists of superstition. Missionaries, friends of a lifetime, have told me that there is a change from Polytheism to a belief in one deity. But in conversation with Hindus, I have never heard the suggestion of Polytheism. Always the talk is of one god. I have observed no signs of decay, but I can only speak from what I have seen with my own eyes. I have known intimately Indians of great ability and of liberal education. They would talk with the wisdom and intelligence of a highly educated and enlightened Englishman. But when they went back to their family they would hang up the fiddle of free thought in their Hindu home. They are a domestic people and the home and the Bráhman director mean more than the applause of Councils or the conquests of the market.

I had a Hindu friend in Calcutta. He had been sent twice to England by the Government, for he was an expert —indeed, the only expert—on a subject, neglected in India, but very important both to England and to India. One day he took me to see the Temple of Káli, the famous fane from which Calcutta takes its name. I thought it a good opportunity for seeking the secrets of my friend's religion, but he preferred to talk of the penalties of caste. He told me that when he came back from his visit to England he had been heavily fined for crossing the "black water." He had paid the fine and was re-admitted to caste. But when he went to England a second time the fine was very heavy, and he was warned that he must not repeat the offence. Now the Government wanted him to go again and he was anxious to go. I urged him to go and to defy the rules of caste, but he sadly replied: "Would you defy caste if you knew that you and those dear to you would be outcasts, and when they die, dragged by scavengers to the burning ghat?" He was no coward and was highly esteemed by the Government, but he realised that the home came first, and that the Bráhman could destroy him in this life and in the future lives of the reincarnation. The threat of "sixty thousand years in hell" appals the bravest.

As far as I could learn, all Hindus believe in reincarnation, and their almost stoic patience and beautiful acquiescence in their environment may be partly attributed to this belief. Sometimes when the talk grew intimate a chance word or a startled look would suggest the "ebb into a former life," and the thought would come of that strange something which "has had elsewhere its setting and cometh from afar." They would never discuss their future chances, and never comment on the lot of their neighbour who had passed over, and would never tell me whether it was good or evil for a Rája to become a fish when he ceased to be a King. I often noticed their indifference to death. They were sorry when a young man died, but rather rejoiced when an old man passed away. It was a misfortune to die without leaving a son, but otherwise death was no great thing, as there were so many lives to come. There would be rivalry and envy among men of the same class; but I have never heard men of a lower class speak jealously or bitterly of the class above them.

I have said above that I saw much in Hinduism which was admirable and wholesome, and though I look on the Bráhman system much in the same light as a lizard might view a moraine, or a beetle a steam-roller, it is fair to enumerate some of its good results.

The Hindus are frugal, good to their young and their old folk; they are industrious bread-winners, loyal and devoted to their homes. They are very patient and law-abiding, very obedient to authority when it is apparent and present. I could mention many other admirable qualities, and all praise is due to the Hindus, for they live in a world which most Englishmen would regard as an impossible nightmare. They walk along a lane of bewilderment with terror at many a turn, and often illusion at the ending of the way.

The Hindu is under two authorities: the Bráhman and the *Sirkár*.[1] Both are exacting at times, but of the two the Bráhman is perhaps the less rigid and the easier to understand. In the Bráhman jurisdiction there is great variety, ample scope for free thought, and endless opportunities for the Hindu's ruling passion and preoccupation—worship. He will worship anything or anybody, and as he saunters

[1] *Sirkár*, the Government.

through life there is much to interest him. There are auguries and omens; beasts and birds to be observed; stones and rocks and trees to be propitiated; some holy spring or sacred pool to be visited—"books in the running brooks, sermons in stones, and good in everything." Unhappily there is evil as well as good in the objects which confront him as he passes from his hut to his fields, from his fields to his hut. There are malevolent as well as benevolent deities awaiting him. But I always thought that he got more thrills out of his life than we of the western world experience. With us a visit to the fortune-teller is a rare adventure, with them the astrologer is as common as the tax-collector. We talk about the weather—they know about the weather. They seemed to me to know more about nature than we did, and their knowledge is handed down from immemorial generations in arresting proverbs.

We imagine sometimes that theirs is a dull life. As I watched the oxen turning the Persian wheel at the well, and the buffalo lumbering round the oil-press in the dark shed lit by a feeble lamp, I would read in the steady brown eyes of my companions the reciprocated thought—"This is the common lot. We shall go to our fields, and you must ride on for years to other villages."

Still, the life of the villagers is not altogether that of Mr. Mantalini at the mangle: "I am perpetually turning, like a dem'd old horse[1] in a demnition mill, my life is one dem'd horrid grind."

When he is not busy in his fields, arguing with his moneylender, or expostulating with some unwelcome emissary from Government, he is communing with a spirit world rich in variety and charged with surprises. He has ample leisure, for there are seasons—calculated by some observers to cover six months in the year—when the fields must be left to themselves. Then is the time for the temples, the religious fairs, the wedding feasts, and above all for paying homage to the men of religion, and to those ascetics who have given up the world—the Faqirs.

Many of us who have lived in India are apt to look

[1] Cf. Anatole France. "*Est-ce que par hasard que l'humanité ne ferait autre chose que tourner comme un cheval autour d'une meule?*"

askance at the Faqirs, but Sir Denzil Ibbetson, who knew more about life in the villages than any Englishman and who taught me how to observe,[1] has a good word for the religious orders. "Many of these are of the highest respectability: the members are generally collected in monasteries or shrines, where they live quiet, peaceful lives, keeping open house to travellers, training their neophytes, and exercising a wholesome influence upon the people of the neighbourhood. . . . Some travel about begging and visiting their disciples. . . . There is an immense number of these men whose influence is almost wholly for good."

In such a large flock there must be black sheep. I can only judge by the faces and the mien of the Faqirs, whom I paused to observe, by the faces of the men who made them gifts, and by the life and the conduct of the country folk who held them in reverence.

Their livery of ashes, their paint-smeared foreheads, and their matted locks repel at first sight, but sometimes I caught an expression which almost gained in nobility by its squalid and grotesque setting.

One evening in a wild part of Jammu territory I was overtaken by a heavy storm as I rode up a steep mountain-track. I had gone ahead of my camp-followers, was soaked to the skin, and was thankful to find at nightfall the shelter of a mango grove. Behind the dark trees was a hill-scarp, and in it a large cave, in the middle of which sat a Faqir, his right arm[2] bent, atrophied and rigid above his head; with his left hand he was cooking on an iron plate his evening meal of unleavened bread. Hitching my horse to a branch of a tree, I approached the Faqir, told him of my plight, how that my bed and food were on their way, and that the track was by this time probably washed down the cliff—on which he offered me his leathery pancake. I accepted the food

[1] "Too many of us go about among the people with our eyes and our ears shut, or if we do acquire any information think it too trivial, and too much a matter of course to be worth recording; and every year sees Indian officials, with their heads stored with facts of the most invaluable nature, die, and take their knowledge with them." Ibbetson. "Census of the Punjáb," *para* 246.

[2] "Their slowly wasting joints and stiffened limbs
Jutted from sapless shoulders like dead forks
From forest trunks."—*Light of Asia.*

with gratitude, and he deftly set to work to cook another cake. I sat down on a rock near my host and studied his face. It was the picture of resignation and refinement, gentle eyes and finely shaped head. But like most of his fraternity, he would not speak. I told him of my life in Kashmir: how I had seen the pilgrims at the holy places and had tried, when I could, to help them: how I had often longed to hear of the wanderings of men like him. We were both of us wanderers, and could tell each other much of interest. Fate had brought us to this cave. Surely he could speak. His eyes spoke kindly but never a word would he utter. I suggested that the Hindus were always courteous and that silence on such an occasion seemed discourteous. On this he dropped the iron fork from his hand, looked intently at me, smiled, shook his head but said nothing. Then I told him that my tobacco was useless, as the rain had spoiled it, and he pushed his hookah towards me. I hoped that this would prove a pipe of friendship but he still kept silence. Yet all the time the kind eyes of this ascetic told me that he was in sympathy, and I sat on, hazarding guesses as to his life and wanderings and his hopes —and sometimes there was a look in the eyes, a movement of the lips, a contraction in the throat, which told me when I had guessed right.

At last I exhausted my store of vain knowledge. He still looked at me with his wistful dog-like eyes, all the time feeding with his slender iron tongs the small fire of charcoal and faggots which gave out a grateful warmth and helped to dry my wet clothes. Then I began to think that there can be sympathy and communion of thought without words, and for another hour I stayed silent, but our eyes talked. As I looked at his thin body, his shrunken, withered right arm, the poor beggar bowl now so empty, and the threadbare blanket, I remembered the question: "Doth Job fear God for nought?"

The sound of my approaching followers brought me back to the world, and I said good-bye almost with reluctance, for my naked and forlorn companion seemed to have the power of sending my thoughts far away from my everyday life. He waved his left hand in negation when I offered him silver for my entertainment, and went on counting his beads. I and my camp passed on to the village, which was our halting place. Next day I asked the villagers whether they knew the Faqir—was he famous, wise, or had he occult powers? No, he was just a holy man, recently arrived from Benáres.

Another Faqir interested me. In the winter in Kashmir the rivers and the lakes were frozen and the frost was intense. I skated across the Dal lake to the golden island, and found there sitting on the frozen snow a Faqir almost naked. He looked young, and he too had a good face and most intelligent and expressive eyes. The people from the city, Hindus and Moslems, had flocked out across the ice to see this man who sat there day and night on a leopard skin defying the rigours of the climate. He, too, was silent and remote from us worldlings, but I could tell from his eyes, half scornful, half amused, that he followed our remarks, our speculations as to his charm against cold. One old Kashmiri friend said to me: "He must smoke hashish," but the Faqir negatived this suggestion with a motion of his hand. I noticed that he never acknowledged the alms which the admiring crowd lavished on him. He was a week's wonder, and then disappeared, and I was assured by men whose word I could trust that there was no trick and that he sat there day and night in his ashes.

Years after when I saw the fire walkers in Bikanir there was no trick, and I saw men walking slowly through the flame, unscorched and unhurt. There they told me that the secret was faith, but the more I watched the Faqirs and tried to find out the reason of their influence on the people, the more I thought that their power lay in their absolute detachment from the world.

This is all surmise, for their armour of silence makes it impossible to get to the truth. Sometimes they have talked to me, but long silence seemed to make their words incoherent, and I learnt more from looking at them than from listening to them. I used to question the people as to the causes which led men to give up the world, but I learnt nothing beyond generalities.

Once, just before my ship was leaving Bombay, I was talking with some English friends and we noticed a strange looking Indian with long hair hanging down his back, dressed in curious clothes, half Indian, half European. My friends challenged me to tell them his caste and country, but I was puzzled. I had travelled through every country of India and thought that I could distinguish the different races. I said I could not make him out, but he might be from Sind. To make sure, I approached him, asked him whether this was his first voyage and whether I could be of any assistance. He responded pleasantly, and then I told him that his garb and headdress were strange to me. He laughed, and then in faultless English told me his story:

"Two years ago I was rich, the owner and editor of a well-known journal in Calcutta. I aped the European fashions, neglected my family, my religion and my caste, and was as bad a profligate as any in India. I had a fine house, a splendid library, and though I spent extravagantly I still had a large income. Suddenly I saw that my life was rotten, and I determined to leave my wife and family and all my possessions and seek the protection of a *Guru*[1] in Benares who was as good as I was bad. But the holy man saw what I was and repulsed me with contempt. Again and again I besought him to take me as his *chela*,[2] but he drove me away with abuse and blows. After some weeks he relented and took me in, and when my probation was complete, sent me to wander through the jungle. Night by night I would sleep where the dead were burnt, never speaking, and watching the stars in my solitude.

"Two days ago I was told to come to Bombay as I was wanted to go out to America as a lecturer. I washed off my ashes and paint, bought some European clothes, and came on board this ship."

The next night I saw him in the saloon in evening dress, and later he wrote to me from Paris telling me of his plans in America.

I had often met elderly Hindus who had given up office and wealth to live in solitary contemplation. One of these

[1] Spiritual preceptor: the Moslems also have their preceptors—*Pir*.
[2] Neophyte; disciple; lit. a servant.

was the famous Sir Dinkar Rao,[1] and he told me of the comfort of getting out and away from the fever of life.

In Rajputána there is a temple far away, beautiful, shady and secluded, where rich gifts come from all parts of the East, tokens of gratitude to the gentle Kṛishna. In Tod's time it was a sanctuary for criminals and a haven to those "whom ambition had cloyed, superstition unsettled, satiety disgusted, commerce ruined, or crime disquieted."[2] Before they may gain admission to the shrine and share in the food of the god, they must give up family and friends and make over their wealth to the Pontiff of the temple. When Tod knew this famous shrine, the personal income of the high priest was £10,000 per annum. It was impossible to estimate the value of the rich caravans which brought the offerings of worshippers, costly gifts from distant Samarcand and from the ports of Arabia. Merchants dwelling beyond the Indus and as far as the Caspian sent their tribute to this happy backwater of life where "no blood-stained sacrifice scares the timid devotee, no austerities terrify or tedious ceremonies fatigue him."

To the strenuous active mind of the Englishman, this may seem a poor ambition, a limited ideal, but to the Hindu buffeted by the blows of two conflicting worlds, the peace of Náthdwára passes our understanding. There are many similar shrines in India, where men escape from "too much love of living, from hope and fear set free."

We shall never understand the Indians, never gain their sympathy nor win their confidence, while we deal with them purely on official lines. We shall never get near their hearts while we dismiss with a superior smile the strange beliefs and fancies which mean so much to them and con-

[1] Sir Dinkar was one of those notable Indians who make their mark in the congenial environment of Indian States. In the Mutiny a doubting Rája of a great State asked Sir Dinkar's advice as to whether he should side against the British Ráj. "What should I get," he inquired, "if I joined the rebels?" "Six foot of rope," said Sir Dinkar.

One day he was with a friend of mine at the Calcutta Zoo—Zoological Gardens are very popular with the Indians. They call them *Chiriya Khana* (birds' houses). My friend and Sir Dinkar were looking at some fine tigers, one of which had been a famous man-eater. "What would happen," asked my friend, "if the British left India?" "Exactly what would happen if you removed all the bars of all the cages in this garden," was the reply. That was an obvious truth sixty years ago. It is equally obvious to-day.

[2] Tod's "Rájasthan," Vol. I. Chap. XIX.

stitute their way of life. A system such as Bráhmanism, which has lasted for 2,500 years, barely touched by Western ideas, and practically unimpaired by our efficient administration, cannot be lightly dismissed. We must reckon with our host. Social reforms, indeed all reforms, will fail, if the Bráhman shakes his head. Just as he is a director and arbiter of the Hindus in matters of the other world, so he is the controller of their affairs in this world. It is equally unwise to ignore the Faqirs. Some of them stand for what is highest in most of the religions of the world. They represent, often dramatically and worthily, renunciation and self-sacrifice, believing that their woes

> "Shall purge
> Sin's dross away, and the soul, purified,
> Soar from the furnace of its sorrows, winged
> For glorious spheres and splendour past all thought.

Nor is it wise to laugh at any of the universal beliefs of an old and grave civilisation which has long since lost the faculty of laughter. We smile[1] now when we hear of the astrologer, but he plays an important part in Eastern life. Sometimes the astrologers, like others in similar professions, are inclined to hedge, and perhaps much is heard of their successful predictions and little of their failures. But I have known many cases in which their forecasts seemed to be substantiated and accurate. I sometimes notice in our papers that a fortune-teller has been convicted for telling fortunes for money, and I wonder, when I think of the astrologers, "Soothsayers like the Philistines," who also tell fortunes and take money in India. They base their predictions on the true and never-failing stars, and many wise and great men whom I have known in India are guided in their actions by the monthly gazette of their family astrologer, the quiet man, possibly living at Benáres, who watches the wondrous firmament and tells his clients what they may expect. Not only do the Hindus believe in the science of the astrologers, but the Moslems, too,[2] know that

[1] In the sixteenth and seventeenth centuries astrologers were the fashion in England. Charles I and Cromwell both had recourse to the astrologer.

[2] Cf. "The Adventures of Hajji Baba."

the stars have their influence. I could give many instances to show the extraordinary accuracy of the astrologer, and I grew so accustomed to the implicit belief which my friends had in astrologers that I never expressed a doubt, though I sometimes ventured to cross-examine and to obtain corroboration from Englishmen.

One friend of mine, an Indian Chief, received his monthly programme of events from his astrologer. "Jotish Ji," as he always called him, sent a warning that my friend's heir would be seized by a strange fever on the 27th March. The Chief was going with his family into camp for shooting, and he had with him an English doctor and an English nurse. Having learnt that a specific drug was the chief remedy for the disease predicted, he told his English doctor to procure the drug, as on the 27th March his heir apparent would be attacked by this unusual fever. The doctor had no belief in astrology and neglected the warning which was given him on the 2nd March, but my friend ordered the drug from Bombay. All went well till the 27th March. The whole party were in good health and spirits, but that day the heir apparent was attacked by the fever. The Chief asked the doctor whether he had the drug, and he admitted that he had not carried out orders. My friend produced the remedy and his heir apparent is still heir apparent.

The same astrologer one clear, starry night was sitting on the veranda of my friend's chalet in the hills. He had been entertaining some British officers, and after dinner they went on to the veranda where in a corner they saw the astrologer muffled up in a blanket, for he lived in hot Benáres and felt the chill of the air, in June, 1914. "What do you see in the stars, Jotish Ji?" asked the Chief. "I see five great nations at war in Europe," replied the astrologer.

I have told elsewhere how the astrologers of Kashmir came out to me when my eldest son was stricken by typhoid. The English doctor who daily came out to my camp had little hope of the fever breaking. The astrologers offered to cast the boy's horoscope and kindly sent me after two days the rough and incomplete forecast, as it would take a month to prepare the full horoscope. The draft predicted that the fever would break on a certain date. My wife took down the date, and the fever mercifully ceased on that very day.

There are many strange fields of thought and experience in which the Indians move, ignored or taken for granted by us matter-of-fact people from the West. Astrology is one such field. There are charlatans among the astrologers, as there are knaves among the ascetics, and they are evil and do harm. I have heard of instances where the quack astrologer ruined lives and brought about marriages of misery. But there are many Indians whom I have known who believed with Varaha Mihira[1] that "As the night without a light, as the sky without a sun, so is a King without an Astrologer." The Indian sage postulated great qualities in the astrologer and had no respect for the star-gazer. He regarded the sun as the fountain head of astronomical science, and in his view the astrologer was naught if he were not a student of astronomy. "A person who without knowing the science exercises the profession of astrologer, is a wicked man and a disgrace to society. Consider him to be a mere star-gazer." I fear that many of the fortune-tellers who travel through the villages are "a disgrace to society" and a pest to India, "circumforanean Rogues and Gipsies." But it is unwise to ignore or contemn a code which guides hundreds of millions from the casting of the horoscope to the funeral pyre. Perhaps Robert Burton, most learned of Oxford men, was wise in his opinion. He did not "apologise for Judicial Astrology." As for the stars, "They do incline but not compel: no necessity at all, *agunt non cogunt:* and so gently incline that a wise man may resist them, *sapiens dominabitur astris:* they rule us, but God rules them. The heaven is a great book, whose letters are the stars wherein are written many strange things for such as can read." Burton quotes Paracelsus and notices that Hippocrates, Galen and Avicenna held that physicians without astrology were butchers—*homicidas medicos astrologiae ignaros.*

There are many mysteries in India which I cannot explain yet cannot ignore. I have been the unwilling patient of collective hypnotism, a kind of *illusion consentie.* I have

[1] A great astronomer, died A.D. 587.

never seen a man fling a rope into the air, climb up it and disappear. I have never seen a man lift himself and a chair from *terra firma.* But I have read of these things, and have met men who solemnly assured me that they had seen these miracles. When I was with Lord Curzon in India an Englishman wrote to an important newspaper saying that he and two British officers had seen the rope trick in Karachi. I at once asked the writer to place me in communication with the two officers, but he declined to give their names. Later, a famous conjurer came from England and gave a performance at Government House. He had a French name and a Welsh accent. I asked him about the rope trick. He said: "I have a cheque for £700 which I will gladly give to anyone who will do the rope trick in my presence, but, so far, I have failed to find the man."

I often pondered on the way news passed in India, faster than the *fama* of the Romans. I remember how the news of Cavagnari's murder reached the bazaar in Peshawar two days before the tragedy was known to the authorities in India. Travelling to Gilgit on a mountain track in the high Himalayas I noticed that my guide was talking to himself, as I thought. But he was really talking to a man on the other side of the precipitous valley—it seemed to me to be miles away—but he was talking and receiving answers. It was nothing strange to my guide, and I sent messages through him to the little figure across the ravine and received quick and intelligent replies. I think many who have lived in India, and have observed, will agree that the Indians have some strange method of transmitting intelligence which cannot be explained by bonfires on mountain tops nor by any method of signals.

CHAPTER X

"The gifted few of matchless breed"—LOWELL

Indian States Contrasted with System of British India—Huge Size of British Provinces—Personal Touch Between Rája and His People—The Daily Durbár—Education of Chiefs—Inherited Knowledge of Rája—Indian States a *Terra Incognita*—One of the Two Real Indian Institutions Left—Better Suited to Indian Temperament—Bright Life in Capital—Idiosyncrasies of a Few Abnormal Rájas—The Jewel Houses—Historical Gems—Treasure Forts—Isolation of Rájas Disappearing—System of Indian States more Suitable for India than Any Form of Democratic Government—Impossible for Indians to Work Bureaucratic System—Better to Adopt as Model for New System a Well-governed Indian State—Possible to Constitute Indian States throughout India—Recent Case of Benáres—Due Safeguards of Existing Interests Necessary—Sketch of Maharája of Jammu and Kashmir.

THE Indian States always interested me. They were to me the real India, rich in variety, types and contrasts. I seemed to pass into a new world when I left the land of regulation for the country of chance, colour and charm; when I passed from British India into an Indian State. In British India the machine of law and regulation moves on like the Car of Jagannáth, and all is well for those who keep clear of the wheels. There is a time for sowing and reaping, and a time for paying in the land revenue: there are *Táhsils*[1] and *Thánas*[2] dotted about the country, and the dweller in British India, wherever he may go, will find the same law-court, the same school, and the same gaol, all of the same pattern. If he likes monotony, it is there. But the Indian dislikes monotony in excess, and seeks at long intervals for the fun of the fair, and travels great distances to the mighty *Melas*,[3] where he can meet his fellows in the old fashion. But nowadays in British territory even the *Mela* must be regulated. In British India there is now very little personal touch between the people and the

[1] Subdivisional Revenue Office. [2] Police Station.
[3] A fair connected with some religious celebration.

British members of the administration, and the tendency is still further to discourage the personal element in Government. The increasing office work of the British officials in the Districts, the decreasing opportunities for the tours, the camp life and for the interviews with Indians, who come to Headquarters, as their fathers came, to pay their respects to the Sahib; the use of motor cars which rarely leave the high road, and the disuse of the languages of the people; these combined are destructive of that touch of nature which leavened and lightened the heavy regularity of our rule. This same tendency has made it easy for the agitator to spread his anti-British propaganda through the villages. There is no one now who can refute the slander or expound the truth. If the District Officer be far away from the villagers, Delhi is still further, and the old saying "*Delhi dur ast*"[1] applies to all the Provincial capitals. The Provinces are so huge, so unmeaning to the millions of men who, jumbled together in a Province, are dissimilar in race, religion, customs, language, that there is small blame to them if they do not know, and do not care who sits in the seats of the mighty. He comes and goes, and they have never regarded him as their Protector and Providence. Once, in Calcutta, some villagers were gazing at the fine statues which line the Red Road, and one of them, pointing to the effigy of some Viceroy, asked what it represented. "*Koi Rakshas hoga*,"[2] was the reply.

In Indian States it is all different. It is important to realise the extent of the territory ruled by the Rájas. I use the word Rája[3] for convenience, but there are many variations of the kingly title. In Hindu states the ruler is known as Maharája, Maharána, Maharáo, Ráwal, Rái and Ráo. In Moslem States the usual title is Nawáb, but the greatest of the Moslem Princes is the Nizám. There are also the titles of Mir, Khán and Jám.

[1] Delhi is far.

[2] Peradventure some demon or other.

[3] My old friend the present Maharája of Bikanir in a recent speech said: "I have humbly endeavoured in all earnestness to live up to the ancient Hindu ideal of Kingship. Etymologically a Rája is only he who *pleases* his people and keeps them well content; protection is the very kernel of kingly duties according to the Mahabharata, and of the six citadels of a kingdom mentioned in our Holy Scriptures, the citadel of 'ready service and the love of the subjects' is the one most impregnable."

There are some six hundred and seventy-five States in India, of an area of eight hundred and twenty-four thousand square miles, and containing a population of seventy-two millions. Of these States seventy-three have rulers who are entitled to salutes of eleven guns or more, and are addressed as "His Highness." From a geographical and strategical point of view the States are of great importance, and though seventy-two millions of people seem insignificant when compared with the vast population of British India, it must be remembered that in quality the people of the States are the thoroughbreds of India, and some of them possess a real nationality. Five of the States are in direct relations with the Government of India. The two largest of these are Haidarabad in the South, eighty-two thousand, six hundred and ninety-eight square miles, and Jammu and Kashmir in the North, eighty thousand square miles. In the former there is a Moslem ruler over a people mostly Hindus; in the latter, a Hindu ruler over a people chiefly Moslem: and it is interesting to notice that the regrettable fights between the two religions, which in late years have become so common in British India, are almost unknown in the Indian States. The States have their Charters in their Treaties, which give them sovereignty qualified by the fact that they are under the Suzerainty of the King Emperor. In a hundred and seventy-five States the Suzerainty of the King Emperor is exercised by the Supreme Government of India in the person of the Viceroy; while in five hundred States it is entrusted to the Provincial Governments.

Whatever may be the outcome of Indian reform, provision must be made for the fulfilment of the obligations towards the Indian States which are contained in the various Treaties. They are recorded in a convenient form in the eleven volumes of Aitchison's "Treaties," a work which used to be known to the officers who aspired to service in the Political Department of India, and is very well known to the Rájas and their advisers. They were made, for the most part, when the British swept in full and powerful tide over the great Peninsula, and brought peace—The *Pax Britannica* —to the distracted and almost exhausted States of India.

Throughout these States, which present even more startling diversity than can be found in the two hundred and fifty millions of people who are huddled together in the fifteen[1] Provinces of British India, there is found always, and everywhere, the strong personal link between the Rája and his people, for he is with them for life, and when he is gathered to his fathers, his son or his adopted son will carry on the traditions and customs of the State. The Rája himself is bound by these traditions, and knows that his people dislike innovations which clash with custom. All, even the humblest, can have access to the Rája, and the daily Durbár is at once the refuge and the remedy of the people, the rein and curb of the officials, and the *raison d'être* of the Rája. So much is the Rája a part of the Hall of Audience, that the people speak of him as "Durbár," or "Durbár Sahib." It is curious that our predecessors did not borrow the institution of the daily Durbár. The only example I ever saw in British India was the Durbár of the Indian Cavalry Regiment. It was an admirable method of inquest, and a grand device for clearing the air.

In Indian States it has many uses. It affords an opportunity to the Rája for speaking directly to the people, and for learning from them their homely wants and preoccupations. It gives the people a chance of seeing and hearing their Chief, and of judging what kind of man he is. It is a fine safety valve; and one result of the Durbár habit is that the Rája knows more than his officials about the personalities and the conditions of his State. As a boy he has listened to his father, and even to his grandfather, telling of the problems and incidents of past generations. The Rája is proud of his stored-up knowledge of customs, precedents, proverbs; he has a memory for faces and names, and knows the value of prompt and laconic decisions. Legends grow up of his wise and pithy judgments; and on the whole I should say that Durbár justice is prompter and less ruinously expensive than it is in India, and in the long run just as fair; for the Rája knows the facts, and understands the people. The Rájas—and I have known many

[1] There are nine large Provinces, three of which, Madras, Bengal and the United Provinces of Agra and Oudh, have populations of over forty millions.

of them—are men of great courtesy and dignity, and these qualities appeal to all Indian hearts.

I was at the opening of the Mayo College for Chiefs at Ajmere; helped to draw up the rules for the Chiefs' College at Lahore; have visited the College for Chiefs at Indore, and the famous School in Kathiawár hallowed by the memory of Chester McNaghten; and have seen the effect of the education, and the change which has come in the outlook and capacity of the Indian Princes of to-day. I have watched the change with close interest, and have also studied the effects of visits to Europe, and the formation of Western habits of life, fearing that these might weaken the old strong link between the Rája and his people. But there has been no real or permanent rupture. One of the Rájas, whom I have known for long years, one of the ablest and most successful administrators of the present time, is absolutely unspoiled by foreign travel, and is as devoted to his people, his family and his religion, as any home-staying Indian Prince. In spite of such change, and in spite of legislation and material progress in British India, which have their echo and their effect on the Indian States, the relations of the Rájas to their people remain unimpaired, and the Indian State still depends on the personality of its Chief, and on the maintenance of personal touch between the Ruler and his subjects. It may be that some of the Rulers of the seventy-three more important States would not be regarded as ideal administrators if judged by Western standards. But it is unwise and dangerous to appraise Indian institutions in terms of Western opinions and prejudices. I have known Rájas who outwardly might have been regarded by casual observers as lacking in some of the approved arts and methods of Government, yet were looked on by their subjects as a father. They might have seemed to the Western mind old-fashioned, but their people held them to be wise and just in their decisions, esteemed them for their courtesy, and loved them for their knowledge of the country-side.

Perhaps the people in Indian States are more tolerant and less exacting than the folk of British India: yet, after all, the Rája is one of themselves, eats the same food, wears the same clothes, and thinks the same thoughts. The Rája, moreover, knows what his people want, and, unconsciously, perhaps, is more swayed by public opinion than are the rulers of British India, who find it very difficult to know what the people really desire. They think that they know what the people ought to want in the way of sanitation, education, popular franchise and swifter progress; but the people are too polite and too fatalist to say that in their hearts they care for none of these. But the Rája, whether in his palace, or in his progress through his State, comes into touch with the humble villager, knows his languages, can read his face, and understands a chance allusion in the local patois. He is not dependent on the officials of his Court, nor is he the slave of administrative shibboleths. He often likes short cuts, likes dramatic justice, and, above all, likes to emulate some predecessor whose name is still remembered as the rival of Naushirwán.

Very little is known about the Indian States. The number of British officers who serve in the States is small, and to the officials of British India, the land of the Rájas is indeed a *terra incognita*. Hasty observers who have read Reports, or have seen with their own eyes the great public works of British India, and many other signs of material progress, are apt to regard the Indian State as an anachronism. They do not reflect that an institution indigenous, Indian in spirit and genius, and ancient, is not necessarily an anachronism. The Indian State is one of the two institutions still left in India of the real Swaráj type. The other is the Indian village with its Council of five.[1] Both have survived, unimpaired by political cataclysms or economic changes. The framers of the new order for British India might with advantage have remembered their existence.

I regard the average Indian State as better suited to the happiness and temperament of the Indian than the huge unwieldy administrations which are responsible for the vast Provinces of the Indian continent. And I believe that the average State ruled by Rájas of the standard which I have

[1] "The Council of an Indian village community most commonly consists of five persons . . . the Panchayet, familiar to all who have the smallest knowledge of India."
"Early History of Institutions."—MAINE.

known, is better calculated to bring content and opportunities to the people than is the present system of British India, a bureaucracy of British mark, largely administered by Indians. The Indian is rather a fine and sensitive subject for experiments in government. Spiritually he moves in regions wider than are known to us; but materially he likes limits and prefers to live with his own fellows within those limits. His ideal is for small, homogeneous units. It gives him no gratification to feel that the King's writ runs through British India, and that everywhere he can find the same law, the same school, and the same gaol. The Indians love differences, variety, and some opportunity for excursions from the monotonous tenor of their lives, and dislike having drab monotony forced on them by the Government.

Now, in an Indian State, there is some escape from monotony. One can see the bright life of the capital, which is within the reach of all; can watch the Rája and his courtiers clad in the immemorial robes of splendour, the gorgeous elephants, the prancing horses with painted points, the stately carriages, the yák tails and the peacock feathers, the gold and silver maces, the mail-clad horsemen and the musketeers, with their pieces wrapped in red cloth, loud music and enthusiastic greetings of the Father and Mother of them all: then in the Square the gossip and the sugarcane and the sweets.

> "Ah such a life, such a life as one leads at the window there,
> Bang-whang-whang goes the drum, tootle-to-tootle the fife,
> Oh a day in the city square, there is no such pleasure in life."

There is gossip, too, in British Territory, but it is gossip about something impalpable. In the Indian State the Rája is flesh and blood, and can be met coming round the corner at any moment. He is real, he is theirs. There is infinite and delightful variety among the Rájas, but there is a remarkable similarity in the administration of their States.

In many respects the character and outlook of the Ráj-put Chiefs of Rajputána differ from those of the Mahratta Chiefs of Central India, and such differences can be noticed in other groups and in individual States; but in all the system of Government is very much the same. It is personal rule which postulates personal relations between the ruler and his subjects.

Sometimes in so vast a galaxy trouble may come from the idiosyncrasies of Rájas who are not true to type, to custom and tradition. But these departures from the normal are rare, and they yield quickly to the treatment which the Suzerain Government is bound to apply. I have known such cases. One Rája loved cruelty; another loved a woman, and for her sake removed a censorious Uncle; but the most dangerous form of love in Rájas is love of money or love of ease.

I have seen great misery caused by an avaricious Rája; but I have seen greater misery caused by an easy-going Chief who left his country to the mercy of his officials. These are the two dangers, and when the signals go up, the Political Officer, of whom I have spoken, of whom little is ever said—the good Political Officer—comes on the stage. He is there, the Representative of the Government of India, to advise when his advice is sought. He never interferes, but when the Barons of the State[1] go out in arms because their avaricious Chief asks for more; or when the people cease to cultivate their fields because the officials take all the harvest, while the drowsy Rája says, "A little sleep, a little slumber," why, then the Political Officer drives up from the Residency to the Palace to ask how His Highness is. His Highness was never better, but he is not quite at ease. There is trouble. Then, with his best "bedside manner," the Political Agent says that he too had heard of trouble, and, indeed, had seen outward signs of trouble, and can he be of any assistance? Though, of course, the Rája himself can deal with any difficulties, which will arise in any State; indeed, have arisen in another State, where the Government of India were reluctantly forced to interfere. Then a Council is appointed, reforms introduced, and the State is lifted on the rails again. When the Rája dies, and by good fortune is succeeded by a minor, a Council of Regency is set up and there is a thorough overhaul of the

[1] The *Thákurs* are of the same Clan and often of the same family as the Rája.

finance and administration of the State. Such incidents as these are the rare exception, and as a rule the State runs on quietly and smoothly, and roads, irrigation works, and sometimes railways, add to the prosperity of the ruler and his people.

The Rája who loved cruelty was an eccentric, and, unlike any of his rank, he was lacking in the courtesy and the dignity which distinguish the Rájas as a class. His father before him was caustic in his humour and coarse in his English speech, probably coarser in his own tongue. Many stories are told of him. A great and overwhelming British official paid him a visit. The railway station and the triumphal arches were emblazoned with the great man's name and titles, and underneath in larger letters were the words, "God help us." The son inherited his father's mordant wit, and spoke English more fluently than his sire. The chief objects of his cruelty were the rich bankers of the State. He would, at seasons of the full moon, harness them to his carriage, or make them row his pleasure barge. His dislike of the money-lending classes was peculiar, because he himself was a sound financier, and his State was well managed. He also disliked many of the British Political Officers accredited to his Court. One of them, he said, "always gave him the sensation of a rat in his pyjamas." The inevitable end came, when he tendered his abdication. I saw him in his capital shortly before the Delhi Coronation. He was pleading for concessions. Lord Curzon sat in a high chair: the Rája on his right front. I sat opposite. The conversation was in Hindustáni. The Rája opened the proceedings by saying that it was all a mistake; that he had never meant to abdicate; on the contrary he had looked forward to the Delhi Coronation with pleasure as he had counted on some special honour in recognition of his services. To which Lord Curzon, gazing with unmoved face over our heads, replied in forceful English that this was mere waste of time. I interpreted the reply, though as the Rája spoke English well and fluently, he might well have thought that my interpretation was also "mere waste of time." But interpretation on occasions like this has its usefulness. It gives time, and firm decisions uttered in two languages have a kind of emphatic finality. Next, the Rája asked that his allowance should be increased. "Tell him," said Lord Curzon, "that in my opinion the allowance ought, in justice to the State, to be diminished." Then followed other requests, all of which were refused. While we were sitting in this triangular tragi-comedy, outside others were anxiously waiting, for there were rumours that the State troops would rise in behalf of their ruler, and the British Cavalry in a garrison some miles away were held in readiness. But when it was known that no concessions had been made, there was no rising. It was a painful interview. I saw the Rája soon after this at Delhi, to which place he came in a private capacity. I saw him in a crowd, looking on at the procession of elephants which carried the Ruling Chiefs of India. He had ceased to rule. He paid a visit to the one of the few men who knew how to manage him. He was received in state and ceremony; but he crawled from his carriage to my friend's tent of audience and said: "Why did you leave me? You knew I was only foolish old fat fellow." Later, when this friend of mine was leaving Bombay, the erstwhile Rája rushed down to say farewell, and his last words were: "Now I'm poor old Jumbo, roving round India."[1] Though I felt sorry for him, I realised that roving Jumbos are dangerous and he had trampled on too many of his subjects. He still had his shafts, envenomed shafts, of wit with him in his retirement, and when Lord Curzon left India for ever, he sent him a telegram of condolence, "I deposed greet you deposed."

In the vast assembly of Chiefs there were all kinds, but they were nearly all great gentlemen, sure of themselves, and with traditions: some, indeed, with a past. But in India the past can always be retrieved, and I have known many, who, making a poor start, finished most successfully.

It takes two years to know something of an Indian, and then, perchance, the ice is broken and conversation becomes easy. They all have their special subjects, but the wisest conversation is silence, friendly communication of silent goodwill. There are curious things to be learnt

[1]It is as unusual for a Hindu to rove and be restless, as it is for an Englishman to sit still and brood. Both are dangerous signs.

about their institutions. I was once dining with a great Rájput Chief, and he urged me to drink more champagne. I was young, and had had enough. "You must drink," said my kind host, "until your head goes turning, or you will never appreciate the Nautch we are going to have in the Palace to-night: until your head goes turning round and round you will not like our dancing." I saw Nautches in all parts of India and never appreciated them; but they mean much to the Indians, and perhaps the stolid Englishman requires stimulant in order to understand the slow swaying of the artistes "with rings on their fingers and bells on their toes," "that chime light laughter round their restless feet."

Some of the Rájas possess fabulous wealth; not the wealth of the European capitalist, but visible, tangible, ready-money wealth in the shape of coins and jewels. Many have seen the *tosha-khánas* [1] and the bewildering and dazzling disorder of the pearls, diamonds, emeralds and rubies, which lie jumbled on the floor, as though some rude pirate-chief had flung them out of a sea-stained iron chest in careless and contemptuous mood. But the ever present, lynx-eyed man, who smiles and says nothing, can tell you the number of the pearls and the weight of each gem. And his assistant can tell you the jewels the Rája wore yesterday. He can tell you where the Rája went, for he always goes where the jewels go. This great splash of colour and light is a State heirloom and is sacrosanct, not for the common robber, but food for his masters, the swart Paynims, who in bygone days have hacked their way to power and its gauds.

There are wicked jewelled daggers, and, in diamond-encrusted scabbards, thin, curved blades of steel from Toledo and Sirohi;[2] one is notched by the fierce stroke of a parricide; another ended a dynasty. There are great emeralds, once the gleaming eyes of a Hindu god, and rubies, not the pigeon's blood of the Farnese jewels, but gems incarnadine, on one of which some bright-eyed dwarf with tiny graving tool has carved names and dates. Two of these are of dread import to India, telling a story which in certain eventualities may be repeated—1398 when the "sturdy Scythian

[1] Jewel-house. [2] Sirohi, a State in Rajputána famous once for its fine steel.

thief" swooped down on Delhi and spilled the blood of India for seven months; 1729 when another cruel hawk swooped down from Persia, and Nadir Shah proved as ruthless as was the Tartar Taimur. There are dates, too, of softer memories. Jehangir (1605-1627), in spite of his lady's remonstrance, carved his name on the beautiful gem, and though in the East the man wears the jewels, I like to think that the woman wore it sometimes, and that this world of limpid light bedecked Mumtaz-ud-Dowlah, the lovely consort of Shah Jehan (1627-1658). He could scarcely have refused anything to her in whose memory he raised the most exquisite of all buildings—the Táj. Jehangir, in answer to his wife's remonstrances, said: "This jewel will more certainly hand down my name to posterity than any written history. The house of Taimur may fall, but as long as there is a King the jewel will be his." And so in 1848 the ruby came into the safe keeping of Queen Victoria.

I have heard many a story of pearls of price, of famous emeralds and diamonds, but must pass on to the real treasure-houses of the Rájas, which few of us have ever seen, for none may enter the old remote forts, where gold and silver, accumulations of ages, lie torpid in rusty strong boxes. At Amber, the Rája, on accession, is admitted once to see the treasure of the State, but it is said that the monastic soldiers who guard the fort will not even let him see the labyrinth which leads to the chamber. He must be blindfolded. The Rája never sees the hoard again.

When I went to Kashmir in 1889, the Rája had just been deposed, and as I have already recorded, the State was practically bankrupt. No payments were made, and as an emergency the Representative of the Government of India decided to explore the resources of one of the distant forts in the Dogra hills. There were gold and silver, gold coins which would have made the numismatist tremble with excitement, and in a corner, in muddy sacks, were loads of sapphires which a great English jeweller pronounced to be the finest stones in the world. But I remember that this necessary violation of the old Fort was regarded in the countryside as an act of sacrilege.

Just as the treasure is far away, so is all thought or word of money far away from the preoccupations of the Rájas. In England, not long ago, the talk of money was the mark of the unrefined. I have never heard a Rája talk of his wealth, still less boast of his fortune. Nevertheless, sometimes money looms large when it is a question of dowry and dignity, and one such case greatly interested me. A great Rája had a son and heir of whom he had every reason to be proud, and he was formally engaged to a charming Princess of a distant State. The son had never seen the lady, but by what was regarded as a breach of all etiquette, he had seen her photograph, and he fell very much in love. But unfortunately the father had received the offer of another lady possessed of a richer dowry, and he ordered his son to break off his engagement. This the son declined to do, and he was married to the charming Princess and an heir was born. I met the son when I was on tour, and was greatly struck by his manners and conversation He was in dire straits, as his father had exiled him and cut off all allowances. I suggested that he should pay his father a surprise visit and present his little son. "Alas," he said, "I have already done this, but my father will not forgive me." Two years later, Lord Curzon interceded with the father, and reconciliation followed. The father was a fine character and was devoted to his son, but the son had broken a tradition, and to a Rájput, tradition is dearer than a son.

Up to the end of the last century the Rájas rarely met save at some great assemblage held in honour of the Royal House of England. But though there was no intercourse there was a system of news letters, and remote Kashmir would hear of what was passing in the distant States of Rajputána and Kathiawár. In the present century this isolation is disappearing, and the Council of Princes and other developments are changing in some respects the outlook and the evolution of the Indian states. But they will remain for long institutions which rest on personality rather than on regulation, unless, indeed, the turbid waves which are beating on the bar of British India spill over into the happy lagoons of the Indian States. I can conceive a natural union of the States of Rajputána and Kathiawár, and unions of other Indian States which might stem the flood from British India. But if the two systems must clash I should prefer to see the system of British India reverting to the type of the Indian State rather than to see the last of real India submerged in the dead and levelling waters of democracy.

Democracy, like most forms and fashions of man, is very much a matter of climate. In the West we praise it, sometimes from the heart, and often from the lips. To make the world safe for democracy we have staggered under a heavy and cruel burden, and it is natural that the English, so pledged to this form of governance, should desire to pass on its boons to the peoples of India. But so few know how different India is, how unlike in temperament, outlook and experience. There are certain essentials to happy stability in the East, among them continuity and cohesion. Democracy does not always assure these, even in the cool and practical countries of the West.[1]

We look too much from Western windows, and ignore the strange, strong Eastern light. We imagine that we breathe the same air and think the same thoughts. It may be too early to appraise the results of the democratic experiment in China, but I have always remembered the Memorial of the Censor Wu K'o-tu in 1873, a liberal man, urging that Ministers of foreign nations should be excused from kneeling when received in audience. He writes:—

"They have made some score of treaties with China containing at least ten thousand words. Is there a word in any of them concerning reverence for parents, or the cultivation of virtue, and respect for the nine canons of rightful conduct? No!

"Is there one word in any one of them as to the observance of ceremony, as to duty, integrity, and a proper sense of shame, the four cardinal principles of our nation? Again No!

"All that they speak of is national profit. Such and such a clause implies benefit or profit for China. They think only of profit, and with the meretricious hope of profit they beguile the Chinese people."

[1] Anatole France enumerates as the vices of a Republic: "*Le manque de continuité, le manque de responsibilité, le manque de cohésion.*"

This was the outlook of China in 1873. This, in altered phrase, is the Hindu outlook to-day.

We are told that the system of British India is out of favour, and that the people of the three-fourths of India which we have painted red on the map require some form of Government more congenial and more national. I believe that the British system as it existed up to the end of last century was benevolent and in a material sense a monument of just, progressive and prosperous government. It was perhaps too rigid and somewhat uneventful, but it was successful while it was controlled by the English. At any rate it was a possible system. But it is an impossible system when the Indians themselves take control, for they cannot work a Bureaucracy of the European model. If they are to succeed, they must get back to some system of their own. They must start from the village and the *Panchayet*—work up, instead of trying to force down. None cares to work a machine which they have condemned, and if the machine is faulty and too intricate, the change from British to Indian control is no remedy. There must be danger when two men try to drive the same engine, and if the Indians who are for change, and desire, as many very naturally desire, to see their beloved Bharatavarsha—that most lovable land, governed under national or rather Indian auspices, let them take as their model for the administration of the provinces a well-governed Indian State.[1] Fortunately in the Provinces there are still the heads of the old Families, who would be regarded as the obvious and natural Rájas of the new States. Recently the new State of Benáres was constituted, and it would be easy to find in every part of India names as suitable, such as Durbhanga, Burdwán, in Bengal; and Jeypore, Vizianágram

[1] I addressed the Royal Institution on this subject in March, 1914. I gave details which would be out of place in this book. The scheme would be gradual and would aim at the division of India into two equal parts. The first would consist of Indian States: the second would remain like the present Provincial Governments, but smaller in area and more homogeneous in race and language. To the first part should be restored and added the territory which lapsed to British territory in the time of Lord Dalhousie.

I advocate variety in the forms of Government, though I consider that limited Monarchy is best suited to India. It should be remembered that India is as large as Europe, omitting Russia, and infinitely more varied in races and religions, and there ought to be some variety of treatment. There may be Republics, and on the North-West Frontier a Republic seems obvious.

and Ramnad in Madras. Moreover, if it should happen that the present road of reform leads to an impasse, it might be deemed advisable not only to create new States, but in addition to enlarge the boundaries of the old States. The Capital cities of the existing Provinces should form an enclave under the administration of the Government of India.

In the twenty-one years I spent in India, I became acquainted with the Rájas of many States, and I have known the grandfathers of many of the Chiefs now ruling. Though education and progress in many directions have brought changes, yet I notice no great change in character or conduct, and, so far as their respective States are concerned, it is safe to predict that the grandson will very frequently take the same line as his grandfather when dealing with the problems which recur with remarkable regularity. I could describe what I have seen and known in many States, but will confine myself to a few of the interesting Chiefs with whom I have been associated. My experience may be useful to those who are doing the same work as I did: or, if the old school pass away and the new school, contrary to my anticipations, develop a new type, it may be of use to place on record a picture of some of the Chiefs as I saw them in the Victorian time.

Pratáb Singh,[1] Maharája of Jammu and Kashmir, a Jamwál Rájput of the Dogra Hills, comes first. I can remember him in 1880, when he came with his handsome father, Maharája Ranbir Singh, to the Durbár at Lahore. I noticed then that the father seemed prouder of his two younger sons than he was of the heir apparent, the Mian Sahib, Pratáb Singh. Ten years later my services were lent to the Kashmir State, just at the time when Pratáb Singh was temporarily deposed, so my acquaintance with him was resumed at an embarrassing juncture. He was of small stature, always wearing a turban too large, and he had an inquiring eye. He suffered from ill-health, and a very able doctor told me in 1894 that the Maharája could not live for more than two months. But he lived for another thirty years, and his

[1] Lieutenant-General His Highness Maharája Sir Pratáb Singh, Indar Mahindar Bahádur, Sipar-i-Sultanat, G.C.S.I., G.C.I.E., G.B.E., born 1850, succeeded 1885, died 23rd September, 1925.

activity grew with his years. Not many years ago he suddenly took up cricket and engaged an eleven of professionals. The game as played by Pratáb Singh was described to me by a Kashmiri, and as far as Pratáb Singh was concerned it was a curious game. It was understood that he was to make a certain number of runs, and for the rest of the match he would sit watching the wonderful game of "clicket." It was just his way of showing his sympathy for English institutions.

His constant letters, written in a tiny, difficult script, full of quaint saws and kindliness, latterly urged me to pay him a visit and entered into the smallest details to convince me that the journey to Kashmir should be made easy. But I had grown to look on him as immortal, and thought that there was still time to carry out his wishes. In September, 1925, I spent a day in Geneva with a great Indian Chief, who was attending the League of Nations. He was going to speak on the subject of opium, and we talked of the many men we had known and respected who seemed to take opium with no baleful results. Pratáb Singh was one of these, and my host, who, like the rest, admired Pratáb Singh for his loyalty to his religion and his customs, agreed that opium in a large measure accounted for his long life and his ever fresh interest in affairs and the fashions of mankind. He added that the astrologers had recently predicted that if Pratáb Singh survived 1925 he would live another fifteen years. Alas! on the night of September 24th, when I returned to England, I found a long telegram from Rája Hari Singh announcing the death of his uncle on the 23rd September.

Pratáb Singh was the most inscrutable man I have ever known. During my six years' service with him in Kashmir and Jammu we had many a long conversation. He knew all that was passing in his State, and he took a keen interest in India and in England. He asked sudden and sometimes embarrassing questions, and he was delightfully curious as to our English ways and habits. But he was always courteous and never said an unkind word. One day he asked me bluntly what I thought of him. I replied that he reminded me of one of our English Kings. Like all Indians he had a profound veneration for the Royal House of England, so my answer pleased him, and he only laughed when I said that he was like the English King who never said a foolish thing and never did a wise one. I had been urging him at this interview to give an order to cancel the fictitious arrears of Land Revenue which hung like a cloud over my Settlement of Kashmir. The conversation went on. After an hour he said: "And so you think that I never say foolish things. This is true. Many tell me that it would be unwise to cancel the arrears of Land Revenue, and that if I do so, the Kashmiris will get out of hand. You think it would be wise?" "I have thought so for three years." "Then call a writer." And there and then he dictated the order which saved my Settlement.

He was the soul of hospitality and gloried in the fact that King Edward, King George and Queen Mary, and the Prince of Wales had all visited Jammu. His scale of entertainment was lavish, even for an Indian Chief, and when the Resident in Kashmir, who had listened to the Maharája's regal programme for a Royal visit, ventured to suggest that the expenditure was heavy, and was saying, "I think——" the Maharája interrupted: "yih *think* ke bat nahin hai, yih Riwáz to hai," which means, "this is not a matter of thinking, it is a custom."

One of his favourites was cut to pieces near Jammu as he drove out to take the air. The assassination caused a great stir and the Maharája was much concerned. One day he asked me whether I went to church. I said I was usually out in camp. "Yes," he replied, "but when you are in Srinagar you do not always go to church." He said it was right to go to church and his people thought better of an Englishman who attended church. He suddenly asked: "What do you think is the best thing in the Prayer Book?" I could give no answer. "Ah," he said, with the recent assassination in his mind, "this is the best—From plague, famine and sudden death, Good Lord deliver us."

A German Prince of high degree paid a visit to Jammu with a large Staff, and the Maharája prepared one of his usual lavish State banquets, and asked me to represent him at the feast. When the toast of the King Emperor was to be drunk the Maharája entered the room and sat on a chair. After the toast had been drunk, the Maharája retired, and soon afterwards sent for me. "I noticed," he said—apparently he had been watching the feast through a lattice—"that you did not eat tinned asparagus, nor *pâté de foie gras*, and that you did not drink champagne: why was this?" I replied that I did not care for these things. "But," said he, "you have not eaten nor drunk eighty rupees' worth, which is what I pay to the Contractor." I then explained to the Maharája that it was impossible for any Englishman, however competent, to consume eighty rupees' worth at a meal. "Not if he dined entirely off tinned asparagus?" he asked.

Neither he nor his brothers, owing to their strict adherence to Caste rules, ever visited England; but the Maharája had a map of London and used to picture the route by which the King would go from the Palace to Parliament, and was delighted if he ever caught us making a mistake about the geography of London. On the occasion of King George's visit to Jammu, in December, 1905, the Maharája questioned me very closely regarding the voyage to England, and I rather hoped that he was contemplating a visit. He knew all the details of the voyage, and all went well till he came to the subject of the Channel. Then he shook his head and said, "*bahut vomiting hai*," which was his way of saying that there was much sea-sickness on the Channel crossing. I did my best to reassure him, but he gloomily said: "*bahut vomiting hoga*"—"there *will* be much sea-sickness"—and this was the end of his venture.

Though lavish in his hospitality the Maharája was very simple and frugal in his own life. He rose early and left the Inner Palace at about 7 a.m., and in the Outer Palace would listen to the Reports of the Officials, and to the extracts from the newspapers. At 10 a.m. he took his bath, and then began his prayers (*puja*[1]). This *puja* is more than prayers, it is worship and meditation and conversation on religious subjects with the Pandits, representatives from distant Holy places and pious pilgrims. High officials

[1] *Puja* is literally Idol worship, but it is used for rites generally. *Jhanda ki puja* is the translation of "Trooping of the Colour" or worship of the flag.

of the State, provided they are Hindus, may attend the Rája's *puja*, if their business be urgent. The *puja* lasts till 11.30, when the Rája takes the first of his two daily meals; his second meal was at 10.30 p.m. He was a vegetarian and avoided all alcohol. They set before him some fifty or sixty dishes of various kinds of bread, cakes and rice, vegetables, sour and sweet, and sweetmeats of every description. There was butter in everything: but his favourite food was curd and pickles. The breakfast lasted an hour, and then came the Durbár, when the real business of the day was transacted. The Durbár closed at 2 p.m., when His Highness retired to the Inner Palace, and was busy with cases of a personal and private nature. At 5 or 6 p.m. he would go out in boats, or riding, and would return to the palace at 8 p.m. Then more private letters, and solitary *puja* until 10.30 p.m., when he had his second meal. At this meal there would be jests and jokes and laughter, and perhaps our oddities, mistakes and Western gaucheries would keep the floor (for they do not use tables) in a roar of merriment. At midnight, the Rája retired to the Inner Palace. On Sundays, at noon, he would listen for an hour to his musicians. He was very generous to the religious mendicants and pilgrims who swarmed to Kashmir, and as a good Hindu was much influenced by the clever, insidious, and at the same time, charming Bráhmans of Kashmir, known all over India as the Pandits. In his heart I think he trusted me. I had fought for him when I represented his State in a dispute with the Punjáb Government over the boundary between the Jammu territory and the Punjáb. I won the case, and as the Pandits had told the Maharája that I as an Englishman would assuredly surrender to the British Government, Pratáb Singh was doubly pleased.

I delighted in my talks with him in the palace on the river. Usually he led the conversation to religion, philosophy, English customs, and past Viceroys and Commanders-in-Chief whom he had known. If there were a pause I would endeavour to mention the object of my visit, to me of importance, as I never went to the palace unless there were some crisis in my Department. He was always convinced that he was right, and I always felt that he was wrong:

but he had a way of stating the case which would have impressed anyone who was not vitally interested in the decision. And, looking back on all these discussions, I have discovered the curious point that I was right as regarded the immediate problems; but the Maharája was right if one could only look forward ten or twenty years. I do not suggest that he had powers of prophecy, but he thought in centuries, while I thought in calendar years. He was the quintessence of Hinduism, "*plus ça change, plus c'est la même chose.*" Out of sheer courtesy he would sometimes agree, though he saw the futility of my well-meant reforms. It was all very difficult for him, since the Pandits in the Outer, and the ladies in the Inner, Palace were waiting for his return when I had left the postern gate on the river.

When a Rája rises after audience he has ample time for reflection before he reaches the Inner Palace, the home of his family, for the way is long, and is barred by four *deorhis*, or portals. At the first there is a military guard; inside there is a large open court, through which he passes to the second *deorhi*. This is guarded by old retainers of the palace, who murmur, "*Andáta*"—"giver of bread," "*jey deo*," or some such greeting, to their Chief, as he enters the winding, dimly-lit corridor, dull red in colour, smooth as marble, smoothed by little, hesitating hands, scented by generations of otto of roses, and haunted by the frou-frou of silks and muslins. He comes then to the third *deorhi* and is lost to mankind. This is in the hands of maid servants of the palace, who are allowed to go into the outer world when it is necessary. The fourth and the last *deorhi* forms the entrance to the home of the Maharánis, and this is guarded by the maids-of-honour, or the *Khwases*, who come with the Maharáni or the Ráni at the time of marriage. These may never leave the palace unless they go in attendance on their mistresses. When a message is sent to the outer world they may pass out to the first entrance and deliver the order to the chief of the *deorhis*—an office of anxious and vigilant trust. The message is given from behind the screen (*purdah*) and the maid-of-honour may not be seen by any outside person. No male, unless he be a member of the ruling family, may pass the first *deorhi*, and when occasion demands the presence of a doctor or a Bráhman priest, they must be heavily veiled. They can just see their way through the dim passages with red walls, but they cannot look up nor around, and they are always led into the presence by the Názir of the *deorhi*. If any questions must be asked, the Názir is the intermediary. The visitor never sees, nor is seen by, the ladies of the Inner Palace. And often before the Rája has reached the fourth *deorhi* he may regretfully doubt whether the reform to which he has assented in the Outer Palace will be favourably received by the second chamber of the Inner Palace.

I have mentioned how the Maharája signed an order which wrote off all the arrears of Land Revenue and saved my Settlement. Overjoyed, I suggested a large meeting of all the heads of villages and their eldest sons, who should hear from the Maharája's own lips the blessed news. He at once said that I could far more appropriately announce the news myself, as I was responsible for this measure. I then told him that everywhere and always, even during the period when he was deposed, I had acted in his name. He knew this to be true, and he then agreed that I should assemble the Headmen of the villages of Kashmir on a certain date when he would attend. I sent out the invitations that very day, and my office, knowing the importance of the step, worked through the night. When the great day arrived, I went to the Ruby Palace on the river, above the Maharája's palace and saw with pride all the Headmen arrayed in dazzling white, with their sons, seated on the grass, quiet and expectant. I also saw my right-hand man, Keshu Rám, who looked the picture of woe. The meeting was fixed for noon, and it was now 11.30 a.m. I asked Keshu Rám if he was ill, and he said: "His Highness is not coming." "Oh, yes, he is," I said in a loud voice. "He is waiting for me to escort him," and I went off in a light boat to the Maharája's palace. There was no sign of the State barge, but Hamira, the chief of the palace boatmen, was on the postern steps. He was a friend. "Where is the barge?" I asked. "It has not been ordered." "Get it ready at once!" I said. I rushed up the steps and entered the courtyard, which was full of soldiers. I passed along by a high blank wall to the narrow staircase which led to the Maharája's apartments. The staircase was barred by two *Bandúkis* (Musketeers), but they saw I was desperate, and so, mercifully, they let me pass. The first room was empty, but in the next room I found the Maharája, surrounded by his courtiers, and I saw among them the old Pandit, Zan Kák, the leader of the reactionaries, an old, very courteous and most dangerous man. I shook the Maharája by the hand, and I never let go his hand till we were seated in the State barge. "Just in time," I said; "they are all there, waiting to hear from their Maharája and Father the joyful news. If your Highness had been unable to come, all our faces would have been blackened." The Maharája never said a word, but when we reached the lawns of the Ruby Palace and the villagers rose from the ground like white geese rising from the Wular Lake, he said to me: "You tell them that the arrears are remitted in Kashmiri, I do not speak Kashmiri." I replied: "Your Highness, it will do as well in your own Dogri tongue, and the effect will be entirely lost unless you announce the news." Then Zan Kák wriggled his way in and said that he would speak for the Maharája; but I laughed and led the Maharája to the raised terrace of the Palace, and he spoke the words which freed Kashmir from extortion and misery. And since then and for ever I shall praise Pratáb Singh, for he did a very difficult thing. He braved the Bráhmans and he defied his family, and, incidentally, he made a country.

Our friendship grew until I left Kashmir, and was revived when I returned to India with Lord Curzon, and again when the present King Emperor visited Jammu. Pratáb Singh had a strange life, and I wish it had been happier. It is a misfortune, if one is born to be a Maharája, to have brothers. I was in the confidence of Pratáb Singh and of his younger brother, Rája Amar Singh, who was one of the most brilliant men I have ever met. The Maharája loved and admired his brother, and Rája Amar Singh was loyal at heart to the Maharája: but the miserable *Bandúkis*[1] and the courtiers kept them apart and hostile.

[1] Literally Musketeers. They played the same rôle as the followers of the King and the Cardinal in the famous novel of Dumas.

Pax Britannica, blessing as it has been to British India, has somewhat enervated the Indian States, and in my time the life of a Chief was often one of dull boredom, tempered by intrigues and occasional assassinations. In Kashmir one of the windows of the State opened on Central Asia, and there were possibilities of an intrigue of the first class, but I always thought that the temporary deposition of Pratáb Singh was a mistake, for I know that he was the most loyal of the loyal. He had no son, and this was a grief to him. He was kind, courteous and generous, and in some ways, brave. Ask the splendid Church of England Mission in Kashmir what they thought of Pratáb Singh. And be it remembered that the Bráhmans have no love for missionaries, nor for Hindus who support them. Ask anyone who knew him well, and they will all speak with kindness and affection of a very complex character, who knew much and suffered much. Much was written about his death in the English Press, and it may be of interest to record what did happen when Pratáb Singh was passing. It is, of course, incorrect to say that all the Maharája's jewels were burnt on the pyre. Some are destroyed because they form part of the national costume in which he, like all his race, must be dressed when passing through the fire.

Perhaps the most striking incident in the obsequies of a Hindu Prince is the moment when all the vast throng of white-clothed mourners are shaved of all but their eyebrows. At the funeral of the late Maharája of Jaipur over two thousand barbers were busily engaged.

When a Hindu dies, he goes neither to eternal heaven nor to eternal hell. He merely goes to *Preta Loka*, the "world of the departed," a world very similar to this world of ours. He remains till he is re-born, either as a better being or worse, according to his *karma*, in this or some other world. To provide comforts and to remove difficulties in the "world of the departed," the dying man gives alms at the moment of his death, and those alms take the form of articles which he was fond of or commonly used in this world, such as food, apparel, money and so forth. When he is too weak to make the effort of giving and the gifts are many, a kind of magnetic current is established between him and the gift by means of a thread, one end of which he holds in his hand while the remainder of the thread encircles the gift. This is the *Sankalpa* thread. Before the actual death, the dying man is taken off the bed and placed on mother earth or the floor of his room, which is covered with *Kusha*, a holy grass. When Pratáb Singh was lifted from his bed he was placed on the floor, which was covered with five lakhs of rupees' worth of gold, with Kusha grass over it.

Four vessels filled with water and containing some sesamum and a certain amount of money were placed in the corners of the room: large lamp-stands with numerous wicks, besides the lamps on the four water vessels, were kept burning, for there must always be a light to illumine the dark path to the *Preta Loka*. These lamps are known as the *Mandali*, or circle of light. The *Sankalpa* thread enclosed a large number of cows, horses and buffaloes, and also foodstuffs, utensils and clothes. After death, the body was dressed first in a silk cloth bearing the print of Ráma's name; next in full royal dress; and lastly in the winding-sheets which numbered one hundred and one and were valued at about 60,000 rupees. These were mostly given to the temples, but some were burned with the body on a pyre of sandalwood. And thus, according to the ordinance of his creed and the dignity of his house, the spirit of Pratáb Singh, Maharája of Jammu and Kashmir, was sped to the "world of the departed," and in the dim vista vouchsafed to mortal ken, I picture him awaiting the reward of one who was ever true to his traditions, kind in his endeavours and loyal to his friends.

CHAPTER XI

"Make ready, my scribe, a pen full fair,
And write a goodly thing
A charter first among my chiefs
For my true son Pertab Singh."

—Sir Frederick Pollock.
The Sin of Sir Pertab Singh.

Sketch of Sir Pertáb of Jodhpur—*Sati*—Becomes Maharája of Idar—Adopts Me as Brother—His Curious English—His Hatred of the Moslems—Sketch of the Maharája of Jaipur—A Great Rájput—His Generosity—His Embittered Youth—Story of His Spiritual Adviser—His Visit to England—Shorter Sketch of the Maharána of Udaipur—His Divine Manners—A Prince of Courtesy—The Melancholy of the House of Udaipur.

IT was in 1895 that the other Pratáb Singh, Lt.-General His Highness Maharájadhiraj Sir Pratáb Singh Bahádur, G.C.B., G.C.S.I., G.C.V.O., born 1845, died 4th September, 1922, known to all as Sir Pertáb of Jodhpur, hobbled into my hot tent at Agra. He sat down in a long cane chair and took off his pugri, and then asked if he might have someone to draw off his long black boots. To my mind an Indian never looks his best when he has taken off his handsome head-dress, and what lent special charm to the Rahtor turban Sir Pertáb wore was the sacred miniature of Queen Victoria set in pearls. But head-dress or no head-dress, Sir Pertab was striking and noble. My servant drew off with effort the glossy riding boots. "My legs," said Sir Pertáb, "are often, often, broken," [1] and then he called for a drink, and prayed me to go on with my work. But I fell under the charm of the beautiful eyes and the wistful face, and we talked. We had never met before, but I recalled the old days of Rajputána and remembered Colonel

[1] An Indian biographer writes: "He has received numerous hurts in several parts of the body, whether at polo, the chase or pig-sticking. . . . No less than on the field of battle he had either his leg broken, ankle dislocated, thigh pierced, biceps munched, or fore-arm shot, over and over again."

Bradford's hopes and fears regarding the splendid young Rájput, who, summoned to the Abu Residency after some wild escapade, had ridden his camel two hundred miles, to arrive fresh and debonair at the audience. Sir Pertáb passed bravely through the trials and temptations which beset all young Rájputs of the ruling families, and made good. He was a typical Rájput, a great horseman, a gallant soldier, a very astute administrator. He was a shrewd judge of character, a great disciplinarian, and though he spoke little Hindustáni and less English, he never failed to make himself understood. He had a wonderful way with the Indians and was universally loved by the English. But though popular and seemingly easy of approach, as he was, I never saw anyone ever try to take a liberty with Sir Pertáb, and behind the kindly eyes and the beautiful face there was always the inherent dignity of the Rájput. I often watched him and other Rájas when they visited British India, and the profound respect and reverence shown by the leading citizens of the various capitals for a ruling Chief impressed me. These leading men—leaders of what was spoken of by the Chiefs as the *Vakil Ráj*[1]—so free and easy in the British and official circle, were humble and deferential in the presence of a real Rája. Their manner and attitude changed at once—instinctively they recognised their natural leaders and were glad and proud to see them. His English to the last was peculiar, and though he was diligent in the study of mankind and of Indian affairs, he never seemed to care about languages. He rather studied faces and carriage. He was dramatic in gesture and in phrase, and wherever he went he was a central figure. He told me afterwards, when we became close friends, of his childhood and his youth. He remembered as a young boy going out from the Capital of his family to the funeral of his grandfather, the Maharája of Jodhpur. He went with his grandmother (*Mámi*), to whom he was deeply attached. She fondled him and wept, and the child asked her why she cried. She repressed him for daring to ask questions, clasped him close and wept

[1] "Vakil" means attorney: *Vakil Ráj* signifies Government by the lawyers, and the word expressed an exact and important fact—the overpowering influence of the lawyer class in British India.

again. And then the boy, who had heard stories of *Sati*, suspected, and began to cry. At this the grandmother laughed and called him a poor Rájput, and when they reached the grove where the Maharája's funeral pyre was set, the beloved lady went through the fire, and into the same fire the Maharája's old barber cast himself and perished in the flames.

Many a brave lady of the Jodhpur House left her fortress home to pass to the same distant pyre. Some lovingly touched with henna-dyed hands the Palace for the last time, and the marks of the little palms can still be seen red on the wall of the old fort. One such incident is described in Tod's "Rájasthan." It was the funeral of the great Rahtor Prince, Ajit Singh, in 1780. The Rahtors are a brave, proud race, but no less brave are the other clans of Rájputs from which the Rahtor must take his wife. Six queens followed Ajit Singh: "they were the affianced wives of their lord," for whom death had no terrors, and with them went the "curtain wives of affection" to the number of fifty-eight. They would listen to no expostulations. One and all declared that "Without our lord, even life is death." While thus each spoke, Nathoo, the Názir,[1] thus addressed them: "This is no amusement; the sandal-wood you now anoint with is cool: but will your resolution abide, when you remove it with the flames of Agni?[2] When this scorches your tender frames, your hearts may fail, and the desire to recede will disgrace your lord's memory. Reflect, and remain where you are. You have lived like Indrani,[3] nursed in softness amidst flowers and perfumes; the winds of heaven never offended you, far less the flames of fire." But to all his arguments they replied: "The world we will abandon, but never our lord." They performed their ablutions, decked themselves in their gayest attire, and for the last time made obeisance to their lord in his car. The ministers, the bards, the family priests (*Parohits*), in turn, expostulated with them. The chief queen (*Patrini*) the Chohâni, they told to indulge her affection for her sons, Abhya and Bukhta; to feed the poor, the needy, the holy, and lead a life of religious devotion.

[1] The Názir (a Moslem epithet) has the charge of the harem.
[2] The god of fire. [3] The queen of heaven.

The queen replied: "Koonti, the wife of Pandu, did not follow her lord; she lived to see the greatness of the *five brothers*, her sons; but were her expectations realized? This life is a vain shadow; this dwelling one of sorrow; let us accompany our lord to that of fire, and there close it."

An eye-witness told me of a *Sati* in Jammu territory when three Ránis accompanied their dead lord to the pyre. With them went a queen of song and dance, a Musalmáni. They were all dressed in their best and gayest robes, and as they passed slowly down the hill and along the valley they bowed smilingly to the reverent crowd. They uttered prophecies; for at this great moment they seemed inspired, and their prophecies are still remembered. But when they came to the pyre the heart of the Musalmáni failed, and the three proud Ránis shrugged their shoulders.

> With a scream remembered yet
>   Out there sprang the Musalmáni.
> Said the Bráhmans, piling logs:
>   "She's a quean, but not a Ráni."

My informant added that she died not long before he told me the tale, regretting in her old age that she had not passed through the fire.

Later Sir Pertáb told me how the Maharája, his father, was loving and stern, and how he never allowed his sons to remain more than half an hour in the rooms of the ladies of the house. In those days a young Rájput was brought up on Spartan lines, taught to be brave and abstemious; and Sir Pertáb was a great believer in making youth fit and hard. He often inveighed against the system of giving powers too early to the Princes of India. He said: "You giving Princes powers when they first drinking and being married, you putting lighted straw under bears." He was full of wisdom.

Wherever there was fighting Sir Pertáb was there, and his great ambition, which he cherished to the end, was to fall in a cavalry charge, wearing Queen Victoria's icon on his helm. His devotion to her and to the Royal House was beautiful and sincere. He came home for the celebrations of the first Jubilee and was greatly impressed by his reception at Windsor. It was on that occasion that he secured the precious miniature set in pearls. Ten years later he came to take part in the Diamond Jubilee rejoicings, and again went to Windsor, but on his way back to London he sat silent and depressed and would speak to no one. Later in the evening a great friend asked him: "What has happened? Did Her Majesty disappoint you in anything she said?" "No," said Sir Pertáb, "I seeing Queen Sahib ten years ago. I seeing Queen to-day. I not seeing her again, so not talking."

In 1905 Sir Pertáb was Chief of the Indian Staff attached to the present King, and at one place a statue of Queen Victoria was to be unveiled. The day before the ceremony I was going to church, as it was Sunday, and I asked Sir Pertáb what he would like to do. "I going church too," he said; "I going to Queen Sahib's statue." I explained that the statue was veiled, but this did not impede Sir Pertáb, and he sat like a statue himself in silent meditation for two hours.

He was the soul of chivalry, and held English women in reverence. But he was first of all a soldier, and I always thought that Sir Pertáb leading the Imperial Cadet Corps in that splendid uniform of white samite, on their black chargers was the picture of martial beauty. He was very popular with our Army, and when he was Regent or Prime Minister of the Marwár State, Jodhpur was the Mecca of the Cavalry officer, the polo players and the horsemen. At one of the gatherings a young Englishman fell sick and died. Sir Pertáb fought for him in the struggle against the typhoid, and watched over him like a father. He insisted on being one of those who carried the poor boy to his grave. But the Bráhman priests objected and pointed out that Sir Pertáb would lose caste. "Caste!" roared Sir Pertáb. "He soldier, I soldier! I soldier caste, Rája caste!" And the Bráhmans retired hurriedly.

Sir Pertáb, however, was always rational in such matters. A friend of mine once saw him shooting pigeons as they came out of a well, and said: "I am surprised to see you shooting pigeons. I thought it was contrary to your religion." Sir Pertáb replied: "Yes, Sahib, you are right; not good religion, but making good pie!"

This indifference to Bráhman opinion was very rare among Hindus. One rather old-fashioned Rája was greatly upset when a Bráhman in his State committed a very brutal murder. He assented after long resistance to the sentence of death, but could not bear to stay in his Capital and posted off to Benáres to expiate the sin which attached to the punishment of a Bráhman. When the Bráhman was hanged, the old Rája telegraphed to a friend of mine, the Political Agent to the State, "Without hanging no good Government."

When Sir Pertáb was out in China, during the Boxer rising, he wrote to me saying he was the next heir to the State of Idar. I made over his letter to the Foreign Office at Simla, and was somewhat surprised to hear next day that Sir Pertáb had strong claims, and when the Maharája of Idar died Sir Pertáb succeeded. He took up his new dignity with hope and set to work with characteristic energy. But after a time he wrote me a rather despondent letter: "You have placed my head in the heavens, my feet in the mud," in other words, the revenues of the Idar State were small. He asked some of his friends in the Household Cavalry to be his guests at Idar. When they had exhausted the sporting resources of the State, they went to Meerut to pursue the wild boar. They telegraphed to Sir Pertáb to come up and join them in pig-sticking: to which he sent the laconic reply: "I first catching revenue, then catching pig."

When he returned from the war in China he came straight to my house in Simla. He left his followers at the foot of the mountain and arrived in Simla dusty and travel-stained, without any baggage. We were dining that night of his arrival at a large party given by a high official, and I excused myself to Sir Pertáb, saying I could not well cancel the engagement. Sir Pertáb settled this by saying he would go too, although he did not know my host of the evening. Tired as he should have been, and clad only in his khaki dress, in the "Jodhpur" breeches of his own invention, he was the figure and the centre of the party. He was not the uninvited guest; he was the charming and delightful entertainer. Few understood his English; fewer his Hindustáni. But his beautiful manners and his kind, dignified smile won all hearts.

After a visit of some days, when I came in from my morning ride, I found that Sir Pertáb had departed without a farewell, and as I pondered in the porch of my house, a man clattered up the hill, carrying a white *pagri*. He handed this to me and said I was the "*Pagri badle bhai*"[1] of Sir Pertáb, and that I must at once send him some hat I had worn. I got a straw hat and the man galloped off to catch Sir Pertáb on his way down the hill. Then came letters from men of the Rahtor Clan congratulating me on my adoption, and from one of them I inquired what the new relationship involved. The answer came: "If Sir Pertáb dies, you will be responsible for his family. If you die, he will look after your sons." It was a complicated relationship, for from this time Sir Pertáb in his letters always spoke of my wife as his mother, and my sons as his nephews!

Though he liked the English and was tolerant and broad-minded, he was true to his traditions and customs. His feelings for England were once expressed by him in a conversation: "*Lekin* (but), Lady, I every time happy this England. Horses gentlemen, ladies is gentlemen, and grass is gentlemen!" He wisely never wore English dress, and from many observations he made to me it was evident that he realised that the East and the West could never be one. He was very observant and was a shrewd judge of manners. He was once discussing the splendid pageant at Delhi to celebrate the coronation of the King Emperor and he took exception to the elephant procession. Dining at Idar with some English officers, he said: "You eating knife and fork, I eating knife and fork. I not knowing this knife and fork. Great Mogul he knowing how mount this elephant. You not knowing. You sitting howdah in uniform with English lady. Great Mogul he mount properly, he dressed in white muslin and squat by himself on elephant's back. You sitting howdah, we laughing, you not knowing." In vain the Englishmen asked the mystery of mounting an elephant, but all that Sir Pertáb would say was, "I not knowing knife and fork." He had a remarkable knowledge regarding

[1] It is an old custom of the Rájputs to adopt a friend as a brother by the interchange of head-dress, and there is another custom by which a Rájput lady can count on a stranger to be her knight by sending him a *rákhi* (bangle).

custom and ceremonial, and he and the other Rájput Chiefs knew from tradition exactly what the Great Mogul did on great occasions.

Tolerant as he was, he hated the Moslems. But I never realised the depths of his hatred till I was leaving India. Sir Pertáb had come up to Simla to be present at a farewell dinner Lord Curzon gave to my wife and myself the night before we left, and after dinner Sir Pertáb and I sat up till two in the morning, talking of his hopes and ambitions, and one of his ambitions was to annihilate the Moslem people in India. I deprecated this prejudice and mentioned Moslem friends known to both of us. "Yes," he said, "I liking them too, but very much liking them dead." I have often thought of this conversation. One may know Indians for years and suddenly a time comes and they open their hearts and reveal what is in them. Sir Pertáb, good Hindu and Rajput as he was, had travelled and had rubbed shoulders with men of all countries. He knew the English well; he had met many nationalities—he had a kind of cosmopolitan civilisation. But down in his generous heart there dwelt this ineradicable hatred of the Moslems. I had often, on the Frontier, heard Moslems longing for the day when they could shout the battle cry of "Deen, Deen!" and massacre the Hindus, and I know that they, like King Abbas, who engraved these words on his sword, held that "the work of the Lion of God is good and pious." But I never realised that the Hindu nourished similar longings. And here was Sir Pertáb, my brother by adoption, the great and courteous Rájput gentleman, telling me with terrible truthfulness that now he had only two things to live for, to fall leading a charge of cavalry against the foes of the King Emperor, wearing the beloved brooch, and to wipe out the Moslems from India. Perhaps it may be said that higher education, with which he was not endowed, might have softened his inexorable attitude towards Islám; but I doubt whether education will change the outlook of the two religions and permit it to be less ferocious. Wise Hindu friends have told me that one thing only will remove the trouble and that is the prohibition of kine-killing. But, if this education there are other deep-seated causes of hatred. The ferocious would perhaps suggest that the right of playing music before mosques, which the Hindus claim, is one chief cause of trouble; and when I recall the horrid clang of the cymbals and the conches and the hideous hum of the drums which make up their music, I can understand what it means to the devout Moslems at prayer time. I can also understand—for I have witnessed it—what it means to the Hindus when a Moslem flings a joint of beef into the Hindus' well. I can also sympathise with a Hindu legislator, who was discussing the savage outbreak of the Moslems[1] of Malabar, which horrified all Indians in recent times. He said: "I am all in favour of self-determination and local self-government, but I object to compulsory circumcision."

During the Great War in France, I saw much of Sir Pertáb, where he sat like the brave wild boar of India—that foeman to his practical spear—gnashing his old tusks idly, for he saw that this war was not for charging squadrons. I often tried to persuade him to leave the Western front, but he clung on, hoping there would come the gap through which he might lead his lancers to the goal of his desire. And in the end his one consolation was that his Rahtor troopers proved their quality in Palestine, where his kinsman and their English leader met the soldier's death he craved. He died full of years and honours, and in him passed a soldier, sportsman and gentleman, gay, wise and fearless, with a magnetism all his own.

Mádho Singh,[2] Maharája of Jaipur, was the exact opposite of Sir Pertáb. He belonged to the Kachwaha clan of Rajputs. He was in every sense a fine Rájput, though his ambition, after he had been selected to succeed the famous Maharája Rám Singh, was for the victories of peace and improvement of his State, rather than for glories of the field of arms and sport. He made his Capital one of the most beautiful cities in the East and encouraged the arts and crafts of his people. His apathy for horses aroused

[1] Moplah. The indigenous Moslems of Malabar.

[2] Born 1861, and given the name of Kaim Singh, succeeded in 1880, and was named Mádho Singh. His sonorous titles announced by the shrill clear-voiced nomenclator of the Court were "Saramad i Rájaha i Hindustán Ráj Rájendra Sri Mahárajadhirája Sawai Sir Madho Singh Bahádur." He was Grand Commander of four Orders. He died in 1922.

the sharp criticism of Sir Pertáb, and as I had a great liking for Mádho Singh I often had heated discussions with Sir Pertáb. Towards the end Sir Pertáb admitted the fine qualities of the Maharája of Jaipur; but there was never any cordiality between the two, neighbours though they were. Sir Pertáb had for a time been brought up by the great Maharája Rám Singh of Jaipur, and he may have disliked the idea of an unknown young man being chosen to succeed the famous Rám Singh.

I met Madho Singh soon after his accession, and a curious incident won me his friendship. I had gone to Calcutta with the Agent to Governor-General for Rajputána, and on my return at dawn I found the Secretary of the Maharája awaiting me in my tent. He said that the Maharája was in a great difficulty. He had been invited by one of our Staff to attend a pig-sticking meet on the morrow, and as His Highness had given up riding he was in a dilemma. If the Agent to Governor-General rode, he, too, must ride, and he was out of practice. I at once assured the Secretary that the arrangement for pig-sticking was the spontaneous and unauthorised idea of the zealous Assistant; that the Agent to Governor-General had made other engagements, and that there was no necessity for the Maharája to inconvenience himself. The Secretary asked me to convey the welcome news in person, so I went with him to the Palace. We passed through the courtyard down a narrow passage leading into a walled and shaded garden. At the door of the garden the Secretary asked me to wait while he warned His Highness, who was taking an al fresco bath and preparing himself for the business of the day. As he spoke, an American tourist rushed by me, and made in the direction of the enclosure in which the Maharája was ensconced. The Secretary, aghast, remonstrated; but the forceful lady said: "If this young man is admitted, I, who have come thousands of miles, claim my right to admission," and she rushed to her fate. I hastily retreated to the courtyard and listened to the minstrels in the *Naubat khána*,[1] who play day and night, so that His Highness may always awake to sweet music and may know that while he has been sleeping all evil spirits

[1] Minstrel gallery over the inner gate of the Palace.

have been kept at bay by the gentle, drowsy minstrelsy. Then I saw the American lady pass hurriedly through the courtyard, and she must have left Jaipur convinced that even Maharájas should have a few minutes of privacy. She speeded on to the great gate, but did not see in a recess on her right hand a scholarly scribe, who writes, in an exquisite Hindi script, the name and description of all who pass in. The chronicle of the *Deorhi* goes back to immemorial times and is always consulted for precedents. I feel sure that there is in this chronicle a gentle comment on the danger and inconvenience caused by the curiosity of Western travellers. Incidentally, the enterprising Assistant also left Jaipur that same day. Twenty years later the Maharája recalled the incident to me with a smile.

He was large in stature and very dignified and reserved, and I, like most others, looked on him as a model of orderly and level life. He was most generous in his charities, and any good cause might count on his open-handed largess. But much as I liked him, I should have liked him more if I had known what he told me, when I was leaving India, as I thought for good, because I never suspected that the stately, decorous Maharája had had romantic and even lurid experiences before he was called on to rule the fair State of Jaipur. He came to meet me at Agra, on my way down from Simla to Bombay, when I left Lord Curzon. We spent the day together, and at night he asked me whether I should ever return to India. I said "No." "Then," said he, "I will tell you of a wonderful man to whom I owe everything and count as divine. He was a Brinjára drover, happy and prosperous, when he discovered that his wife was unfaithful. So wretched was he that he mounted a hill and flung himself down a terrific scarp. But he was caught half-way by the stump of a tree, and when he recovered his senses he found himself in the hut of a pious man who was on the point of visiting sacred Brindaban. When he was able to move, deeming himself under the special protection of God, he went with the pious man to the great shrine, where he spent the rest of his life. He acquired a great reputation for sanctity, and became the *Mahant*, or Master of the temple. Now I—I was the son of a noble family of the Jaipur State, and heir by right to a principality in that State. But by an intrigue at Court my rights were ignored and another man was unjustly preferred. This embittered me, and I became a 'barwatia.' I took to the road, robbed, and I am sorry to say, killed, when there was fighting. The Jaipur authorities set a price on my head, so I fled to Brindaban and threw myself on the protection of the great Master, whose name I had often heard. He was kind to me and I stayed with him for two years, meditating and living the life of a recluse. The Jaipur State sent a high official to demand my surrender, but the Master, before all the crowd, chased the officer down the steps, with a slipper in his hand, and I loved him all the more for his brave championship of a friendless outlaw. Later I was held a prisoner in the Palacew here now I rule; and then, after service in another State, I was summoned to succeed Maharája Rám Singh. When I had been one year on the cushion[1] of power, I sent a mission to the Master, begging him to pay me a visit, and when he came, I received him with the honours that are given to a Viceroy, and I embraced him as he reached the appointed place on the carpet. But he was very quiet and unresponsive, took no notice of my gifts, and said he must return to his Shrine next day. I besought him not to despise my gifts, and begged him to stay some time, otherwise my people would think that I had neglected a Holy Man. But he only smiled kindly and said that my world and his world were separate and apart, and that I must stay in my own world and never revisit him in this life. And there it ended, and when he died I went in great state, with elephants and troops, to do him honour. He was the greatest man I ever met, though he was not a Rájput, just a Brinjára, a carrier of salt and grain."

Maharája Mádho Singh came to England for the Coronation of King Edward. He chartered a ship to bring himself and four hundred followers, and sufficient water from the sacred Ganges, drawn from the river at Hurdwár, to last them four months. The water was stored in copper vessels and was sweet and good till they returned to Jaipur.

[1] *Guddee* is the Indian equivalent for the throne. It is a cushion against which the Rája reclines.

The Maharája did not incur the great expense of a special ship without due thought, and it is possible that the expense was not greater than the fines for breaking the rules of caste exacted by the Bráhmans would have been if he had travelled over the "black water" in an ordinary ship. He was delighted with England and the English people. He paid me a visit at Thorney Abbey, near Peterborough, which is the centre of great wheat farms and is celebrated for its breed of shire horses and its beef. As I knew that the mere mention of beef would make him ill, I arranged with a leading farmer to show him nothing but Shire horses. He was greatly impressed, as anyone would have been, by the splendid horses, many in number, which my friend kindly showed us, and asked me to inquire what the full price for the whole lot would be. Mr. Topham was puzzled, and said he could not name a price. The majority of the horses had won prizes. Pressed to give an approximate price, Mr. Topham quoted a large sum. "I will take them," said the Maharája, and walked on. As the Maharája spoke no English I acted as interpreter, and told Mr. Topham that it was out of the question as the horses would die in the heat of Jaipur. I then rejoined the Maharája and asked him what use he could make of the horses in Jaipur: "For ceremonies and *tomashas*." I then told him how a Governor-General in past times had imported shire horses for Ranjit Singh, "the lion of the Punjáb," and how these horses had died from the heat of Sind on their way up country, and that he, as a merciful man, ought not to doom these splendid animals to a similar fate. The Maharája at once assented, and I told the greatly relieved Mr. Topham that the sale was off.

The Maharája brought up a few followers on his special train. I made them welcome, but my duties as host were simple, for Mádho Singh provided his cooks and cooking utensils and his beloved Ganges water and his food. I noticed that one of the Staff never left the Maharája. His face was familiar to me, but I had forgotten his peculiar office, and I asked him, when I had a chance, what he was. "I am the jeweller of His Highness," he said, "and responsible for the jewels he wears, and wherever he goes I must go. I never lose sight of the jewels."

The Maharája had paid a visit to Kedleston, to see the home of the Viceroy, Lord Curzon, and he said this to me: "I watched the rabbits"—he called them "hares"—"playing on the green turf, and I thought I could sit watching these little creatures gambolling in the sun, and could rest there for ever, playing a flute, and I wondered how English Sahibs could ever go to India."

He and his four hundred men returned in safety to Jaipur, but they were forced to remain four days outside the city, as the astrologers, whom most Hindus and nearly all Rájas implicitly obey, had decreed that the omens were unpropitious.

My first acquaintance with him arose from an incident of sport in 1882. My last meeting, also, was connected with sport. The Prince of Wales, in 1905, visited Jaipur and spent an afternoon stalking black buck, the Indian antelope, for which Jaipur is famous. Mádho Singh, as host, insisted on accompanying the Prince of Wales; but his presence, with his obligatory followers, would have been fatal to the success of the sport, while his limited powers of walking would have delayed the party. So he was greatly relieved when on arriving at the ground the Prince of Wales kindly suggested that his host should not go farther, and it was arranged that I should accompany him to the Palace. As we drove along he suddenly asked me whether I intended to return to India, and I said "No." "You said you would not return when you left in 1903, but you came back." I assured him that there was no likelihood of my return. "Then," said he, "I will show you what I have never shown to anyone," and he gave an order to his coachman. After some time we came to a large square building into which we drove over a drawbridge. The gate was guarded by soldiers, and inside was a large courtyard surrounded by buildings of two stories with spacious verandas and latticed windows. "This," said the Maharája, "is the residence of my ladies," and we sat in the carriage in a somewhat embarrassed silence. I could not in honesty congratulate him on the beauty of his bower. It was solid, square, and possibly hygienic, but there was no architectural charm about the place. So I thanked him for the honour he had conferred on me, and then we turned and left by the drawbridge, the only entrance to the building. I remembered that in 1882 Colonel Bradford had told me that there were 2,000 inmates of the Zenána of Jaipur. In the twenty-three years which had elapsed the axe had been applied, for the building which I saw could not have housed more than one hundred.

Mádho Singh died in 1922, and I hope that in the incarnation of a Brinjára Saint he is now listening to sweet music on a green sward by a running stream, for heaven lies in contrast, and no contrast could be greater than that of the country under the burnished sun which he ruled so wisely and so well, and a vale in old England.

But in some respects the most striking of all the Rájput Chiefs was the Maharána of Udaipur, the Sesodia Fateh Singh,[1] legitimate heir to the throne of Ráma, the vice-regent of the great god Shiva. I have attempted to describe his beautiful capital elsewhere, but it is useless to attempt a description of the Chief himself. To the Indians he represented not only all that was oldest and purest in lineage and in chronicle, but he was besides holy and sacred by reason of his peculiar status, to which I need not refer in detail.

To the English, to the few who had the good fortune to meet him in Udaipur, for he was ever reluctant to leave his State, and his forebears had stipulated with the Mogul Emperors that they would not render personal service, he seemed possessed of the most perfect manners in the world. I have watched the effect of this wonderful manner on diverse people. When I went out to India with Lord Curzon, having served for sixteen continuous years in India without taking furlough, he used to rally me on my judgment of men, saying that most of my swans were geese. So when we went to Udaipur, and Lord Curzon met the Maharána for the first time, I watched him closely and saw with pleasure that he, who was no respecter of persons, fell at once under the charm. He did not press the Maharána with questions of administration nor point out weak points in the State, nor suggest reforms. In such an atmosphere of charm and

[1] His Highness Maharájadhirája Maharána Sir Fateh Singh, Bahádur, G.C.S.I., G.C.I.E., G.C.V.O., born 1849, succeeded 1884. He is still living, and I had a letter from him dated 13 December, 1927. He always writes to me in Roman *Urdu*.

courtesy it would have been almost profane to touch on subjects so commonplace, so out of place. Little was said, for the Maharána, like most great Indians of that time, believed in golden silence, and the most voluble of his visitors seemed disinclined to be talkative in that gracious and noble presence. I often tried to think out the secret of these divine manners. I do not think it was to be found in the attributes which his Indian worshippers claimed for him, but rather that it lay in his great desire to be courteous to all, and that his simple idea of courtesy was not to encroach, to impinge, nor to interfere. It has been my good fortune to see many good and distinguished men in all walks of life—men of great and men of lowly position—but I have never met anyone with the manners of Fateh Singh. In fiction one often comes across passages where a very witty character is introduced, but he never says a witty thing. So, too, I say that Fateh Singh had the most perfect manners in the world, but I have given no instances. I can only remember that it was a delight and a privilege to sit with him, and perhaps, after all, manners are negative rather than positive, and a noble and kind face, and an understanding smile may count more than courteous words.

I was Chief of the Staff when the present King and Queen visited Udaipur in 1905. There was a State dinner in the Palace, and afterwards, on a still and perfect night, they went up to the roof of the Palace and looked over the exquisite lake to the ring of hills where for miles were thousands of lamps fed by an army of men who ran from lamp to lamp with jars of coconut oil. They sat in silence looking at the beautiful scene. The Maharána sat behind them and never said a word, but he watched the faces of his Royal guests, watched them, and never looked over the lake. The lamps burned on, for the order was that they were to be kept brimming till a rocket went up from the Palace. After a long time the Prince of Wales asked me how long the illuminations would last, and I interpreted this to the Maharána. "As long as their Royal Highnesses sit here," was the reply, and the illuminations went on.

A prince of courtesy, and though one never knew what he thought of this world and of the strange folk who came from over the sea, one knew that he was a loyal supporter of the British connection, as was his predecessor in the dark days of the Mutiny. And though he was always gracious and exerted himself as a host, there was in the background the melancholy which in the House of Udaipur dated back to the death of the beautiful Princess Krishna,[1] the Flower of Rájasthan, who, sought in marriage by the rival Princes of Jodhpur and Jaipur, was sacrificed for the safety of the State. The curse still lives, and in fact it was an accursed deed, execrated by all chivalrous Rájputs.

The Maharána has had troubles and anxieties. His only son fell ill and an operation was necessary. The English surgeon who operated did his work in a marble hall, and was unaware of the fact that frightened, doubting eyes were watching him from the white marble latticed windows in the gallery. As he got ready, the surgeon whistled gently "The Wearing of the Green," and when the operation was over and the son was out of danger, an official asked the surgeon again to whistle the air, and begged him to whistle it into a cone for the gramophone, "for," said he, "the ladies of the Palace say it is an incantation which must be preserved." And so in the Palace there is still an old cylinder of wax which might perhaps revive, when needed, "The Wearing of the Green."

The story of Krishna Kumari is told in Chapter XVII of Tod's wonderfu book, "The History of Rájasthan." One reads there of the infamous Nawab Ameer Khan, and of the renegade Ajit Singh—that stain on the Sesodia race "cursed by the brave Sangram," "may you die childless and your name die with you." The horrors and the misery suffered by the State of Udaipur in the days preceding the Treaty with the British in 1817 bring home to us what *Pax Britannica* meant to Udaipur and to all Rajputána. The people of British India have forgotten the evil days in the long years of peace and prosperity, but the Rájputs remember.

CHAPTER XII

"And the elements
So mixed in him that Nature might stand up
And say to all the world, 'This was a man!'"
—*Julius Cæsar*, Act v. Scene 5.

Leave India March, 1895—Three Happy Years as Agent to Duke of Bedford—Decide to Return to India with Lord Curzon as his Private Secretary—The East a-calling—Lord Curzon's Untiring Industry—Sketch of Lord Curzon—Printing of Confidential Papers—His Patience with my Criticisms—The Clever *Bons Mots*—His Desire to do Things for Himself—Thirst for New Problems—His Power of Acquiring Technical Knowledge—His Wish to be Head of the Civil Service—His Interest in Indian Chiefs—His Love of Pageant and Ceremonial—His Reluctance to Pledge Himself or Successors Regarding the Future—His Passion for History—His Insistence on Accuracy—His Ardour in the Preservation of Ancient Monuments—His Religion—Always Working at High Pressure—His Oratory.

I LEFT Kashmir and India in March, 1895, and thought I should never see that fascinating land again. I had at that time served sixteen years in India in the Indian Civil Service, without taking furlough, which most men take after eight years' service. From 1895 till the latter part of 1898 I was busily engaged on my new work in England, most interesting, delightful, and in every way congenial. But, inasmuch as this book relates only to India, I must not stray over the very pleasant fields in which my path lay for three happy years. I gained valuable experience, found that after three months with a chartered accountant, and by constant inspection of the Bedford estates, I could carry out the duties of agent-in-chief, and settled down with content to a permanent life at home.

In the autumn of 1898, Mr. George Curzon, who had been appointed Viceroy of India, wrote to me asking whether I could suggest someone to be his private secretary. Up to this time private secretaries had been selected from England, and no Viceroy had, in my recollection, chosen a

Secretary from the Indian Civil Service. But it seemed to me that it would help a Viceroy to have with him someone who knew at any rate the puzzling terms and technicalities with which Indian administration bristles. I suggested at once my great friend, Major James Dunlop Smith, who had been private secretary to Sir Charles Aitchison, Lieutenant-Governor of the Punjáb. I added that I wished I was available myself. To this he replied that I was denser than he imagined, and that in his first letter he had indicated me in his description of the qualities he required in his Secretary. It was, however, not easy to arrange matters, and if the Duke of Bedford had not been the most unselfish and generous of friends, I should have hesitated to ask him to let me throw up my work. Luckily he had served in India on Lord Dufferin's Staff, and knew what the lure of India meant. Many of my friends pointed out the unwisdom of giving up a most delectable post in England for a five years' appointment in India, on much smaller pay, and with no prospects of employment at the end of five years; for I had resigned the Indian Civil Service in 1896 and could not be reinstated.

But I had heard the "East a-calling," and in December, 1898, I started for India with the Viceroy designate. We spent Christmas at sea, but there was no holiday for him or for me: work was continuous after our ship left Marseilles. Day and night he toiled in the Captain's quiet cabin: day and night he wrote, and talked, and when he was not extracting facts from his formidable collection of books, he was extracting information from all on board whom I had mentioned as experts. I, who had regarded voyages as intervals of forced rest, wondered how long the pace would last; but it seemed to quicken in the heat of the Red Sea, never slackened in the dust and glare of the Indian tours, and to the end of the five years it grew faster and faster. Yet so infectious was his cheery and boisterous industry that I never tired. But I was well and strong, while he was seldom free from pain.

Much has already been written regarding his strenuous Viceroyalty. He arranged with me in 1899 that I should be his biographer. But the late Mr. Lovat Fraser asked Lord Curzon whether he might write a book on his Indian administration, and the Viceroy, who had never met Mr. Lovat Fraser, agreed on condition that I passed the proofs. At the same time, by my request, he absolved me from the task of writing his life. In the year before his death he again asked me to be his biographer, but after careful consideration I reluctantly declined. Another and more able pen than mine will give to the world the biography of this rare and most devoted public servant; but I may be permitted to offer to a smaller circle a sketch of one who was to me a great Chief, and a "tremendous companion."

It was a fact noticed by the late Lord Salisbury that my Chief could write as fast as he could think, and I have watched him long after midnight, racked with pain, which he once described as "toothache in the leg," writing in his clear and beautiful handwriting some speech or dispatch, which he would give me for criticism. I have seen him tear up ten or twenty sheets of foolscap, if the criticism appealed to him, and rewrite the whole note. He never cared to cut out or revise: he would always begin afresh. I have never seen such power of work, such diligence and such accuracy. The trouble was that he expected to find the same energy and application in others, and when I pleaded that long years in the Indian climate are apt to enervate even the most diligent, he would never accept my plea. He held that India and its problems must needs arouse enthusiasm in all officials, and that the man who was not full of an almost missionary zeal for the welfare of the Indians would be better at home.

All of us who have served in India have our ideas, and many of us used to agree that in theory certain changes were desirable. But the usual attitude of Authority was that India required rest rather than change, and there were many good arguments for leaving well alone. Into this calm atmosphere came a young, brilliant and energetic Viceroy, with a passion for problems; an accessible Viceroy, who would listen or discuss, and if he got on the track of a problem would never let go till he and his officials had solved it. After the first year I saw the tragedy of the situation and realised the strain: so instead of looking for problems, I sought rather to bury them out of sight. For in India a problem does not end with its solution; and to the end of his time in India Lord Curzon would take constant stock of the working of his various reforms, great or small, important or insignificant, and, while watching his early efforts, he was always adding to the list of the obstacles to efficiency which must be removed. He used to speak of watching and watering the garden which he had planted, and he often reminded me of a driver of an English goods train with its incongruous variety of trucks driven at express speed, and I could see him looking anxiously back to see if any of his wagons had left the rails.

Lord Curzon was unlike all the Viceroys I had known. He was younger—a young, resolute man, with a Council of older men who had won their position by ability, character and hard work. But this young Viceroy, very sure of his facts, could beat them all at work. His predecessors had not been Parliamentary fighters, and had mostly held high administrative office before they came to India. Lord Curzon came out fresh from the fray, ready to argue, to convince, and always determined to prove his case up to the hilt. Unlike those who had held office during my time, he had some personal knowledge of journalism, and paid more attention to Press criticism, with the inevitable result that the newspapers responded and paid more attention to him. He rather courted publicity for his actions and reforms, and wished to create a public opinion, appreciative and auxiliary. He was more outspoken than his predecessors, outspoken in his minutes and in his conversation. When we first came out he asked me whether he should guard his conversation at luncheon and dinner in his own house. I thought this would be too great a strain, but I fear that I was wrong, for the free and natural talk of a Viceroy is always repeated and usually exaggerated. He was a curious mixture of full dress and undress. In public, he was the great, stately Proconsul, sonorous and formal. In his own house he would often throw off the mantle and be natural. But the roots of his nature and his culture were down in the soil of past times, and his diction and his attitudes were strange to Simla and Calcutta. Some of his phrases sounded pompous, and a visitor from another world who had read the literature of the eighteenth century might have thought that he was listening to some magnate addressing the rascality of the neighbourhood. He would say things in jest—often taken in earnest by those who watched the handsome strong face and were ignorant of his love of laughter and joke. For the brief interval between work, continuous till 8 p.m., and starting once more at 11 p.m., he wished to be himself, listening to the fine band in which he delighted; but his guests never saw George Nathaniel Curzon, but always saw the Viceroy. When he said that no self-respecting woman would allow cold tapioca pudding to be served at luncheon, there was a sensation in Simla. He was filled with enthusiasm, as he talked on any subject. I remember one night his talking to a young chaplain who had made up his mind to leave India. It was a kind of rule that guests who had conversed with the Viceroy told me afterwards the purport of the conversation. This chaplain told me how encouraging and kind the Viceroy had been, and next day, fired by the Viceregal predictions of promotion, he wrote to say that he had decided to stay in India. It was all illusion. Lord Curzon could be the most charming of hosts, and was so to the end. He delighted in hospitality, but there was a dangerous hypnotism in him. Many men who came to Government House full of fixed purpose, went away full of the Viceroy's purpose. He had great power—perhaps charm—and in the five years of my diary I can find but few instances of men whom he failed to win to his views.

But, with all this power or charm, there was often intolerance, and his fault was that on occasions he regarded the average man as invertebrate. He could not suffer fools gladly. After what he would rather pathetically call one of his "angry days," when things had gone persistently wrong, proofs from our always overworked Press not forthcoming, bad news from the Frontier, hostile articles in the newspapers, English and Indian, unwelcome suggestions from the India Office, collisions between Europeans and Indians—there were no communal clashes in the Consulship of Curzon—he would ask what was amiss, and I would always answer: "Too much ὕβρις." To which he would reply, "I was born so, you cannot change me." If he could have been a little more patient, a little more understanding, he would have been a very perfect Viceroy. For, quite apart from his striking ability and his untiring industry, he had noble qualities. His love of justice, his hatred of tyranny, his contempt of meanness and his scorn of inefficiency or apathy would have made him perhaps the greatest of the great line of Viceroys, if only he could have recognized that the officials were not sprinters, but long-race runners. He had an intense admiration of the work of the Indian Civil Service, and believed that England had been singled out by Providence for the greatest mission in history; but, while he admired their work, he had little sympathy for the hardships and trials of the workers. He had a contempt for climate and environment; his zeal for study and industry acted like a drug and made him impervious to heat and cold. Perhaps a week in the plains of the Punjáb in the hot weather would have made a difference; but, ill as he often was, he could stand the sun and the heat better than any of us.

As a rule, for the first two years of office, a Viceroy is popular: the third year sees a pause and questioning, and the last two years are often charged with adverse, if not hostile, criticism. At first the omens were auspicious, and from the first day in Bombay—that glorious and welcoming city—Lord Curzon aroused the interest of all classes in India. His promise that he would endeavour to hold the balance fair between the Indians and the British was well received. The British had a good conscience, for the balance had never been deflected to their advantage. But the Indians, who are always looking for a sign, perhaps read more in the Viceroy's words than was intended. Lord Curzon had no illusions as to the difficulty of holding the balance fair; but he little thought, in those first glowing months of welcome and applause, how delicate were the scales, and how dangerous and baffling was the racial question. An old friend of mine, one of the Secretaries to the Government of India, was talking to a merchant of Calcutta. The latter said: "This new Viceroy will hustle you Secretaries." "No," said my Secretary friend, "he will be paper-logged in three months." But he was wrong.

In the offices of Government every paper is printed.

Printing is cheap in India, and perhaps one of the reasons for the extraordinary length of the reports and letters which came up from the Provinces, and of the equal prolixity of the notes which were written in the Secretariat on these reports, was that the writers knew that they would be immortalised in print. It was interesting to look through these heavy files of print—to read Lord Lawrence's laconic orders, and Lord Lytton's perfect and arresting notes. It is pleasant also to know that just as I read Lord Lytton's exquisite English, so do the men of the Secretariat of to-day delight in Lord Curzon's scathing and illuminating homilies. He revelled in files, and was never paper-logged, and by the end of the first three months of Calcutta it was the Secretaries who were paper-logged, while the Viceroy sat at his unencumbered table asking for more.,

The Private Secretary of the Viceroy has his own Press. I was enjoined by the India Office to consider very carefully the question of printing the mass of letters and notes which were sent and received. It was suggested that the private letters from the Viceroy to the Secretary of State, and other very confidential matter, should never be printed, and I was offered the services of two men from England who could help me to keep important papers confidential. Among other leakages, printed copies of Queen Victoria's letters to the Viceroy had been sold in the Calcutta Bazaar. It was an anxious matter, because I realised that nothing was safe or confidential if it went to the Press. But Lord Curzon swept aside the suggestions of the India Office. His predecessors had done their work in print—why should he be condemned to reading endless reams of manuscript? But the letters of Queen Victoria were never printed again.

I found that my Press was in the hands of a Bengali family. The Superintendent was an excellent man, Grish Babu, and the Staff were his relations. When I remonstrated with him on his nepotism, he remarked that he could trust his own family, but could not be responsible for outsiders. The family of Grish stayed on and worked always at high pressure, for copy poured in very early in the morning and very late at night, and it was usually accompanied by a blue slip which signified that it was very urgent. Poor

Grish Babu! toiling in Calcutta, which he loved, for it was his kindly home, and in Simla, which he loathed, for it was cold, foreign and expensive. He never failed me. He was told that if any act of leakage were proved, he and the other Grish-lings would go. There was no leakage during my five years; that is, no leakage which became public.

Lord Curzon loved Calcutta. He was proud of the stately Government House built in the image of his own home of Kedleston, and he told me years before, when he made his first journey to India, that he resolved when he next visited Government House to enter it as Viceroy, and to have me with him. Later he came again to India in the Viceroyalty of Lord Elgin, and went straight to Kashmir. He was at that time writing articles on his travels for *The Times*. He was on his way to the Pamirs, and was afterwards received in Kabul by the great Amir Abdur Rahmán. The then Government of India did not approve of the visit to Kabul, and George Curzon had written an article inveighing against the timidity and general delinquencies of the Government of India. He asked me to read this very vitriolic, but very interesting article. I handed it back to him without comment and gazed out from my veranda upon the lovely valley of Kashmir. He flushed and then said: "Don't you think it is good?" "For what?" I asked. "It will make them sit up," he said. "Yes," I replied, "but if you are coming out as Viceroy, you would not like some young M.P. to go jumping the Frontier and flouting you?" "Do you know what *The Times* pays me for these articles, and that you are asking me to tear up what is of some value to *The Times* and of much more value to me?" "I don't care what they pay you," I replied, "but I know that it will pay you better not to send that article home." He grumbled, and said I was as timid as the Government of India, but he went into his room and wrote another article. This was one of his charming qualities, that he never resented my criticisms, although they often entailed heavy labour on him.

The post of Viceroy of India is essentially lonely. He can have no friends. He is not *primus inter pares*, he is *primus* and apart: yet Lord Curzon craved for someone to be with him, and hated solitude. Even when he was writing he would often ask me to stay on in the room and silently pass the pages to me. He rarely made mistakes, and I always felt a kind of pleasure if I could find an error. In one branch of literature I knew more than he did. He was addicted in his letters to quotations from Dickens, and invariably went wrong. (No writer is more quoted than Dickens and no writer more misquoted.) When challenged, he would at once ask me to fetch the book in question. He knew where every book was—he knew in which drawer a letter would be. His brain was like a splendid and perfect index; yet to the end he would mix up Micawber and Dick Swiveller. It would have been better for him and for others if he had known more of Dickens and less of logic.

Though while he loved Calcutta and the riverside park of Barrackpore, liked driving through the vast crowds of the packed bazaars and the green humid lanes of the suburbs—liked, too, to see new faces and learn of new enterprises, he always regarded Simla as the real work-room where he could work undisturbed save by the weekly visits of the Secretaries and the weekly meeting of the Executive Council. But he never liked Simla, and just before I left him in 1903 he said: "I congratulate you heartily on one thing—on leaving Simla so soon. How I hate the place!" It was too cramped for him. If he left Viceregal Lodge, it was to drive along the narrow ridge crowded with officials or summer visitors. There was the retreat at Mashobra and the beautiful camp under the deodars at Naldera. But after a time he would grow restless and come back to the work-room, where the work he had himself initiated grew like the proverbial snowball. After six months he said: "I have worked on your lines of conciliation and of deference to official susceptibilities. I must now put on the pace."

The gossip of the Club and the clever *bons mots* of Simla society reached me, but never penetrated to the still work-room. Officials rather resented the young man in a hurry, who had discovered that all was wrong before he came; they also resented the quickening of the pace. I come across this entry in my diary, December, 1902: "Viceroy talks in despair about the work and the machinery. I tell him that India is all right half-speed, but it breaks down full-speed: look at Railways, Posts and Telegraphs now that the Durbár is approaching. They will all break down and so do the Departments, when the Viceroy is a man who goes full-speed." An old journalist, a man of excellent judgment whom we all trusted, said to me: "It is a mistake for your Chief to come down into the arena. If he comes down, he must expect trouble." He was right, and the trouble was aggravated by the fact that my Chief was not content with the rôle of Espada, but wanted to take the parts of Picador and Banderillero as well.

He was greatly irritated by the Press correspondents in Simla. Their plain tales from the hills were always based on our very excellent amateur theatre, on balls and picnics and race meetings. Not a word about the toil and the efforts of officialdom, and the Viceroy feared that India sweltering in the heat and dust of the plains would think that we were Olympians, careless of mankind. But the Press correspondents, when I remonstrated with them on their levity, replied with some truth that in the hot weather India is sick of toil and efforts, and longs to hear of revels and junketing. How weary I grew in the conveyance of admonishments, but the cheerful good humour of the admonished made the task easy. Yet, in spite of some awkwardness in starting, the officials responded nobly, and would often say that hard as the Viceroy worked them, he worked himself far harder.

Famine and plague were our portion in the first year, and I suggested that if a tour were made in the worst afflicted districts, without a following, with myself and only one A.D.C. (a Viceroy has eight A.D.C.s), he would see the real facts, and also see what officials could do in times of stress. This tour was of greater benefit than any progress of pageants and huge camps, when the Viceroy only finds India *en fête*, whitewash and illuminations. He came away from this tour with his already high opinion of District officials greatly enhanced. There is nothing finer in the record of our race than the determined efforts of these devoted men to save Indians from death by famine and plague. Many of them died at their posts. There was only one contretemps on this most useful tour. At the capital of one of the provinces, the Viceroy was asked to visit a new plague camp which the City Fathers had erected. It was a beautiful camp, most orderly, clean and new. At the door of each room was a card giving the name of the plague-stricken man and the date of his entry, and it appeared that all the sufferers had entered on the day of the Viceroy's visit. I noticed one patient shivering violently under the blanket, and pulling down the blanket I asked him his story. As I talked to the man, who seemed remarkably composed, the English official in charge looked in and exclaimed: "This is my gardener!" On inquiry the gardener admitted that he was in rude health and was merely occupying a bed to oblige the City Fathers, who had given him fourpence for his trouble. Unluckily Lord Curzon also looked in and grasped the situation. The unfortunate notables, who had watched with pleasure the Viceroy's obvious approval of the camp, were astounded when, turning on them, he denounced them as impostors who had brought him a long way in the burning heat to take part in a sham. It was a case of over-zeal. The camp was perfect, but it lacked patients, and so patients were procured. I attended many such ceremonies, but having lived in Kashmir I knew that underlying the sham there was often reality and worth. But Lord Curzon had not lived in Kashmir.

He used to speak of India as a University in which no one ever took a degree. There is profound truth in this, for the wisest of Civilians always told me that the more they learned of India, the less their knowledge seemed to be. If ever any Englishman deserved a degree in the great University of the East, Lord Curzon deserved it. He had studied, travelled, and had noted, and he came out a Viceroy knowing more than most of the glacis that stretches out beyond the confines of our Eastern enceinte. He had travelled round the Frontiers, which were known to most officials merely through books. Yet he never obtruded this personal knowledge and always paid the greatest deference to the last traveller who brought news or ideas from Persia, Afghanistán, or from the Roof of the World where three empires meet. He was strangely modest as he sat listening to the explorers. But though he believed in travel, he had a curious indifference for local experience and for technical knowledge; for he believed that anyone who had vision could learn from books. One instance of this will suffice. The only technical knowledge which I could claim was a smattering of the intricacies of the Land Revenue of India. This is the key to India, for the land and agriculture count more than the problems of the great cities, of Frontier defence, of commerce and finance. There was a Committee called to consider the education of the aristocracy of India. Lord Curzon presided, and I was a member of this Committee. I urged, as the inquiry went on, that the young Princes and Nobles of India should be sent for three months to see the work of a Settlement Officer, as I thought that no one could understand the Land Revenue system of India until he knew how the record, the Domesday Book of the East, was made. One day he said after our sitting: "I am amused at your insistence on a Settlement training. If this is essential, how is it that I, who have had no such training, have drafted a Resolution on the Land Revenue system of India?" He said this in all modesty. He had torn up the Resolution drafted by the Secretary, an expert in Land Revenue, and had written a draft which all acknowledged as a masterpiece. He had done this by sheer industry, by days and nights of reading the dry-as-dust reports on the most difficult and technical subject in India. But he did not read all the reports: he only read the reports written by men recognised by the Civil Service as sound.

If, when he first came out, he had devoted himself to what all thought was his special subject—the Frontiers of India—all would have been satisfied. But he seemed eager to explore fresh fields into which others had never strayed, plunged with delight into dark pools and often found bottom.

He loved problems, the more difficult the better, and his great desire was to see things done.[1] He was impatient of delay, fretted at the leisurely yet safe manner in which the business of Government was conducted, and often compared the methods of the Secretariat to two old-fashioned lawn-tennis players returning the ball to each other, but never caring who won the game.

[1] Cf. "*Le difficile n'est pas de donner des ordres, c'est d'en assurer l'exécution.*"

Though he underestimated local experience, he had a craving to see how the machinery of Government was pieced together, and how each part of the machine worked. He was the first Viceroy who ever inspected the offices of the Secretariat. This was regarded by some as a dangerous intrusion, an invasion of the sacrosanct arcanum of administration. But he was not content with giving orders: he wanted to see the various processes through which his orders passed on their way down to the Districts of India. This desire to see for himself what his predecessors had taken for granted, arose partly from the feeling that everything literally depended on him, and partly from the generous and almost boyish sentiment that he was a fellow-worker of the humblest copyist in the offices. He once expressed to me his wish to give an annual dinner to the Civil Services of India at which he would preside as Head of the Civil Service. At first I thought the idea was admirable; but I consulted some experienced Civilians, and they thought it might prove embarrassing. I explained to the Viceroy that at such dinners the Senior Civilian presided, and that as he was not a member of the Civil Service he could only attend as a guest. He maintained that he was Head of the Civil Service, and continued to regard himself in this light, but he abandoned the idea of the annual dinner. Here again he was moved by two distinct impulses—the impulse to assert his all-embracing powers, and the impulse to be one of a Service on which his work and its success depended. It was a case of Jekyll and Hyde, and I never felt quite sure which of them predominated. In those days the telephone was in its infancy, and the Foreign Office, which is directly under the Viceroy, heard with mixed feelings that a telephone was to be installed in their quiet and cloistered home. Next he suggested that a telephone in my office would be of advantage; but I pleaded that this would interfere with my most important work of interviewing the numerous visitors who thronged to Simla and Calcutta. He agreed, and my five years were never rudely startled by the hateful summons of the bell. It all sounds old-fashioned now, and I dare say that much which we did in those far-off days by interview and by letter is now done by telephone. From an

Indian point of view I wonder if it is better done—whether the words over the telephone have the same effect as the words spoken at the interview. So much depends on eyes and the play of the mouth.

Lord Curzon was a very noticeable man. He was always "at the head of the table." I remember when I first went to India I hardly knew the name of the Viceroy, and few Civilians in the Districts took any interest in the personality of the remote Satrap. But somehow everyone in India seemed to be aware of Lord Curzon,[1] and an intelligent traveller once said to me: "I know nothing of your Chief's work, but I do know that he interests people in the most distant parts of India."

He certainly interested the Chiefs and the people of that huge territory which lies in the Indian States. He was an untiring traveller and visited every State of importance; visited States to which no former Viceroy had ever penetrated. He encouraged those Chiefs—and there were many in his time—who devoted themselves to the welfare of their subjects. He looked coldly on those—and they were few—who neglected their duty as Rulers, and spent the revenues of their States on the pleasures of European capitals. He passed an Order and published it that no Chief should be allowed to leave India without his permission; and he let it be known that he disliked absentee landlords as a class and held in contempt the selfish Chief who did nothing for his own people. He called the Chiefs his colleagues in Empire, and he did not so call them in vain: and though hostile critics have challenged his embargo on foreign travel and extravagance, the majority of the Chiefs silently approved, and the Indian Press, ever ready though it was to resent any attack on privilege, acquiesced in Lord Curzon's policy. He breathed new life into these old and slow-moving kingdoms, and the Indian Princes, who in the last fifteen years have played leading and most distinguished parts in the drama of Empire, owe much to Lord Curzon's inspiration; something, perhaps, also to the efforts he made to improve the various Colleges for Chiefs. He did all

[1] Cf. "*La France de l'Empire,*" by Louis Madeley. Like Napoleon, "*Il nous avait donné l'impression sensible de sa présence réelle dans chacun de ses bureaux.*"

within his power by interview and by letter to give the Chiefs new interests, and threw himself into the scheme for giving the younger Princes and Nobles a real chance of a military career. The Imperial Cadet Corps, which started under the fairest auspices, was the first attempt to solve a problem which had baffled Viceroys since the days of Lord Lytton, and though Lord Curzon's successors stepfathered the generous idea, the door through which Indians might pass into the higher appointments of the Army was first opened by him and can never now be closed. But though the Imperial Cadet Corps languished after Lord Curzon left India, he had the supreme satisfaction of seeing at the great celebration of King Edward's coronation the cavalcade of his dreams, four ruling Princes in the leading files, and Sir Pertáb Singh, Maharája of Idar, at its head, an escort perfect in parade, equipment and personnel.

While ever ready and eager to deal with the dullest and most prosaic of problems, this very practical and painstaking Viceroy loved pageant and ceremonial, and was never happier than when working out the details and programme of some great solemnity. There was a general agreement that the Coronation Durbár at Delhi had never been surpassed, and the whole scheme emanated from the brain of him who was first and last a devoted student of history, impelled in all his actions by the historical sense. Living in the past, he could evoke the past; and to any problems he could bring his rich store of knowledge of bygone days. He could readily apply the lessons of the past to the problems of the present; but he was content with this and never attempted to anticipate or to forecast the distant future. Once a great Indian publicist, who used to pay me surreptitious visits in Calcutta (his influence with his people would be gone if it were known that he had been inside Government House), was talking to me about the great question of Home Rule for India. He had a genuine admiration for Lord Curzon, for his justice, strength and energy; but he dreaded his craving for efficiency; for, said this most interesting and patriotic Hindu: "Every step in efficiency is another rivet in the shackles in which we are bound. We do not ask for Home Rule now, nor in ten years, nor in twenty: but all we ask is that he will not shut the door of hope on us. Ask him to say that perhaps in fifty years India may be self-governing." I was so moved by the sincerity and eloquence of his words that I went into the next room, where Lord Curzon passed his days and long hours of his nights, and told him of my friend's plea. He listened with attention, for he had a high opinion of my visitor, who owned and edited the best Indian paper of that time. After long thought, the Viceroy said: "No, I will say nothing, for it might embarrass my successor if I raised any hopes or expressed any opinion as to when self-government will come." I urged that it must come some day, and that it seemed cruel to close the door of hope. But Lord Curzon replied: "It will not come in my time, and I cannot say what may happen in the future." So I returned to my friend and told him that the oracle was dumb.

He never seemed to dwell on the future (though he cared greatly what posterity would think of him), yet, even when satisfied with the immediate results of his labours, in small matters as well as in great, he tried to make his schemes safe and complete, and never omitted a single detail in the elaboration of his plans. One of his earliest measures was the removal of the North-West Frontier administration from the Punjáb Government. There were many good reasons for this change, but as I had been in the Punjáb I knew that the loss of this interesting charge would be bitterly resented by those who had so long watched and warded the passes into Afghanistán, and I was anxious that the wind should be tempered. But Lord Curzon would not bate one jot, and he marshalled every argument he could bring. I pointed out that he had proved his case and that some of the arguments were superfluous and might cause unnecessary pain to the Punjáb Government. But he replied that a statesman should never omit an argument. When the command of the Punjáb Frontier Force was removed from the Punjáb Government and made over to the Commander-in-Chief, there had been no friction and no heart-burning; but unhappily Lord Curzon's up-to-the-hilt method left raw edges. He was always painfully thorough, and once convinced that a measure was beneficial and right would ignore all susceptibilities, and never wore a velvet glove upon his iron hand. He always scorned the balancing mind when he had decided on a policy. Day by day he would collect in large envelopes, trays and baskets, any material which proved his case, and this material was never wasted. He spared no pains to get at the facts, and when not busy with the problems of the moment would, as a pastime, review the events and the verdicts of the history of the past. Directly we arrived in Calcutta, he set to work with pious zeal to establish the actual site of the Black Hole, where, on the night of 20th June, 1756, one hundred and twenty-two Englishmen and one English woman were stifled to death. After two years of toil, he identified the exact site of the tragedy, and paved it at his own expense with polished black marble. The following year at his own charges he erected a replica of the monument which Governor Holwell, a survivor of the Black Hole tragedy, had set up. This monument had been demolished in 1821. Much to his surprise and annoyance a school of Indian writers arose and insisted that the Black Hole tragedy was a myth, and that Holwell had never erected a monument. Busy Calcutta was not greatly interested in the controversy, and I rather hoped that no notice would be taken of the preposterous suggestion of the iconoclast school. But Lord Curzon, burning with historical zeal, proceeded to prove the Black Hole and the Holwell monument, and produced twenty-five authorities to convince the world of what the world was already convinced. For, remembering that the verdicts of history had been sometimes reviewed, he foresaw that unless the Indian writers were at once challenged and refuted, some historian in future generations might return to the charge. He was no doubt right from the historical point of view, but this excursion involved much time and trouble. It was characteristic of his methods. Two authorities would have been sufficient, but he cited twenty-five. The incident is also characteristic of the generous manner in which he spent his money on historical monuments. But he gave more than money: he gave his whole heart and soul to the preservation of the glorious buildings of the past for the benefit of posterity. And, as I recall his untiring activities, in spite of sun and heat, of the long climbs among the ruins, and the long hours spent in recording what could be preserved, I feel now, though I did not feel it then, that his labours were not in vain, and that posterity will be grateful to this wise and altruistic conservative. I shall never forget one scene. In one of the most beautiful of Moslem buildings we found a squalid Post Office, half brick, half adobe, and the Viceroy in his indignation ordered the whole staff to quit on the spot. This might have inconvenienced the postal deliveries for the day, but it evoked the conscience of the authorities and had its effect all over India. This direct action on the part of a Viceroy, a Rája, or an elephant, always appealed to Eastern sentiment. The Indians worship power, and like to watch its display.

He was always obsessed by the idea that he would not have time to do all he wanted, and though he rarely ever spoke of the pain which so cruelly beset him, he more than once told me of the hill-top in Simla where he desired to be buried. He also talked to me sometimes about religion. Few guessed that this forceful man was a true son of the Church, and a humble and sincere believer in the Bible. He was imbued with the spirit of the Old Testament: he felt that he had a mission; and he enjoyed the discomfiture of the Amaleks who fought with him.

The ever-present desire to accomplish made him an exacting Chief, and caused his critics to repeat that he was the young man in a hurry who had found everything wrong in India waiting for him to put it right. Sometimes, when I was sent on some special mission, I thought with relief as I left Simla or Calcutta of the respite from the incessant strain of my work. Yet so magnetic was his influence, that after a few days I always longed to be back with him, and as I drew near his residence I would look with apprehension to see whether the flag was mast-high. For I always dreaded that the high pressure of work would kill him. Once the doctors insisted on his giving up work for three weeks. His illness was kept secret, and I carried on the routine work. But day by day he would ask me for details as to what had passed, and at the end of the first week he said that unless work were brought to him he would die. But I told him that I must carry out the order of the doctors. However, he prevailed, and at the end of the second week the Secretaries brought their cases to his bedside. One of them had questioned me as to when the Viceroy would be able to resume work, and he added: "It is a tonic to me to do work direct with him." He had the same effect on me, and though I was keenly interested in India and in the problems which came every day, I could not have lasted the five years if it had not been for this superman's example.

He loved, or thought he loved, a respite from his toil, and was as joyous as a boy when he was shooting, or watching the races, or admiring some great festival. He delighted in entertaining, but I, who knew his face so well, always had the uneasy conviction that at dinner or balls he was yearning to be back at his work. Once, but never again, during a large dinner party, a servant, unseen by me, brought in some proofs, and at table he deliberately proceeded to correct the proofs. This reminded me painfully of Archimedes at the fall of Syracuse.

His speeches have been published, and I cannot imagine any literature which gives a better idea of a Viceroy's problems. The style is clear, but the readers of the speeches miss the splendid charm of the delivery. He was an orator of the first class. As a rule the speeches were written, and he would discuss them with me before delivery. They were written very rapidly and rarely revised. When speaking he used no notes, and when once he had written a speech he could remember it word by word. To my mind—and I can remember all these speeches—the finest in matter and delivery was on an unimportant occasion on the 12th February, 1903, when the Chambers of Commerce of India met in Calcutta. I remember Lord Kitchener's hearty admiration, and I also remember walking back with Lord Curzon from the Town Hall to Government House. I advised him never again to speak in Calcutta, and to let them long for more, as he could never surpass that speech. It would have been well for him if he had followed this advice, for a speech he made nearly a year later alienated Bengal and offended the Hindus throughout India. At the dismal, drowsy Budget debate, held in the Throne Room in the sultry heat of Calcutta just before the officials of the Government of India fled to the cool heights of Simla, Lord Curzon once read his speech: on that occasion he spoke of the "manuscript eloquence" of the members of the Council, who always read their speeches, quite forgetting that on this single occasion his eloquence was of the same nature. It did not strike him as incongruous, for he was apart, his "withers were unwrung." His ways were not their ways.

If only he could have suffered fools gladly, if only he had been a regarder of persons, it might have been more comfortable; but perhaps the work would have taken longer. Stories clustered around him, but most of them were the clever inventions of the practised wits of Simla. He was a conspicuous target and seemed to invite arrows. But they were rarely envenomed, and when the time came for his departure, generous India remembered, and remembers still, his greatness and his devotion to duty and forgot the little foibles to which all men are prone.

I do not propose to follow him through the acts of the five years of my stay with him; for these will be told in his Biography. But I must allude to two events which seem to me of special interest. One was the death of Queen Victoria, and the other the coming of Lord Kitchener.

CHAPTER XIII

"To be great is to be misunderstood."—EMERSON

Indians' Interest in Queen Victoria—Their Veneration and Love—Tradition of the Great Queen and Mother—Shock Caused by Death—Mourning in Calcutta—Lord Curzon's Devotion—Proud of being Her Last Viceroy—Determines to Commemorate Her Great Reign—His Constant Effort to Carry out Her Wish to be "Kind to the Indians"—His Personal Attention to Petitions—Endeavour to Remove Grievance, however Small—Interference with Man on the Spot—Decides to Build a Great Memorial to Queen Victoria in Calcutta—Incessant Toil till His Death for its Success—India His Home and the Pivot of His Life—Lord Kitchener—Lord Curzon's Delight to have Him as Commander-in-Chief—Lord Kitchener's Interest in Transport and Supply—Comes out Determined to Control these Departments—Bides his Time for a Year—Threatened Resignation—Lamentable Breach between Viceroy and Commander-in-Chief—Similarities and Contrasts of the Two Characters—Criticisms of Lord Curzon in England.

WHEN I first went East in 1879, I was taught my work by wise old Indians. I thought them old, for an Indian of forty seems old to an Englishman of twenty-two. They decanted into my thirsty mind their ripe and crusty experience, and were always the most courteous and patient of teachers. They told me of the simple facts which make up the life of the people; told me quaint stories and taught me pithy proverbs.

Sometimes my Indian teachers would shyly ask me about my own country, and they often begged me to tell them about the great Queen Empress of India. They approached the subject with veneration and awe, and I learned how they worshipped in their homes her effigy on the silver rupees. In the simple huts of the villagers I would often see some poor and tawdry representation of the Queen. It was the only ornament of the home; but it was very sacred, and more benign than the red-smeared idols in the Temple. As time went on, this interest in the personality of the Queen Empress seemed to grow, and later, in Kashmir, I remembered how the whole countryside was moved when a Pandit in the service of the State said in a speech that the Queen Empress was human like himself. He was forthwith stripped of office and banished. He pleaded that it was a slip, just a jocular remark, but public opinion did not tolerate jocularity when the Queen Empress was concerned. To India she was divine and sacrosanct. Her hold on the imagination of the people was wonderful and secure. It was not the result of clever statecraft or political design, but was spontaneous and natural. As sovereign of India, Queen Victoria was venerated by reason of her high office. But transcending this official attachment was the simple love of the many millions for the Royal Widow who had reigned over them so long, a great Queen, descended from Kings more ancient than the sun and moon-sprung Princes of Rajputána. There was a dim consciousness of some famous Proclamation, but a very clear and constant certainty that she was their steadfast and never-forgetting friend and mother. She had learned their language at an age when most cease to learn and begin to forget: and though she could not come herself to India, the word passed and repassed round the whispering-gallery of the East that the great Queen's one preoccupation was the happiness of her Indian subjects. It became a legend in the land of Ind that every Viceroy was enjoined by her to be kind to the Indians; and when hard seasons came they looked to her, just as in the nearer East they used to look to the hills. She was indeed to them a very present help in trouble. And as the long Victorian days ran on, bringing quiet prosperity and peaceful content, the tradition of the great Queen and the kind mother grew. What one thinks of most one loves best, and the English Queen was ever in the thoughts of the peoples of India. They had come to look on her as immortal, and thus her death came as a shock to all. The sad news of her passing reached my office before dawn, and all India knew by noon that a great something had gone out of their lives. Rightly in sentiment, though wrongly by rule, the cannon boomed out, not the solemn tale of her eighty-one years, but a fuller salute of 101 guns. This was befitting, for she had indeed given of her best to India, and to the end her letters came to the

Viceroy, always on the same note: "Be kind to my Indian people." Her last letter, dated 14th December, 1900, is now in the Victoria Memorial, Calcutta. On the day when the news came the Lieutenant-Governor of Bengal was an early caller. He said to me: "This is the worst thing that has happened to India in my time," and many of those who flocked to Government House uttered the same thought. The British deplored the loss of a sanction and an inspiration: the Indians mourned as for a mother. On that day of shock and gloom over 800 telegrams of sorrow were received, and my office, always working at high pressure, toiled on long after midnight, dispatching suitable answers to messages, some touching and almost passionate, some simple and quaint, but all very genuine in their grief. In this mournful and melancholy collection it was almost a relief—a relief like the clowning in one of Shakespeare's tragedies—to come across a telegram from some little far-off town:

"In the words of the poet we shall never look like her again."

In Calcutta my house was across the road which ran along the gardens of Government House, and from its spacious veranda I had glimpses of town life, and saw more than they saw in the stately Palace, 200 yards away, which Lord Wellesley had built a century before. Truly in that fine building the wish was fulfilled that "India might be ruled from a Palace and not from a counting-house; with the ideas of a Prince and not with those of a retail dealer in muslins and indigo."

From my veranda in the early morning of 2nd February, 1901, I saw a sight which set me thinking. I saw the greater part of Calcutta's dense population file silently past on their way to the great park (*Maidan*) to sit there all day, without food, mourning for the great Queen Empress who had made them her children. Little marks of spontaneous sorrow on their poor dress; quaint banners: "We poor Mussalmans from Sialdah grieving"; all most simple and improvised, convinced me that the second greatest city in our Empire was sad at heart. Their sadness was contagious, but there was comfort in the thought that this silent stream of mourners was the finest spectacle of co-operation and colour kinship which I have ever seen. On that day of perfect sympathy it would have called for a real prophet to look forward but a few years and to predict an age of non-co-operation.

Lord Curzon was the last of the Victorian Viceroys. He was quick to realise the loss and his busy brain was at work to heal the smart and to carry on the great tradition in a manner which would appeal to the heart and soul of India. I have noted that he was no respecter of persons, but he had a tremendous and innate respect and reverence for Queen Victoria and for the Royal House. He remembered every word she had said to him when he became Viceroy, and he read and re-read her letters. It was her wish that the ceremonial of Government House should be observed to the utmost. The critic saw in the increased splendour of his entertainments a personal love of display—that "pomposity" they so freely attributed to him. For the sake of tradition and continuity he toiled to make the Coronation ceremonies of King Edward a noble and impressive manifestation of India's conception of the Empire. The critics in England saw in this glorious celebration not Coronation but "Curzonation." But he felt sure of the Royal mandate and always regarded himself as the Viceroy of the Empress rather than as the Agent of the India Office. So in the year 1901, a year full of pressing work, he worked harder than ever to commemorate the good Queen Empress and to mark in splendid dignity the accession of the new King Emperor.

I would mention here an innovation of Lord Curzon's administration, which was due to his desire to carry out the wishes of the late Queen Empress. In India, anyone, however humble and remote, can approach the Viceroy by the method of a written memorial. These memorials come in shoals, and the ordinary way of dealing with them was to send the memorial to the State Department which dealt with the particular grievance. But Lord Curzon was not satisfied with this method and insisted that I should read the memorials, and if I found any grievance which called for special redress I should bring it to his notice. This involved considerable labour, sometimes useless; but perhaps it was not entirely in vain. Secrets leak out even in the Government of India, and it soon became known that the Viceroy looked into the memorials himself. From my point of view it was not in vain, for I learned from long discussions with the Viceroy his intense love of justice, his bitter and almost savage hatred of oppression, and his simple and generous sympathy for the man who had gone wrong after long years of apparent rightness. I felt impatient at times when I thought that there was no reason for revision and deprecated a further reference to the Local Government; but his attitude always was: "The Queen has asked me to be kind to the Indians. How can I be kind if I do not look into their grievances?" This desire to get into personal touch with the people was disliked by the officials. It implied a kind of distrust: it seemed to them an act of needless interference and an invitation to groundless complaints. In the series of collisions between Indians and British soldiers, the Viceroy's desire to ascertain the facts was often inconvenient and embarrassing. I pointed out to him that these regrettable "collisions" were no new incidents, and that I remembered them ever since I had been in India. The two races will collide, and as they are often ignorant of each other's language and each other's customs, misunderstandings will arise; but it was a mistake to make too much of what was often an innocent and innocuous affair. So at last he decided that, as in this one point we were not in perfect harmony, he would deal with all papers referring to collisions without my intervention. He asked me my last word on the subject, and I replied by quoting:

> "The time is out of joint, oh, cursed spite,
> That ever I was born to set it right!"

It is very difficult to be a Viceroy, and youth, energy and burning zeal do not make the office easier. Lord Curzon's simple argument, often repeated in our daily conversation, was: "What is the use of my wearing myself out to prove to India that I mean to hold the balance fair between the two races if all my work is to be rendered futile by these collisions?" I would try to cheer him up by suggesting that his splendid and constructive work for India was in no way impaired by a thoughtless scuffle between a bewildered soldier and a benighted peasant. But he declined to be comforted, and I think that in this one line he regarded me as a hopeless bureaucrat. He knew, and often gave generous utterance to the fact, that the British officials were vigilant, just and sympathetic, but he had an idea that he held a special mandate from home, and that it was his duty to make sure that none of the 315 millions of people had a solid grievance. He would have tilted against any windmill, and cared nothing for the critics, who taxed him with trying to do work which could be better done by the men on the spot. He was a past-master of the great problems of the East and a most careful expert in Indian administration; but when he came into contact with individuals and with Indian idiosyncrasies he was naïve, even careless. Sometimes when discussing the case of some hoary offender, who had been caught red-handed providing for his old age by peculation, Lord Curzon would urge that no man would endanger his official position for a bribe of twopence. I had to explain to him that the experienced bribe-taker in the East treats all alike, and that twopence multiplied by 30,000 and paid annually was a considerable addition to the offender's salary. At times he seemed so simple and so ignorant of mankind that I thought of him as an Oxford Don who had slipped out of his College rooms and gone for a frolic in the East. But though he never got into the skin of the Indians, he had a surpassing knowledge of Indian affairs, and nothing escaped his vigilance. All classes in India respected and realised this vigilance, and though the garrison of India was seriously depleted by the dispatch of troops to the Boer War, and to China for the Boxer rising; though India was visited by famine and plague and their attendant miseries and hardships, the country remained quiet and steady. There was no breath of sedition, no clash between Hindus and Moslems, and no assassination of officials—a great record for any Viceroyalty, and proof, perhaps, that Lord Curzon's patient endeavour to hold the balance fair was not in vain.

Before we had set out for India, Lord Curzon had discussed with me the idea of a Valhalla for London, where the men and the achievements of Empire might be commemorated, Westminster Abbey being full and overcrowded, and St. Paul's filling up. I find an entry in my diary, 25th

January, 1901, where this idea is again discussed, and the idea takes the shape of the Queen Victoria Memorial Hall in Calcutta, where the history of our Indian Empire could be seen in statuary and on canvas. He set to work at once; and endless interviews and correspondence followed. By 2nd February the scheme was ready. At the outset it looked somewhat unpromising. The Provinces clamoured for Provincial Memorials: the various sects claimed that they had a special interest in the late Queen Empress and were entitled to commemorate her in their own way: Medicine urged that fine hospitals were the one and befitting memorial for her splendid benevolence: Education insisted that any money which might be subscribed should be earmarked for colleges: Agriculture put in a plea for experimental farms: and, if I remember aright, the Veterinary Department applied for consideration. To all these claims Lord Curzon was deaf. He scorned the utilitarian idea, and at a great meeting in Calcutta he silenced the utilitarians by quoting the late Queen Victoria, who had once expressed the opinion that a memorial should be personal. All February and March of 1901 he strove by speech and letter to persuade and convince India that an all-Indian memorial was the best form of expression for the love and gratitude felt for the late Queen Empress, while the prompt and generous responses given by the Ruling Chiefs made it obvious that Calcutta, the seat of the Government with which they were associated, was the proper place for the Memorial. So generous were the gifts of the Princes of India that a limit had to be placed on their munificence. One had offered £100,000: another £50,000, and many £30,000; but the limit was fixed at £16,000, and this large subscription was only accepted from a few. All classes were invited to subscribe, and the Viceroy scanned with eager interest the lists of the subscribers. He started a journal of the Queen Victoria Memorial Fund, and wrote most of the articles of the early numbers. Before he left India the subscriptions amounted to £400,000. But he was not content with money subscriptions, and gave much of his time and energy to obtaining objects of historical value from East and West. Everyone was brought under contribution. He has told the story of the Queen Victoria Memorial in his work, "British Government in India," told us of the obstacles and opposition. But to-day the beautiful Memorial Hall stands serene in Calcutta, and, like the Táj at Agra, has its message and its moral. It is the seal and the consecration of the devotion of many millions to a great and altruistic sovereign, who by constant and homely kindliness had won the heart and captured the imagination of India.

Up to the end of his life, Lord Curzon toiled for the success of the Memorial Hall. Though he had never seen it, he knew where each object of his fine collection was placed. And at all times I would notice on his work table in London or at Hackwood, a bulky file of papers with the letters "Q.V.M." It was no mere hobby; no special keenness for a congenial object; it was a part of his life. He clung to it in spite of discouragement and of the cold fits that so often follow great enthusiasms; and he won, for he was inspired from the beginning to the end by his devotion to the Queen Empress and by his pride and faith in the work and achievements of Her representatives in India. He never tired of reminiscences of his predecessors, and I used to think that in the spacious halls and corridors of Government House, Calcutta, he communed with the ghosts of Warren Hastings and Dalhousie. India was his home, and the East had called him early. He always maintained that India was the pivot of the British Empire. It was certainly the pivot of his life, and when he should have laid down office at the end of the term which custom has so wisely prescribed for Viceroys, he lingered on, saying to me: "I have not finished my work." He could not have finished his work in ten, nor in twenty years; but it was a tragic pity that he stayed on beyond the appointed term. Whether his career in England would have been different if he had left India on the completion of the five years, it is difficult to say. But the unfortunate, and, as I think, the unnecessary quarrel with Lord Kitchener would have been avoided, and the people of India would have been spared the shock of learning that the Viceregal office was not so sacrosanct and infallible as they had always imagined. I have often thought that the spectacle of the contest between the *Mulki Lat*

Sahib and the *Jungi Lat Sahib* weakened for ever the once great influence of the Viceroy of India.

Some time after Lord Curzon became Viceroy, Lord Kitchener had expressed a wish to join his Council as Military Member; but at the time the idea was not welcomed. Later, when it was suggested that Lord Kitchener might become Commander-in-Chief, Lord Curzon supported the appointment with delight and enthusiasm. Indeed, he regarded the appointment of so great a soldier as a deserved compliment to India, and talked to me with high anticipation of the relief it would be to feel that he could leave the Army to so competent a Commander. In the summer of 1902, I came to England for the coronation of King Edward, and met Lord Kitchener. He talked much about India, and told me that he was not interested in matters which concerned the Adjutant-General, but cared only for questions of transport and supply. I said that he ought to have taken the office of the Military Member of the Council, and that he would find, when he reached India, that the Military Member "devilled" for the Commander-in-Chief, that the system had worked well when Lord Roberts was Commander-in-Chief and Sir George Chesney was Military Member, and that it still worked well. But he said that his information was that the Military Member was now the stronger, and that he usurped some of the functions of the Commander-in-Chief. There was some truth in this, but it was due to the accident that the Commander-in-Chief had been ill and died, and his successor was only a locum tenens. I thought that the balance of authority would soon be restored when Lord Kitchener took up the office of Commander-in-Chief. All went well when Lord Kitchener arrived in India, and the most cordial relations existed between him and the Viceroy. In the early part of 1903, Lord Kitchener asked me to breakfast in the Fort of Calcutta, and handed me a lengthy note proposing the abolition of the Military Department. He would not let me take it to read at leisure, and said all he wanted to know was whether Lord Curzon would accept his proposal. I said that as Lord Kitchener had not yet seen the Frontier, and had not really seen anything of the

Army, or of the work of the Military Department, the obvious criticism would be that the proposal was founded on ideas formed before he had reached India, on which he put his note in his pocket and said he would wait for a year. He did wait, but when the Government reached Simla, I noticed in the electrical atmosphere of the Hills signs of a coming storm, and I find in my diary that I was urging Lord Curzon to retire at the end of the five years: that he should not tempt Providence by overstaying his time, and that a collision with Lord Kitchener was inevitable if he stayed on. The situation recalled the story of the two Kings of Brentford, and reminded me of two tigers in the same jungle. He laughed at my fears, and was confident that he could manage Lord Kitchener. But the latter, in the summer of 1903, chafing at being over-ruled by the Viceroy and the Council, twice threatened resignation. I always thought that Lord Kitchener came out to India with a mandate for the abolition of the Military Member and his Department, and that he was confident that he would never be allowed to resign. He was quite ready to hold his hand for a year, but when he knew that Lord Curzon was extending his term of office, he quickened the pace.

I left India in October, 1903. The subsequent breach and the recriminations were an unhappy ending to a splendid and most useful Viceroyalty. Lord Curzon sent me long letters, and as I was then writing weekly articles for *The Times* on Indian affairs, I kept in touch with passing events in India. I am convinced that the question of Indian Army administration could have been settled by compromise, and if these two really great but intensely simple and naïve men had been left alone to settle the question, there would have been harmony and, most certainly, efficiency, for both lived and strove for efficiency. It was an old-fashioned Army for an old-fashioned continent—an Army for police and defence, and in no way a force for foreign adventure. Whether a long line of Kitcheners could have changed the Indian Army into an Imperial force is an open question, and it is not fair to test Lord Kitchener's reforms by the experiences of the Great War. The test will come in India itself; and then perhaps it will be found that the old-fashioned, homely constitution of Military Member of Council and Commander-in-Chief had its peculiar merits in a land of peculiar and almost provincial requirements.

Later, I was again associated with Lord Kitchener, for in 1914, soon after the outbreak of war, he appointed me to be his Commissioner to look after the Indian wounded in France and England. I heard the news of his death at Lord Curzon's house. I often wished that I could have reconciled these two men; for both would say kind things of one another, and I believe the reconciliation would have taken place if death had not come. However, death reconciles all.

There was a likeness between these two remarkable men. They both lived for work, and cared nothing for the susceptibilities of others. Neither could tolerate inefficiency nor be lenient to failure. Lord Curzon was the greater student and could work longer than Lord Kitchener. Both were equally impatient of criticism or opposition. Both loved pageantry, loved beautiful surroundings, and took an almost feminine interest in the details of domestic arrangements. Both were determined and acquisitive collectors, and both had an extreme reverence for rank. Lord Curzon loved debate and revelled in logical and masterly minutes. Lord Kitchener distrusted and despised all such official exercises. The conflict between them was like a fight between an elephant and a whale. Both were great lovers of their country and devoted to duty. Many probably regarded them as hard, strong men; yet I saw Lord Kitchener in tears as he watched some old veterans of the Mutiny totter by at the Delhi Durbár; and I knew of a case where he had punished an offender harshly, and soon after had found him congenial work on better pay. From the old Balliol days to the time of his death, I knew how gentle and affectionate Lord Curzon could be when he was off duty. The world saw him in caricature, and unfortunately he was apt to play up to the caricature.

Officially I left Lord Curzon in 1903, when he came down in pain to preside at the farewell dinner which he gave to my wife and me the night before we left Simla for ever. Knowing his habit of jocular allusions when he said good-bye to those who had worked with him, I expressed the hope that he would not jest. "Jest!" he said, "I am far nearer to tears." And so was I, for, after five years of closest communion, it was a wrench to leave. After dinner, he crept back to his bedroom, and there, long after midnight, and after singing "Auld Lang Syne," with Lady Curzon on one side and Lord Kitchener on the other—false auspices, so it turned out, of peace and good will—I went up to wish him a final farewell, and found him hard at work, writing a long note on education. He was the same when he was on his death-bed. He wrote on till the end.

Since 1903, I have heard much criticism of my old Chief; many satirical anecdotes, mostly without foundation, and sometimes definite suggestions that he was lacking in certain qualities which the English esteem. I have often succeeded in convincing the critics that they were wrong, for they did not know the exact circumstances. But men whom I admire and respect have told me that he was ungrateful. He was grateful enough for a kind word or for any little act of sympathy. But he was not grateful in the sense of giving rewards for official efforts; for he held that the work itself was its own reward. He always appreciated good work, but he regarded it as part of a man's duty, and it was a surprise to him when men failed to do their duty, or did careless and inefficient work. He had fought against his own physical disability, and by sheer grit and grim purpose had trained himself to be fit for any work and ready for any strain. And it was this knowledge of what he had himself surmounted that made him contemptuous of weaklings and slackers. He was not consciously ungrateful, but he lived so much in his work that he had no time to think of or care for the little springs of life, the hopes, the anxieties which for ever beset the English in the East. His roots were well down in solid old soil, and he never remembered that all of us in India were deracinated, without roots in India or in England.

One other tendency made him a man apart. History was in his bones. He was always thinking of the verdicts of history. He knew that he was making history, and perhaps his eager and constant thought of the judgment of posterity made him impatient, and perhaps inconsiderate, of the opinions of his contemporaries. He had a quaint desire to create a public opinion in India, and alternately he was belaboured by the Indians and by the British in India, as he pursued his noble aim to hold the balance equal. And at the end of it all, his splendid industry, his success and his final defeat, none could deny that in very truth he had "loved righteousness and hated iniquity."

If I have failed to give some idea of the real man, it is from lack of skill rather than lack of knowledge, for five years' close and constant intercourse enables anyone to form a shrewd opinion of character. I saw him in all moods and in a great variety of circumstances, and after he had left India I was with him whenever there was a crisis in his life. I can only repeat what I said of him in public in 1903, at a farewell dinner at Viceregal Lodge, Simla:

"A great humourist has said that no man is a hero to his banker, his lawyer, or his valet. And he might have added —ten thousand times less is he a hero to his Private Secretary, unless in very truth he be a hero. Well, I have found my Chief now, as I found him years ago, to be a man to whom the test could safely be applied. Scarcely a day has passed —and I say this not as a pleasant exaggeration at a pleasant dinner party—not as a courtier, but I say it as a deliberate diarist of long standing, and I say it after verification— scarcely a day has passed without some striking act on his part of generosity, high-mindedness, of active and practical sympathy for those who were in trouble, or overwrought with work, of righteous indignation for anything that was mean, cruel or oppressive—hardly a day has gone by without some signal proof of his indomitable energy, his cheery pluck, and his remarkable prevision. These are some among other great qualities which have commanded my admiration, but what has most endeared him to me, and has won my affection and my absolute devotion, has been his invariable consideration. My work has been a daily pleasure, a daily tonic."

This speech was made before an audience, many of whom had been my friends for twenty-one years. In such an audience it is well to be accurate and sincere. I wrote an appreciation which appeared in *The Times* on the day of his funeral, and death makes us think and ponder our words.

When, in the year of his death, he asked me to write his biography, I said I would consider it on two conditions. One was that in the preface I might say that I had never asked for nor received a favour at his hands. He assented to this condition, and said it was a true statement of fact. I mention this, as I wish my readers to know that all I have set down has been based on the observations of an independent writer, no partisan, no led-captain. He interested me. I admired him, and yet was often very sorry for him, for he never knew the meaning of rest and contentment. He was a great artist, who never found perfection. He often reminded me of Dr. Johnson in his accuracy, rapidity of composition, and in his love of explaining and expounding. He had many of the qualities which are associated with John Bull, and on occasions would *toss* a rival in conversation. He was at the same time very sensitive, very desirous of appreciation, and would have liked to be popular. He frequently embarrassed me by asking what people said of him, thought of him, and was not altogether satisfied when I invariably replied that he was looked on as a great public servant. If he was no more than that to the general public, it was partly his own fault, for he never took off the mask in public, and he was nearly always in public. In conclusion I would quote from a charming work, "Life in the Indian Civil Service," recently published. Sir Evan Maconochie writing of his thirty-two years' service says that Lord Curzon was "the greatest Indian Viceroy of our times—possibly of all times—fearless, creative, ardent, human . . . his were great days, and to us who knew and served under him they are a treasured memory." Sir Evan has said in these few words what I have sought to say in many pages.

CHAPTER XIV

"Kings are like stars, they rise and set, they have
The worship of the world, but no repose."—SHELLEY

Leave India Again—Write for *The Times*—Old Policy of Keeping England in Ignorance of India—Importance of Correcting Misstatements, not only in England, but in the United States—Rudyard Kipling Quoted—Asked to Accompany the Prince and Princess of Wales to India as Chief of Staff—Busy for Next Nine Months Preparing Details of Tour—Prince and Princess Fulfil every Engagement—Great Enthusiasm in India—Contrast between Respect shown to Viceroys and Affection for King Emperor's Son—Possible that this Influence in some Permanent Form might Solve Many Difficulties—Notice Great Changes since I left Lord Curzon—Activities of Anti-British School—Movement no longer Confined to Great Cities—Risks of Tour—Story of the Two Detectives—Position of Indian Women.

THIS was my second time of leaving India, as I thought for ever, and the sadness and regret were enhanced by the knowledge that I was going home without plans or any certain hope of occupation. But the kindness with which my friends sped me on my journey kept me free from present care, and the drawbacks of being a rolling stone only intruded themselves when I reached London and reality. It was necessary to work, as I had twice forfeited my right to pension, and it was a little difficult to determine what I had to offer. My varied experience in India was of little use in London. I had no technical knowledge, and at the age of 46 it was too late to enter a profession. I began to think that it would have been wiser to have remained in a safe groove, and realised that to live in the Indian Civil Service was easier than to make a living in London. But work came, and the first offer was from *The Times*. That generous national institution wanted someone to write weekly articles on Indian affairs, and the idea thrilled me. I was prouder of this new employment than I was of any of my previous occupations, saving only my work in Kashmir. It was all so novel and so fascinating to see one's own thoughts printed in the then fine thick solid pages of *The Times*. It was in the days of Buckle, Moberly Bell and Valentine Chirol, and all three were charmingly courteous, encouraging and patient. I lay stress on the honour of writing for a paper the material of which we shall never see again, and I remember Moberly Bell showing me a letter from a butcher in Norfolk who, on hearing that *The Times* contemplated a publication rather smaller in size, wrote to warn Printing House Square that he would cease to be a subscriber, as *The Times* was the only paper in which he could wrap his joints! Sometimes, to my joy, I would be called on to write a leading article, and I remember that though I tried by hints and questions to ascertain the subject of the leader, they would never tell me till 11 p.m., when I found myself in a room without any books of reference. And then I wrote the leader. And as I walked home along the Embankment idea after idea would come into my mind, and I bitterly regretted that I had not been told in advance. But *The Times* knew its business, and the articles would have been heavier than they actually were, if I had stuffed into them all the ideas which came to me in the early hours on the chill Embankment. I have always read the leading articles in *The Times*, and it seems to me that the recipe for a useful leader is two ideas thrice repeated with variations. I was very proud of this work on *The Times*, and looked on the very high remuneration which they gave me as the highest form of reward. It was the spoil of my own spear.

When it was known that *The Times* was going to publish articles on Indian affairs, a great man at the India Office asked me to have a talk and inquired the object of the articles. I replied that they would attempt to describe India to people in England, who knew nothing of India. "And do you think that this is wise?" asked this clever and experienced man. "In my opinion the less England knows of India the better." I suggested that we had nothing to conceal of our acts in India; that, on the contrary, we had much of which we might be proud and that British administration in India was the finest achievement of our race. I therefore held that the more England and the world knew about British India the better. Later, in 1918, when I came back from France after the Armistice, the then Secretary of State for India invited me to undertake the task of explaining Indian conditions to English people, and offered me large facilities. But I declined, and told him it was too late, and quoted the opinion of the experienced man who held, as did his department, that "the less England knew of India the better."

It is not easy to give to English readers real pictures of India. But it would be possible sometimes to prevent them from forming unsound and dangerous opinions as to British Administration in the East. This misunderstanding of the problems of India is serious enough in England: but the grosser misstatements can be corrected in this country. But in America, the misunderstanding is extremely serious, and twice after visits to the United States of America I have urged on the authorities that they should have agents to refute the wild and unchallenged charges of England's high-handed tyranny in the East. Theodore Roosevelt, who understood our aims and objects in India, and admired our administration, often talked to me of the danger caused in America by daily misrepresentations of England's action in India. But we shall go on in our ostrich fashion and comfort ourselves with the lulling words "*Qui s'excuse, s'accuse.*"

I liked the work on *The Times*. It was easy to find a subject each week, and I might have gone on for ever in my harmless efforts, since the kind folk of Printing House Square never criticised and always accepted my articles. Fate, however, was to take me again to India, and though on my return *The Times* asked me to resume the articles, I reluctantly declined. I feel sorry now, that I did not give better measure to my generous employers, but it came too easily and involved too little effort. So easy to turn the tap of yeasty memory. Valentine Chirol told me that my articles would never flagrantly impede the Thames. Still, one misguided enthusiast offered to reprint the whole series at his own cost; and, better still, Sir Alfred Lyall, to me one of the most charming of writers on India, sent me words of praise and encouragement. But as I am writing my reminiscences in the hope that they may be useful to other men, I will make one observation on writing for the Press. That is, that the beginner like myself will never go far if there be no consciousness of labour or effort. Rudyard Kipling was once discussing his early life with me, and he extracted from a cupboard a mass of manuscript and handed me an article entitled "An essay on the Horse."[1] I read this without admiration or pleasure, and told him so. "Exactly," he replied, "it is a translation of a French essay, which my editor gave to me one hot stifling night in Lahore, and I sat there with fever and a French dictionary and produced this thing. If the editor had allowed me to do the fancy work, which I could do without effort, I should never have made good. This 'Essay on the Horse,' and many other such essays which were never printed, and were probably never meant to be printed, made a man of me. You cannot build without quarry work, and they kept me hard at it in the quarry."

I went on writing my tale of two-and-a-half columns until 11th December, 1904, when to my surprise I was bidden to Marlborough House, to be received by the Prince of Wales. He told me that he and the Princess were going to India at the end of 1905, and he asked whether I would undertake the duty of Chief of the Staff for the Indian Tour. A wiser man, thinking of the responsibility and the delicacy of such a post, might have hesitated, but the Prince's manner was so charming, and so kind, that I accepted the invitation with fervour, and proceeded to give a sketch of what happened when a Viceroy was on tour. I told him of the arrival at the Railway Station of an Indian State; the long rows of notables on the platform; the distinguishing dress of the Hindus and Moslems, the niceties of the head-dress; the drive to the Palace; the interests of the host and the chief features of the administration of the State. When I had finished my recital, the Prince asked me to repeat it to the Princess; and again I told the story of the long, long Indian day, so full of interest and variety, but also so full of exacting repetition. In every Indian State there is some

[1] This was a translation from the *Novoe Vremya* of a paper on Prjevalski's wild horse.

legend of note, and some event in history, of which the people and their Chief are proud: and these were never forgotten by the Prince and Princess when the time came for remembering them.

At this interview, the first of a long series which continued up to the date of departure for India, I was so encouraged by the manner in which they listened that I was carried away by enthusiasm into little details. But they showed no signs of being wearied, and their marvellous memory, their charming sympathy, and desire to throw themselves into an Indian atmosphere made my task easy and delightful. Happily, the facts were so fresh in my mind, that I did not make many mistakes, for I found later that both the Prince and the Princess never forgot the smallest detail. From this conversation the scheme of the tour in India was formed. But if I had then known the effort and strain which the tour was to involve on the Prince and Princess, I should have been less confident. But in an English December it is easy to forget the heat, the dust, and the glare of Indian travel, and difficult to realise the fatigue of nearly 9,000 miles journey by rail alone, and the discomfort of 28 nights spent on the trains, comfortable though the carriages were, thanks to the efforts of the Railway officials of India.

Drawing up the programme for the Royal Tour, it seemed practicable to arrange ceremonies which would enable the Prince and Princess to fulfil their desire to see the people of the various and varied countries of India through which they passed, and at the same time to keep intervals for rest and quiet. But during the nine months' preparation of the programme every mail from India brought pressing requests for further ceremonies and for more interviews, all most reasonable, most natural, and very difficult for Their Royal Highnesses to refuse. Thus the days of the tour became crowded with engagements, and when the Royal visitors arrived in India, there were still further invitations and eloquent and appealing calls for more. There were no detailed records of the Indian Tour of King Edward to serve as a precedent, and in the thirty years which had elapsed places of great interest, then inaccessible, had been brought within reach by the Railway system of India. There was a new and very important feature in this second visit of the Heir to the Throne, for the women of India were to see, for the first time, a Princess of Wales.

Each Province, each Indian State, possessed its own peculiar interest and its own particular charm, and the Prince and Princess wished to see all that was characteristic, historical, and of social and political, or economical importance. In a word, they desired to acquaint themselves with the conditions of some 320 millions of Indians, of whom one-fourth live in Indian States ruled by Princes of their own.

It was an ambitious desire, but their fresh, keen interest, and their genuine sympathy enabled them to carry out every detail of a most exhausting and comprehensive programme. The obvious course in framing the scheme of the tour was, as far as possible, to avoid repetition, and to endeavour at each halting-place to bring before Their Royal Highnesses the distinctive features of the peoples of the neighbourhood —a wide neighbourhood, indeed, for men, women and children travelled hundreds of miles to see their Emperor's son and heir. It was specially desired that the tour should be so planned as to allow of the Royal visitors seeing and being seen by as many of the people as possible, and in all the processions the carriages in which they sat went slowly through the crowds of rapt and reverent eyes. Above all, it was desired that the Indian children should be foremost in the ranks of the spectators.

In spite of the heavy programme, the long, tiring journeys, the endless interviews, the splendid, but I fear sometimes tiresome ceremonial, and in spite of the fact that the promised hours of rest had vanished, their Royal Highnesses never flagged and never failed in their response to the loyal and affectionate importunity of India, from the day they landed in Bombay, 9th November, 1905, to the day they left Karachi, 10th March, 1906. And as I look through the old programme and read my old notes, I often wonder how it was possible to fulfil without a break all those engagements made a year before.

The history of the tour can be read in the admirable book

written by Sir Stanley Reed. As editor of a great Indian paper, he knew India well, and, as was fitting, the book was printed and published in India. I had the honour of writing the preface to Sir Stanley Reed's book, and among other points I noticed the wide difference between the reception accorded by the Indians to the King Emperor's son and the King Emperor's Viceroy. I have seen many Viceroys on their progress through India, and thought that nothing could exceed the reverence which was accorded to them. But there was to me a new note in the crowds who welcomed the Prince, a note of affection, a sense of almost religious fervour. Everywhere it was the same—on the Frontier, where there is little rule and all are equal, in the Purjáb where men are muscular and thought is free, in Bengal where brains count and ideals are born, in Burma, easy and smiling, and happy in a fine religion, in Madras, old-fashioned but safely progressive, and in Bombay, nearest to the West and perhaps foremost in the race of progress; in all these countries, so unlike in type, in language, in religion, in customs and in dress, there was the same fervour, reverence and affection for the Prince and Princess. Later, when as King and Queen they visited India, this fervour was unabated, and in Calcutta, where Western education has gone further than it has in other parts of India, thousands and thousands thronged to gaze on the seat where the King had sat at a ceremony on the previous day.

I have pondered for years over what I saw in 1905, and without claiming that I have, in the words of the late Lord Morley, ever got into an Indian's skin, I do claim that I can read an Indian's eyes, for daily practice for over twenty years has quickened my vision. And my eyes revealed to me in 1905 that there was a very real, significant, and most compelling influence in the person of the Prince. It seemed to me that this was a power, an influence that might, if it could assume some closer and more permanent form, prove the solution of a problem which has not yet been solved and is rapidly becoming more tangled and more involved.

I had only left India two years before the commencement of this memorable tour, and I had left an India to seemed appearance quiet and prosperous. But in 199 tangled an conditions changed. The Partition of Bengal, Lord Curzon's unconsidered and unintended remarks at the Calcutta University, the treatment of Indians in the Dominions, and the barring of a career to Indians in the Indian Army, had been seized on and cleverly used by the restless, devoted and never-tiring leaders of the anti-British-Government school. I do not suggest that this school did not exist in Lord Curzon's time. It was founded when I first knew India.

I used to think that the villagers regarded me and the others doing the same work as their real representatives. In camp, as I sat by the fire listening to their anecdotes, I felt I was one of them. I knew that I liked them, and felt sure that they trusted in me. But clever and suitable propaganda, never ceasing and never combated and so never defeated, has changed this comfortable, happy official elysium: and I learned on the Royal Tour some startling and disconcerting facts about the anti-British movement. It was no longer confined to the great cities and to the limited class of the educated Indians, for whom there was no occupation and livelihood under our system, but had spread to the villages, those same villages which, in the evil days of the Mutiny, had watched, unmoved, the rebels pass by, and had gone on ploughing. Rebellion and revolution meant nothing to them—they were not politically-minded. But—so I was told by Indians who knew—the villagers are now beginning to dream dreams, and some day may turn over in their sleep.

Among other places visited by the Prince and Princess was Peshawar and the Khyber Pass, and well-meaning persons both in England and in India sent me messages of warning and protest, urging that it was wicked to risk these precious lives. There was a risk all through the Tour, and no one knew this more clearly than the Royal visitors. But they trusted the people, and the people responded. They were safe in that dare-devil city of Peshawar, and safe among the Afridis of the Pass. But when we returned to Peshawar after the visit to the Afghan end of the Pass, I received a budget of letters from Calcutta urging that Calcutta should be omitted from the Tour, as the anti-British feeling ran high and there might be trouble. Always contrasts, always the paradox in India! It was safe to pass through the wild and undisciplined country of the Pathâns: it was dangerous to visit the Capital of India, the second largest city in the Empire. The visit to Calcutta was, of course, made, and not a single item of the programme was altered, though to the last moment there were anxious suggestions that certain functions should be omitted. And I would add that the enthusiasm and affection of Calcutta was one of the most marked features of the Tour, and that men who had advised against the visit assured me that the bitter feelings of the Indians of Calcutta had been sweetened by the kindly and simple charm of the Royal guests.

There had been a great sea change in the Bay of Bengal. Everywhere there was a sense of kindness and goodwill. The kind eyes, courteous patience, and always considerate speech and gracious hearing, won the responsive Indians, and during these six strenuous months there was a halcyon calm throughout the land. The Indians are quick and miss nothing. They saw that the Royal guests wished to be near and among them, and that they disliked the well-meant efforts of the Police to keep the crowds at a respectable distance. On these occasions the work of the Police is very delicate. If any accident occurred, the blame would fall on the head of the Police. During the whole of the Tour the Prince and Princess moved freely through large crowds, and I never saw any hustling or force used by the excellent Police of the various Provinces of India. There were six Indian detectives attached to the camp of the Prince: two Mahrattas, two Sikhs and two Pathâns. Their chief was a remarkable Moslem, an old acquaintance of mine, who knew more of the underworld of India than any living man. But from the beginning to the end of the Tour I do not think that more than three of us knew of their existence, and though I saw the six detectives almost daily, I often failed to recognise them when they put on the dress of disguise.

After some months of travel, the Prince and Princess were staying at the Nadesri House at Benares, a bungalow belonging to the Maharája of Benares. On one side of the bungalow was an old-fashioned Indian rose garden; on the other side, by the front door, was the shrine of the goddess Nadesri, and a park in which were the tents of the Prince's suite. The Prince and Princess had gone out early to give rewards to some Gurkha soldiers who had done good service in saving life in a recent earthquake. I stayed at home to finish some work. As I was waiting for their return I walked up and down the long rose garden, and suddenly noticed a naked faqir hidden in the rose bushes. I beckoned to him to come out of the bushes, but he shook his head. I saw the British sentry pacing up and down the veranda of the Nadesri house, and said to the faqir: "If you don't come out I shall call the sentry, and there may be trouble!" On which the faqir took out from his beggar's bowl his card and photograph of identification. He was one of the Mahrattas, whom I knew well, but smeared over with ashes, with his long matted locks, I did not recognise him. I had always been warned to look out for the faqirs and their begging bowls, for the bowl often held a murderous knife. "You can see everything from this garden?" "Yes," he said. "No one can enter the bungalow from this side without my knowing."

At breakfast the Prince asked me the proper name of the house. I said it was Nadesri. "Well," he said, "I met a Sanskrit scholar this morning, and he told me that the proper name was Na*n*desri." Some years before this, when Lord Curzon was about to visit Benares, I had ascertained from the Maharája of Benares that the shrine after which the house was named was sacred to a local goddess, Nadesri, so I urged her claims against those of the perhaps better known Nandesri. But after breakfast, to make sure, I went to the shrine, and found there, at his devotions, a venerable Hindu dressed in a spotless white tunic. I said: "Rám, Rám," and he, looking beyond me with viewless eyes, replied: "Rám, Rám." "What is the correct name of this shrine?" He answered, to my satisfaction: "Nadesri." "Good," I said; "and how many years have you been guardian of this shrine?" "I came yesterday," he replied. "Then what can you know about the correct name of the shrine?" I asked. On this, without a smile or change of devout countenance, he drew from his tunic his pass and photograph. "Where is the real guardian of the shrine?" I asked. "We have sent him away on holiday," was the reply.

All through the Tour I received letters of warning, some

written by sensible people, some anonymous; and fantastic as some of these warnings were, it would have been unwise to ignore them, since in India strange and fantastic happenings are not uncommon. But nothing untoward happened. In spite of long and constant travel, in spite of heat and dust, the Prince and Princess kept well, active, and keenly interested. My one doubt and fear was in the first week of the Tour. The climate of Bombay was at its worst and the heat was unusual and without the tempering breezes from the sea. Daily receptions of Indian Chiefs and return visits to their residences at great distances, and constant public ceremonies, would have fatigued the strongest. And then at night dinners and late receptions in stifling heat. Maharája Sir Pertáb Singh, who was at the head of the Prince's Indian Staff, realised the situation one night at a late hour, and approaching with his old-fashioned salaam, said: "I thinking, Prince Sahib, time for sleeping."

In the preface to Sir Stanley Reed's book I ventured to describe the Prince of Wales as "dutiful." I have seen many Viceroys and Satraps in India, but I have never seen anyone who rivalled the Prince in his cheery sense of duty. I never met anyone who had a greater love of method and greater power of memory for faces, dates and events. When I was in America in 1917-18, one of my hosts in Kentucky asked me in a somewhat abrupt fashion: "What, anyway, is this King of yours?" As I had a few hours to spare and was in his house, I gave him a sketch of what the King's daily work was, and the long hours he spent in official duties. "Would you tell my fellow citizens this?" he asked. "Certainly," I said; "provided the Press is not present." My Kentucky friend passed on his discovery, and in other States, when I was leaving, after making speeches on the War, they would ask me at the farewell luncheons to tell them of the King and his work. I do not know who invented the truism "that the most loyal Englishman is the King," but after these luncheons I often heard the same idea set out in the racy idioms of the American language. Few realise the never-ceasing labours of our King and Queen: there are no real holidays for them, but every hour some duty, some new incident, some fresh problem to be comprehended. Whatever touches their people scattered over one quarter of the world comes home to them.

Their servants may look to rest and reward: but when is their rest? What is their reward? Perhaps, as they watch, silent and intent, the heart-stirred throng which surges before the Palace Gates in times of crisis, they know that they have won the greatest and noblest of all rewards.

I enjoyed every day of the Indian Tour, and shall never have so happy a chance again. What made it so delightful, and to me so unusual, was the generous appreciation of work, made so easy and simple by that very appreciation and by that charming consideration. I delighted most in the unrehearsed effects, the sudden emergencies, which always seemed to elicit the best, the most natural, and so the most effective of the Prince's utterances.

In Calcutta I was talking to Moti Lal Ghose, the frail, fiery, but most attractive editor of the *Amrita Bazar Patrika*. He was full of grief and said that the partition of Bengal would lead to the abolition of the Permanent Settlement and to the destruction of the High Court. As he lamented, the Prince came in from the adjoining room in which he was working, and I asked permission to present a very special type of Indian. When we entered the Prince's room, Moti Lal was silent. He went down on his knees, kissed the Prince's feet, and bursting into tears just ejaculated: "My future Emperor, remember poor India. She is in a bad way." The Prince tried to console him. "India was not at all in a bad way and the people in other parts of India seemed happy enough." I then gently removed Moti Lal to my own room, and he told me how grateful he was for this glimpse of the Prince.

I used to have long talks with him when I was with Lord Curzon, and he once told me how the Bengalis were a brave, manly people, addicted to deeds of violence. He spoke almost with tears in his voice of their skill as highway robbers, of the songs which were written of the Robin Hoods of Bengal. "And now you twit us as unmanly and unwarlike, and you say that there is not a single Bengali in the Indian Army!" Then he would impress on me the fact that the British had got into India on the shoulders of the Bengali. "Who were the right-hand men of Warren Hastings and the old

Governors? Who did your work of penetration in the North-West and the Punjáb—nay, even to Kabul? And then when you had overrun the North-West and the Punjáb, you threw off your old friends, the Bengalis, and took to your hearts the Northerners. Look at that map of yours on the wall, showing the spread of education, and I will point out one simple fact to you. Bengal shows the greatest spread and your map grows lighter, and the Punjáb is the lightest of all. Study the colour and you will see this, that misery, peculation and corruption follow the Provinces as they are shaded, and you have deserted your old friends, the honest and honourable Bengalis, whom you call 'Babus,' and gone to Provinces where education is only beginning and where corruption is rampant."

There was another such chance interview of importance during the stay in Calcutta. At a huge reception at Government House, the Prince had retired for five minutes' rest to a screened-in alcove on the veranda. I caught sight of Mr. Gokhale, and asked the Prince if I might bring him to the veranda for a quiet talk. Mr. Gokhale was the ablest Indian of his time. He was just then President of the Indian Congress and was newly arrived from Benares, where he had made an important speech which had interested the Prince. "I gather," said the Prince, "that you think that the people of India would be happier if they were governed by Indians rather than by the British. I may be wrong, for I can only read by their eyes, but my impression is that the people I have seen are fairly happy. Are you sure that they would be happier if you changed the present system of Government?" "I cannot say, Sir, that they would be happier, but at any rate they would feel a pride in thinking that they were managing their own affairs, and taking their place among the self-respecting nations of the world." "Ah," said the Prince, "I can quite understand that ambition, but how can you achieve this while the women of India remain as they are at present in the unenlightened dark background?" Mr. Gokhale admitted that this was the blot, the weak point in the Progressive Programme.

The Tour ended in Karachi. Often when an enterprise of labour, risk and constant effort is completed, there is a sense of relief. But in this case it was not a feeling of relief, but a genuine sense of regret to all of us who had accompanied the Royal visitors. In his letter of farewell to the Viceroy, dated 29th March, 1906, the Prince used these words: "We are both genuinely sorry that our visit to India has now come to an end. We shall never forget the affectionate greetings of India and Burma. Everywhere we found the same loving regard for the late Queen Empress, the same loyal devotion to my dear Father, and the same kind and enthusiastic welcome to ourselves. So long as we live we shall remember India with feelings of warm gratitude and sympathy. I hope that this visit which has involved so much labour and anxiety on your Government will under God's Providence be fraught with benefit to India. We wish you and all in authority under you God-speed in your great work. We wish for the Indians immunity from famine and pestilence, steady progress in agriculture and industry, and a safe and material advance in social conditions." The promise in this message has been most amply kept, and India possesses in the King Emperor and the Queen friends who sympathise and understand. The knowledge acquired in India has increased as the years have gone by, and the affectionate sympathy inspired by the warmth of welcome under an Indian sky has not cooled in the more temperate climate of the distant West. Nothing vital which passes in India is unnoticed by the King Emperor and the Queen.

It is rash to make any assertion about India as a whole, and difficult to appraise the effect of the Royal visit on the peoples of that vast Continent. Still, I would say this. As far as I could see during my life in India and during the Tour, the real strength of the British connection lies in the Royal House of Windsor. Just as at home the one national institution, of which all are proud and all speak well, is the Crown; so in India all classes turn to the Royal House with veneration, love and hope. It is right and expedient that they should see their King Emperor at intervals. It is good for India and it is good for England. For there is nothing which England has to offer to India, the Dominions and the World more representative of all that is good and fair in our land and our race than the King and the Queen.

CHAPTER XV

"The true gods sigh for the cost and pain—
For the reed which grows nevermore again
As a reed with the reeds of the river."

—E. B. Browning.

At the India Office—The Council of India—Power Shifting from India to London—Danger of Impairing Authority in India—Appointed Commissioner by Lord Kitchener—Indian Hospitals in Brighton—New Experiences of Indian Mentality—Their Fine Conduct—Two Memorials and a Touching Tribute—End of Reminiscences—Puzzle and Paradox—Hints to Young Men who go to India—Important that the Best of Our Race Should Go—Use of the "Sun-dried" Bureaucrat—India a Fascinating Land.

ON my return to England after the Royal Tour, I had some talks with Mr. John Morley, who was then the Secretary of State for India, and I was appointed by him a member of the Committee to inquire into the finances of the Indian Railways. Later he asked me to join his Council. This I regarded as a great honour, but I begged him to excuse me and said I could be more useful to him talking in his room, than I could be at the Council table. But he urged me to join, adding that, even if I joined the Council, I could still talk to him in his room. Sir Alfred Lyall, who had for many years been a member of the India Council, told me that work on the Council had the same savour to him as that of chewed hay. And when I joined the Council after a visit to Canada, where I saw evidence of the uncomfortable position of Indian emigrants in British Columbia, I realised the truth of Sir Alfred Lyall's remark. There was very little of the Indian atmosphere in the quiet halls of the India Office. But it was a great privilege to be associated with men who had held emigrants in the Civil and Military Services of India, and detached yet to work with members of the Home Civil a Office, who viewed India with detached yet discerning truth After a short time I resigned. The only impression I gained during my brief term of office was that it was unwise to interfere with the Government of India. During the five years that I worked as Lord Curzon's Private Secretary, I can hardly remember an instance of his being overruled by the India Office, but even in my brief experience as a Member of the Council I noticed a tendency to greater interference, and a desire to initiate politics for India. It was obvious that the seat of Government was moving from Simla to Whitehall. It all depends on the idiosyncrasy of the Secretary of State, for the Council, by their experience and traditions of service, are as a rule disinclined to interfere.

The real business of the Government of India was transacted in the private letters which passed between the Viceroy and the Secretary of State. In them was the pith of the matter; the dispatches were often the official record of decisions already made. Much has been changed since I knew the India Office, and many of its old functions have passed into the hands of the High Commissioner for India. In my perhaps exaggerated belief in local knowledge, and in the men on the spot, I used to think that it would have been well if the Civil Servants of the India Office could be deputed for a few years to the East, so as to get the atmosphere and the poise which cannot be learnt from books and reports. But I was always told that the function of the India Office was to give to the Houses of Parliament the English interpretation of the measures of the Indian administration. It was necessary to translate, and sometimes the translation was splendidly free.

It was about this time that the Secretary of State laid down that the Viceroy of India was the Agent of the India Office. Literally this ruling may have been correct; but while I was in India no one, either British or Indian, regarded the Viceroy as other than the Governor-General in Council, and also the representative of the King Emperor. And I rather think that from the point of view of India the Secretary of State was regarded as the Agent of the Governor-General of India, who, once a year to an exiguous audience, told the House of Commons that all was well. But, whether it was correct or necessary to emphasise the precise subordination of the Viceroy and his Government to Whitehall, it is certainly dangerous and unwise to do anything which detracts from the high authority of the Viceroy of India. The Services of India, the Princes of the Indian States, and the peoples of British India had regarded the Viceroy as the sacrosanct and final arbiter of their destinies, and it was an evil day for discipline and order in India when the Indians began to realise that the great "Lord Sahib" was vulnerable, an idol with feet of clay, and that an interview with the Secretary of State might prove fruitful. There is a word in India which is on every man's lips—"*Hukm*," the order of the *Hákim*,[1] and whatever may be the next form of Indian administration, the "*Hukm*" will be wanted daily, and must be prompt, authoritative and unchallengeable. It must be given in India and not from London. In that book so full of Indian insight, "On the Face of the Waters," there is a vivid picture of Delhi in the hands of the Mutineers. "From the Palace to the meanest brothel . . . the one thought was still, 'What does it mean? How long will it last? Where is the Master?'" The Master will always be wanted in India, and it would be fatal at this stage of evolution to tie his hands or to weaken his "*Hukm*."

I thought that this brief sojourn in the India Office would prove the last of my Indian experiences, but in 1914, on the day of the funeral of Lord Roberts, Lord Kitchener sent for me and asked me to act as his Commissioner, to advise and inform him regarding the arrangements in France and in England for the sick and wounded Indian soldiers. The situation was critical, for large numbers of wounded had arrived in hospital ships, and there were no hospitals to which they could be sent, since very special arrangements were needed for water, food, and other requirements, which Religion and Caste Rules demanded. I asked Lord Kitchener to give me orders in writing, but he thought this unnecessary. On my insisting, he asked me my reasons, and I said that as I was ignorant of military matters I wished for written instructions so as to avoid being "jumped upon." He assured me that he would never jump upon me, but he gave me the letter which I wanted. It assured me of help

[1] Judge, ruler or master.

and consideration wherever I went in France or in England, and I shall always remember with gratitude the co-operation and the cordiality of the devoted officers of the Indian Medical Service and of the Royal Army Medical Corps. I saw nothing in the days of the War to rival the cheerful energy and resourcefulness of Sir Alfred Keogh, the brilliant Director-General, and both he and Lord Kitchener gave me every encouragement.

I made up my mind that Brighton would be the best place for the wounded Indians, and though, as is always the case, men advised me that it would prove unsuitable, I went down the day after my interview with Lord Kitchener, meaning to commandeer the two chief hotels. The need for shelter under a roof was so pressing that I was ready to discount the fact that a hotel makes a bad hospital. When I reached Brighton the local authorities pointed out that hotels formed their chief industry, and offered me the race-course and a pier. But I wanted something with a roof, and in one day I secured the Dome and Pavilion, a fine school, and the spacious Infirmary, which was known afterwards as the Kitchener Hospital. In a very short time there were 3,324 beds in Brighton alone for the Indians. Nothing could have exceeded the generous and unselfish attitude of Brighton, and from first to last the people of that attractive town did all they could by their sympathy and by their contributions to the Gift House to cheer and brighten the lot of those homesick and shattered men. But what appealed to the Ind.ans more than the kindness of the Brighton folk was the scrupulous attention which was paid to the requirements of their religions and castes. And, above all, the patients in the Pavilion Hospital gloried in the thought that they had lain in their King's own Palace. Each hospital had its Mosque for the Moslem, and a Gurdwára where the Sikhs listened to their own Chaplain reading from the Granth, the bible of the fine soldiers who may not smoke, and must bear the marks of the five *Kas*, the uncut hair (*Kes*), the short drawers (*Kachh*), the iron bangle (*Kara*), the steel knife (*Khandra*), and the comb (*Kangha*). In the month of Ramazán,[1] the Moslems keep a very strict

[1] The ninth month of the Moslem lunar year.

fast, and in some cases the rigours of the fast were harmful to the patient. It was pointed out to them, that as they were on a journey, they were exempt from observance. But one and all protested that they were not on a journey, but honoured guests in their King's country; and the Moslem inmates of the Pavilion made the point that they were guests in the King's own house. I gained a new knowledge of the mentality of Indians, sitting with them and listening to their strange impressions of this wonderful new world into which they had tumbled. The rain and cold, the mud of the trenches, and the invisibility of the enemy, the mechanical marvels of the new warfare; the submarine, which seemed to them the most wondrous and the most sinister of all the contrivances which puzzled their tired and bewildered brains; the aeroplane and the Zeppelin, which they always called "Jopling Sahib;" and, above all, the novelty of fighting by night, and the *Zulm*[1] of being sent back to the front after being wounded[2]—these were the common subjects of our talk. But sometimes they would tell me of their domestic anxieties, and would ask me to write letters for them to their homes, and letter-writing involved confidences, in which much was revealed of a life which was new to me. Much as I had always liked the Indians in India, my admiration for them was increased by what I saw of them in France and in England, and later in Syria. They were for the most part dejected and disappointed, for, from the first, circumstances seemed to combine against them. They are the soldiers for the desert and the sun-parched mountains; riders of the plains and strong climbers of the hills. The Sikhs and the Gurkhas, so proud of their traditional powers, found that Flanders was no place for them, and although Sir Douglas Haig always gratefully acknowledged that the arrival of the Indian troops had saved the situation by filling a gap, I think that the Indians themselves felt that their hand had lost its cunning; and it was noticeable that the mountain men of Gurhwál and the Punjábi Mahomedans seemed to stand the novel conditions of static and mechanical fighting

[1] This is a great word in India. It means tyranny, but is used by the Indians for anything which is excessive.

[2] In their own words: "For we are as grain that is flung a second time into the oven, and life does not come out of it."

better than the more acclaimed Sikhs and Gurkhas. Yet all played the game nobly in spite of the cruel handicap, and none played the game more steadily than the wounded and shattered men who found their way to English hospitals. I noticed their intense desire to make a good impression on England, their good behaviour in and out of hospital, and their honest adherence to the rules of their religion and their caste, when these might have been ignored if they had been indifferent. Above all, I noticed their genuine gratitude for, and appreciation of, the arrangements which had been made for them. They had come, as they put it, 7,000 miles over the sea from their homes, to fight their Sahibs' enemies, and, as far as I could gather, they had the vaguest idea as to who these enemies were or as to what the war was about. With some reason it might have been thought that if it was a matter of gratitude, England rather than India should be grateful. But, as their representatives stated in a Memorial which they handed to their King Emperor, they were thankful for "the honour you have given us to come to Europe and to fight side by side with the Europeans in the great War, and to give us the chance of showing our loyalty and fighting capacity on this occasion. When we were leaving India we had mixed feelings of pleasure and misgiving: we were pleased as we were coming to serve our kind and great Monarch: we had misgivings as to our being able to keep our religious and caste prejudices which are dearer to us than our life, but those misgivings disappeared when we landed in France."

Their letters were full of simple gratitude. One written from Brighton says:—

"One gets such service as no one can get in his own house, not even a noble. One gets milk, meat, tea and all sorts of fruit, apples, pears and oranges, sweetmeats as much as one can eat, milk as much as one can drink, and most excellent beds beyond description. These are no fables. This country compared with others is heaven."

The Pavilion with its Oriental buildings and its charming gardens on a sunny day was indeed a haven if not a heaven to the Indians after the storm and stress of Flanders.

In years to come, the student of the British Empire may

find in Brighton two Memorials which express a sentiment and record a strange incident of the great War. On Patcham Downs a pillar marks the place where the Hindu soldiers were cremated, and is the gift of Brighton citizens. And at one entrance to the Pavilion is a gate which was presented by Indians. But perhaps the most touching Memorial is away in a churchyard of the New Forest. An untouchable, a humble sweeper, known as the *Mehtar* or Prince, died in one of the Indian hospitals in the New Forest area. There was a burial ground for Moslems at Woking, but at the time the *Mehtar* died, the Burning grounds had passed out of use, as the hospitals were closing. Woking would not give him sepulture, and it was difficult to decide what should be done. The Rector of the parish came to the rescue, and gave him burial in a Christian churchyard. In India, often when one *Mehtar* meets another he salutes him as "Maharája." But if the story of this poor camp follower, who lies in the beautiful God's Acre in the New Forest, were known in India, he would indeed be regarded as a Prince among *Mehtars*.

When the Indian troops left France, they found a more congenial terrain in Mesopotamia and Palestine: and in a campaign of rapid movement they won laurels and renown. I was sent to Syria in 1919, and found Indian troops happy, useful and efficient, in surroundings which seemed very familiar. I saw how superior they were in every way to the natives of the country, and was amused by their comments on Syrian character and conditions. Their chief objection to the Syrians was that they were not clean in their habits.

So ends my story of Indian experiences. But letters still come to me from India, full of character and of clues to the maze of India. As I write, there comes a letter from an old Moslem friend. He is writing in grief, for he has just lost his best and lifelong friend, a great and good Hindu, at whose cremation I was present a few weeks ago. My friend writes thus: "The Hindus and Muhammedans as usual are breaking each other's heads, and in the last two riots in Lahore and Multan the Hindus were the aggressors. The Hindus have got it into their heads that India belongs to the Hindus, and that the other communities either should be converted to Hinduism, or turned out from the country. I am afraid they will regret it because the Muhammedans are being kept back by the Government curb, which if loosened, there will be thousands of Hindus shot in India in a day. To rouse up Muhammedan fanaticism the Hindus have commenced abusing the Prophet of Islam and his religion."

I wish I could have finished on a more peaceful and hopeful note. But here are two men, both typically Indian, old friends of over fifty years' standing, one a Hindu, and the other a Moslem; and what the latter says in his letter would have been said by the Hindu if he were still living, but he would have blamed the Moslems. This letter is dated 21st July, 1927, from British territory. From an Indian State I received a letter dated 19th July, 1927, containing the good news that the Maharája has raised the marriage age of girls to 14 years and of boys to 18 years.

As long as I shall live it will be the same contradiction, puzzle and paradox. Progress in one most unlikely quarter: reaction and confusion in another, where all seemed so hopeful. But the only conclusion I can arrive at is that, though there may be an outward and superficial change in the binding, the contents of the dark book, India, will remain the same; and it is in that belief that I have ventured to collect from the voluminous diaries of a lifetime some of the little straws that sometimes show which way the wind is blowing. But my chief excuse for recording these rather commonplace reminiscences is that when I went out to India I had seen no book which told of the little things which count. The reminiscences of the great teach us that we can make our lives sublime. My humbler object is to help young men who are going to India to make their lives helpful, useful and happy. The first essential is a good knowledge of the Lingua Franca, the excellent and delightful language known as Hindustáni or Urdu—the language of the camp or "Horde." To acquire this it is necessary to study the grammar before leaving England, and now, happily, the School of Oriental Studies makes easy the study of Urdu.

The second essential is to learn the customs of the people

of the District, and this is a fascinating study to anyone who can talk and understand the language.

The third essential is to keep good health and a good and equal temper. Some men, for some reason or other, never like India, and whatever be their work, whether in the Services, or in business or on Plantations, the sooner they leave the better, for the Indians are quick and sensitive, and no man can be useful or happy if the Indians dislike him. Often work goes wrong owing to the blunder or helplessness of an Indian; many things may have gone wrong—the day is hot, the way is long, and the young Englishman's temper may be short. But he should not give vent to his feelings in the presence of other Indians. The man who has made the blunder should be spoken to the next day. For the thing dearest to the Indian after his religion and his customs is his *izzat*, and the man who reprimands or laughs at the humblest Indian in the presence of his fellows makes an enemy for life. Above all, in dealing with Indians it is a fatal mistake to be satirical or superior.

Some years ago I spoke at my old College, Balliol, on the subject of an Indian career. I pointed out the great attractions of India. The Master of Balliol, when I had spoken, said: "This may do good: at any rate it is new; for of late we have been advised that India is a country to be avoided." I made the same kind of speech at Cambridge, where also an Indian career seemed at that time to be unpopular. I had some success, for two undergraduates, who had decided not to proceed to India, went out.

It would be disastrous if the best of our youth turned from the greatest and noblest field of British endeavour. But I hold strongly that while there is greater opportunity now than there ever was for the youth above the average, there is no longer the same opening for the young man of ordinary abilities. I am not thinking of scholarship merely, but have in my mind the boy who shows qualities of leadership and is chosen to be House Prefect or School Prefect. The boy who can help others is the man who in the coming years will help the Indians to manage their own affairs, and to stand equal and unashamed among the self-respecting nations of the world. This is a glorious task, calling for patience and selflessness, and is a far higher mission than fell to our lot in the last century. But no one will succeed if he ignores the experiences of his predecessors, and the landmarks and the danger-signals which saved them from error and disaster. The "sun-dried bureaucrat" had his uses and his qualities. It is impossible to learn the real facts of India without toil under the sun; and the epithet "sun-dried" conjures up to me the good, keen men who scorned the fierce Indian sun when there was duty to be done. I seem to see the hero, John Nicholson, who, burning to be down at Delhi, sat motionless on his horse through the furnace afternoon, while his exhausted followers lay panting in the shade. So long as the British connection lasts, and it will last so long as Great Britain and Greater Britain send their best to India, the white man must carry on the burden under the pitiless iron sky, "when the heaven is shut up and there is no rain," through the famine-ridden tracts, through the ugly crowds maddened by rumour, suspicion and distrust, shouting antiphonally their religious zeal and their murderous desire. Happily, in India there are halcyon intervals, and life in normal times is full of interest, action and delight. I admit that India has changed since my time, and that the Indianisation of the Services has made long strides of recent years. But, as I have noticed in previous chapters, India had changed in 1879, and I was warned by all my elders that the golden age had passed with the Mutiny. But to me, who had not known the golden age, the twenty-one years I spent in that most fascinating and lovable land seemed to me, and still seem, splendid, spacious and happy, and I doubt whether life in any other part of the British Empire can offer what India gave then, and gives still.

CHAPTER XVI

> "We halt for ever on the crater's brink
> And feed the world with phrases, while we know
> There gapes at hand the infernal precipice
> O'er which a gossamer bridge of words we throw."
>
> —WILLIAM WATSON

References to Constitutional Questions Merely Incidental—Indians Talk more Freely with Me after I left Civil Service—Social Reform—Civil Servants Precluded from Subject of Women of India—Standards of Conduct Wholly Different—Religions and Customs Left Alone—Policy of "Better Not"—In Northern India Bad Results of Old Customs not Conspicuous—English Education Begins too Early—Cruel Consequences of System—Stocktaking in 1906—Improvement in Social Conditions should Precede Political Changes—Provinces too Large—Cure for Non-co-operation—Suggestion that a Member of the Royal Family should be Prince Regent of India—Indian States Best Model for New Constitution—Greater Variety Required—Difficulty of Disentanglement—A New System of Government called for—Present System Uncongenial and Beyond Capacity of Indians—Danger of Tampering with Caste and its Social Discipline—Hindus and Moslems—The *Muharram*—The Race for the Vote—Tribute to the Reform Managers.

I HAD set out to record my experiences and had no intention of giving opinions on constitutional problems. But, looking back on what I have written, I find that by accident, and certainly without design, my reminiscences jostle and brush against some of those high and sublimated subjects—synthetic stuff for restless, broken dreams—transcendental, and above the stumbling facts of my pedestrian experiences. My opinions are not second-hand, but were formed when I was alone in camp and away from my fellows. I have tried not to generalise: indeed, my only close, first-hand experiences were gained in the Punjáb, Rajputána and Kashmir. In the Secretariat I came in touch with some of the larger problems and met Indians from every Province—men of all classes. I knew and liked them all. I was just as happy and interested in talking with a *Syce* about a pony or a *Mehtar* about a dog, as I was when a learned Bráhman expounded the meaning and philosophy of some strange emblem, or when a Rája told me of his problems of Government. At that time I was a member of the Civil Service of India. But when I left that Service and came out from England as Private Secretary to Lord Curzon, I noticed at once a great difference in the manner in which Indians talked to me: they talked more freely.

Thus, a member of the Viceroy's Legislative Council, with whom in earlier days I had closely worked, was speaking one day about an Indian official. He said he was a bad man. I reminded him that six years before I had often consulted him about the "bad man," and that he had always agreed that the man might be employed and promoted. He had never expressed any doubts as to his character. "Yes," my friend replied, "that's true, but as I knew you thought highly of the man's ability, I thought it would have been impolite to shake your faith in him." Now this Indian friend of mine was an old and wise man, of the highest character and reputation. He thought so kindly of me that when he died he made me trustee for his three sons; yet in spite of his wisdom, and in spite of our friendship, his sense of politeness would not allow him to prevent me from making a bad appointment. This sense of politeness often prevents a frank interchange of opinion.

During the time I was actually in the Civil Service I had no leisure and no licence to take any part in the social or political problems of India. We were "warned off," and our duty was to carry on as best we could and to give effect to the orders of Government. We were sometimes consulted about questions which came within our official scope, but, with the exception of Lord Ripon's measure for Local Self-Government and the Ilbert Bill, I cannot remember any reference which could be regarded as of a political colour. As regards social reform, I was not in India when the chivalrous Lord Lansdowne attempted to ameliorate the lot of the women by raising the age of marriage from ten to twelve years. But earlier, in Rajputána, Colonel Walter by his personal influence succeeded in persuading the Princes of the Rájput States to curb the extravagant expenditure on

Rájput weddings. It was this which led to female infanticide. Colonel Walter's scheme involved no legislation, and called for no action on the part of the police. It was a gentleman's agreement, and it worked well and created a useful public opinion. Lord Lansdowne, on the other hand, had to wrestle with the orthodox Hindus, and his legislation, modest and obvious as it was, could only have been enforced by police intervention, and this, of course, was impracticable. I alluded to the subject of early mating in a previous chapter,[1] and quoted Kipling's words: "By all the purdah cloaked." It is absolutely impossible to get behind that purdah, or indeed, to form any sound idea of the life that many of India's girl-wives, "old in grief and very wise in tears," lead in their enforced seclusion.

I was always talking to Indians, and they would tell me all about their customs and ceremonials, and repeat to me their proverbs and maxims. But if I had ever asked them about their wives or daughters, it would have been regarded almost as an outrage on decency, as a blunder in form. I once had an Indian acquaintance, a Governor of an Indian State, big, burly and genial; perhaps not an ideal Governor, but a very charming companion in camp, and a very keen sportsman. One day a lady missionary of high character besought me to use my influence with the Governor to release a young girl in whom this missionary was deeply interested. She told me that the Governor was insatiable, and that his house was packed with girls of tender age. She gave me proof that the girl in question was miserable and wanted to escape. It was humiliating to be obliged to tell the missionary that I could do nothing, as I was an official, and as such debarred from meddling in customs. I might have added, for I knew enough of what passed behind the purdah, that miserable as the girl was, it would have been worse for her if I had intervened. By happy chance this Bluebeard ceased to be Governor, and I never went shooting with him again. But I am convinced he would have thought me prudish, if not hypocritical, if he had known my sentiments on this subject.

Their standards of conduct and our standards are poles

[1] Chapter vi.

apart, and the sage men of old who founded the great business of John Company, were wise, or at any rate prudent, when they left the religions, the customs and the superstitions of the Indians severely alone. For these sage men saw what some of their successors see, that it would be useless to deal with one strange custom unless prepared to deal with all the customs which jar on the Western susceptibilities. They are many. Again, our wise forerunners may have seen, as many now realise, that if an assault is made on the Bráhman system and all that that system connotes, there will be trouble and perhaps chaos. For Bráhmanism is the keystone of Indian Society, and India is the land of the Hindus. It must always be remembered that when England first chanced on India, she touched an island of Hindus, insular beyond imagination, an island where curious customs, inexplicable to us, and illogical, had flourished and hardened, unruffled and uninfluenced by any foreign or outside opinion. For some time before the English appeared on the sunlit scene, the Great Mogul had given official direction, but the greater Bráhman had withstood any invasion of his province of social director. The Bráhman baffled the Great Mogul, and still baffles the English, notwithstanding their telegraphs, railways, and bridges over the sacred Ganges.

John Company found an industrious, amenable and docile people, ready to accept, after cycles of misery and misrule, the plain and downright dominance of the white man who came over the black water. But this dominion was acceptable because the principle which guided the new masters was the principle of "better not": tolerance for all religions, and "better not" meddle with immemorial customs. It is sadly true that many of these customs are hateful to the Western mind, but the men who brought India through the nineteenth century, through mutiny, when the evil wind blew over the land, through famine and plague, and handed her over to the men of the present century safe and sound, unharmed by foreign foes, unstrung by civil wars, these men knew that with a mere handful of British officials and an exiguous force of British soldiers, it would have been disastrous to have stirred up these docile peoples by interference in their myriads of religions or by intrusion on the impenetrable and intermingling jungle of customs. "Better not!"

But it may be said that without direct interference the men of the last century might have used the arts of persuasion, might have pointed out to the Indians that in the other parts of the world there is a public opinion with which some day India will have to reckon. To this it may be replied that the outer and visible signs of life, at any rate of life in the villages, did not suggest that the peculiar customs of India led to bad results. In the villages there was everywhere evidence of industry, frugality, kindness to children and tenderness to old age. Healthy, happy-looking children, fine, strenuous men, and graceful, stalwart women, did not suggest, at any rate in Northern India, that there was much amiss. The manhood and the womenkind of Rajputána, the Punjáb and Kashmir, are no mere "babies of a girl." I cannot speak for the towns, or of the Juliets "too soon marred,"[1] behind the tall lattices. But so far as the villagers are concerned, and they are the real India, I can understand and appreciate the great men in India of the last century who decided that the best policy was the policy of "better not." They saw, as we did, that the idle mouths of mendicants, faqirs and religious houses ate the grain, and that useless cattle, which might only die of old age, ate the grass, while often there was too little grain and too little grass for the workers and the plough cattle, but it was custom, and so they let it be.

Nevertheless the great men were not consistent. If they deliberately decided to regard Religions and Customs as inviolable, it was strange that they should admit the solvent of English education. We are proud of English character, which we perhaps rightly attribute to our schools, where boys bring up boys to play the straight game of life. But imagine a school of the English type in which the boys were all married, almost middle-aged at twenty, and possibly grandfathers at thirty years of age. Husband-scholars, with the examinations and the cares and the calls of a family always in their minds, and always the haunting fear that after the examination the "failed B.A." might find no means of liveli-

[1] *Romeo and Juliet*, Act I. Scene i.

hood. Always the pathetic letters which I know so well from the youth of nineteen or twenty years, the "poor familiar man," pleading not for a career but for *Rozgár*,[1] the dish of rice or the cake of millet for himself and his young family. When the great Essayist offered this fruit of Beelzebub's orchard to India, he was indeed providing an "Essay on Man," and the essay might have been less harmful if the English educationists had been content to wait till the Indian youth had settled down to married life. At eighteen, the Indian boy would have passed the distemper of sex, and have fulfilled the great duty of the Hindu, to whom the procreation of a son is the purpose and end-all of existence. At eighteen he might undertake the study of English without bewilderment and disorientation. I have always thought it cruel that young Hindus should leave their families for exile in England in order to qualify for the liberal professions, and have known many a promising and charming young man ruined by the uprooting, and returning to India an embittered man, hating the conditions of his own home, and hating the country which had shaken the basis of his being and the foundations of his belief.

It is all a muddle. And just as in the Monsoon, when the rain-bearing cloud meets and drives back the dry air of India, there is rolling thunder and blinding lightning, so there will be lightning and thunderbolts when the new ideas of the West clash in real earnest with the old traditions of the East. It seems to me that it would have been safer and wiser to keep the horse in front of the cart: that social changes, prompted and fostered by Indians, should have preceded political innovations of Western complexion and origin, foreign and opposed to all that is vital in Hindu policy.

At the beginning of a century there is always a desire for stocktaking, and in 1906 many causes conspired to arouse interest in the affairs of India. I was asked to advise whether some change in the Government of India was desirable. I gave as my opinion that, from the point of view of material well-being, the present system had great merits.

[1] Daily food.

among them the merit of economy.[1] If, however, something more than material well-being was wanted, the Government should declare its policy. I had been twenty-one years in India and had never been told by Viceroy, Lieutenant-Governor or Commissioner whither we were tending. Enough to get through the day's work as best we could. If a new policy were declared it might lay down that, while retaining the Army, Imperial finance and communications in the hands of a British Government, the members of the Indian Civil Service should no longer do the executive work of the country but should leave it to the Indians and act in an advisory capacity. A lower standard of administration should be frankly accepted, but I admitted that the standard at present was perhaps uncomfortably high for the mass of the people.

In order to lead the Indians to the great end of self-government, I advocated popular Assemblies in every Province, consisting entirely of Indians, non-official, and elected, under an Indian President. When any motion involving social or religious issues, or affecting customs came before the existing Legislative Councils, if there was a *prima facie* case for legislation, the measure should be sent to the Assembly to be debated in public and reported in the Press. If approved by the Assembly it should go back to the Legislative Council concerned, and, subject to the veto of the President, and to modifications based on administrative necessities, pass into law. I am convinced that in most legislation, and especially in laws which touch customs or religion, it would be well to make them applicable to a Province, rather than to force them on the whole of British India.

Some such beginning as this would enable the Indians to prove their mettle, and perchance to rise to higher things.

In giving this opinion I was influenced by two considerations. First, I had always thought that there must be some improvement in the social standards of India before there could be any hope of real and healthy advance in political life. Secondly, I had formed the opinion that the Indian in order to develop his full capacity should work with and

[1] It would be of interest to know the cost of the administration twenty years ago and what it is now.

under Indians. I know from experience what Indians can achieve when they have the real chance. Side by side of the British the Indian seems to shrink from initiative. He is very different in Indian States, and there is scarcely an Indian State in which there have not been men of outstanding ability, great thinkers and men of initiative and action: men of the same race, caste and religion as those working in British India, but worlds apart, solely by reason of opportunity. To give this opportunity India should be divided into smaller Provinces under Provincial Governments, composed entirely of Indians. Of late we have heard much of "non-co-operation," and it seems to me that this indisposition, this malady, would disappear if the Indians were given Provincial Governments composed of men of their own kind and their own mentality. The British and the Indians can co-operate in administration, but in Government they are worlds apart. These Provincial Governments, till such time as India can be given some form of Dominion status, should be under a Government of India of British composition.

As regards the first consideration, Mr. Gokhale always admitted that social reform must come first. And another great Bráhman, like Mr. Gokhale, a former President of the Indian Congress, agreed in my suggestions, as they would enable the Indians to show to the outside world that they could place their house in order. There have been many other great and good Indians who desired and strove for social changes, but they were as the pelicans in the wilderness. They all agreed on one point. They said it was impossible for a Viceroy and his Government to take up social reform.

I may quote another social and political reformer—Mr. Gandhi. "By seeking to-day to interfere with the free growth of the womanhood of India we are interfering with the growth of great, independent-spirited men. What we are doing to our women and what we are doing to the untouchables recoils upon our own heads with a force a thousand times multiplied. It partly accounts for our own weakness, indecision, narrowness and helplessness. Let us then tear down the purdah with one mighty effort." I wonder! I wonder whether representative government and self-determination will tear down the purdah, or bring the Bráhmans into harmonious touch with the "untouchable."

In 1906, another thinker, the most valued and the ablest of all my Indian friends, who spoke with great authority and unrivalled knowledge, urged, in view of the impression caused by the Royal Tour, that a Prince of the Royal House should be appointed as Prince Regent of India. He gave many excellent reasons, but the chief reason was that the Prince Regent would be the head of Indian society, and could discharge the social functions for which the overburdened Viceroy had no leisure. He pointed to the many benevolent and beneficial institutions in England: to the Royal Societies: to other splendid movements in the cause of charity and social well-being which owed so much to Royal leadership and encouragement. The Prince Regent would achieve in India what the King Emperor and the members of the Royal Family had accomplished in Great Britain, and would, as time went on, be regarded as the guide, leader and friend of wise social endeavours. The official head of the Government of India would remain, as at present, the Governor-General in Council, selected by the British Government for a period of five years. Among many other advantages which would be gained by the appointment of a Prince Regent would be the enormous advantage of continuity.[1] I was always sorry for the Indians, who had grown to know and trust a Viceroy, when the time came for the Viceroy to leave India. They have often said to me, "Now we have to begin all over again." The Indians who had grown old would say: "It does not matter who the new man is, we are too old to learn a new Viceroy: we have lost interest." In a Prince Regent, who might conceivably outlast many Viceroys, the Indians would have a permanent arbiter and friend, who would know them and their families and their hopes and ambitions. This knowledge is the real source of healthy power in the East: it is a knowledge which no Viceroy, however brilliant and industrious, can

[1] I should prefer the title "Viceroy" to "Prince Regent," and if it prove impossible to bring the Indian States into any democratic scheme of Government, it will be easy to bring them together under the ægis of a Royal Viceroy.

acquire in five years. It would be a tremendous power for good.

All of us who have had the privilege of serving in India hark back to our first District. We are almost parochial. We swear by our first Province, and are Provincial: but I must confess that I lost my heart not to a District nor to a Province, but to the Indian States of Rajputána and Kashmir. They were the real India of my youthful and mature imagination, an India entirely unknown to those who had only served in British India, unknown, and often misunderstood and misrepresented. I was interested in their history, full of real Indian character and romance, a history which ended after perils and misery in the solemn Treaties or *Sannads*[1] made with the fighting masters of India, made with the Crown. Outside and apart from the system of British India, these States have never forgotten the promise in Queen Victoria's Proclamation, "these Treaties are by Us accepted and will be scrupulously maintained."

I have in a previous chapter suggested that the Indian State, with certain modifications and improvements, rather than the British Province, would be a suitable model for the administration of the new India. Of course, this suggestion will not find favour with Englishmen of democratic mind. But India never has been, and never will be democratic. She is Aristocratic and loves Kingdoms, and if her peoples knew the real issues, they would prefer to be ruled by Rájas rather than be coerced by Bráhmans. It has always seemed to me that the way to Imperial Federation should be blazed by the Indian Princes. They are the natural leaders who could bring all India into the equal partnership of the Empire—into the comity of the nations of the world: they are the recognised leaders of Indian society and fashions, who could most safely guide the march of social reform. It will be wise to enlist them as leaders of the advance: unwise to estrange those loyal colleagues by asking them to follow the bidding of a Bráhman oligarchy or the behests of the lawyers and financiers of the Bazaar.

[1] The *Sannads* of the petty Chiefs are as binding as are the Treaties of the greater States, and must be considered if and when the Indian States are to be brought into democratic line.

It should be remembered that the Government of India up to the end of the last century was perhaps the most efficient, and certainly the most economical administration in the world. Without any disparagement of the capacity and ability of the Indian leaders of to-day, I feel sure that an attempt on their part to carry on such an administration on the old lines will fail.

The large size of the Indian Provinces, and the responsibility of the Provincial Governments unsupported by auxiliary and contributory institutions, always seemed to me dangerous. History suggests that from the time of Chandra Gupta (306 B.C.) to our own times, India has been used to a system of despotism more or less benevolent. In those early days there were 118 kingdoms in India. In the Mogul times the great Akbar divided the land into 15 Provinces. At the present time there are 9 Provinces, all of which would be too large for a Government of Indian composition. If it be decided that the Indians are to govern, British India should at the very least be divided on linguistic and racial lines into 25 Provinces. Akbar the Tolerant could rule 15 Provinces: the British, who treat all alike, have been equal to the task, but the Indians, divided by religions and sectional interests, must have more homogeneous, more compact units of Government. I advocate smaller units of administration in fairness to the Indian leaders, who are some day to displace the British. But I also urge it in the interests of the many millions who, though unconsidered and unconsulted, will be chiefly affected by the momentous changes which are coming. I plead in their interests for some variety.

I attribute much of the trouble and unrest in India to our dull passion for uniformity. I can remember the existence of a non-Regulation Province: but it soon became regularised and drab like the rest of them. Is it conceit, the thought that the way of some masterful Viceroy was the only way? Or is it laziness and the line of least resistance which leads the Government to make all the millions of India toe the same taut line? We had Germans in the Forest Department: but if a stranger from the Southern Cross were to visit India, he would say that this wonderful uniform Government must have had its origin in Germany. Why have one and the same system for all the Provinces? Why not have approached the question of political reform by Provincial avenues, some straight, but most of them winding, yet all leading to a supreme Government, which will for some time be necessary for the control of the Army, the conduct of foreign relations, and the internal safety of India.

All Indians with whom I have recently talked, the older and experienced, the younger and ambitious, agree that for a long time a strong British Army will be essential to preparation for full Dominion status. They would retain the British troops, dispensing with the British in the Civil Service. They do not realise that if a British Army is necessary, a British Government is inevitable. They always take it for granted that British Commanders would serve under a Government of Indians, and forget that in certain eventualities these Commanders might be compelled to serve over rather than under.

They should also remember that the British Government of India cannot remove itself and its British Civil Service, without guarantees for many solemn and binding pledges given to the peoples of British India[1] and to the Chiefs who hold two-fifths of Hindustan, without safeguards for British commerce and industries, and for many other interests which have depended on the impartial justice of British rule. Whatever India may wish or the Parliament of Great Britain may desire, if chaos is to be prevented during the preparatory term of transition, a British Army and a British Government in India will be required to keep troth. When the Indians can give proof of their ability to furnish and implement these guarantees and safeguards, the British Government and its Troops can sail homewards with a clear conscience and a sigh of relief.

The Indian leaders in British territory should be patient with us: for it is so difficult to disentangle ourselves. Unlike the clever juggler who throws off the well-knotted cords with one vigorous jerk, we have tied our knots so truly and honestly that they will take some t me to untie. It

[1] Among these pledges may be mentioned the Land Revenue Settlements, which affect over 72 per cent. of the population.

would be easy to cut the knots, but it would be an act of cowardice and bad faith. Then, indeed, our country, which once did hold the gorgeous East in fee, will "grieve when even the shade of that which once was great is passed away."

What the educated Indians want, and what all who cherish the high ideals of the British Empire desire—some Indian form of Home Rule for India—is possible with patient and careful preparation. It must not be unreal and artificial, "insecurely poised on an inverted apex." The ardent builders of the new Jerusalem must come down to some safe and sound foundation. Surely it would be better to adopt and improve the indigenous institution of Indian States, than to travesty and emasculate a system which is only tolerable in the vigorous hands of British officials, detached, impartial, and, to the Indians, inscrutable as the Sphinx. Part of the problem, as I understand it, is that the educated Indians were dissatisfied with the bureaucratic form of government which prevailed to the end of last century. It was a very efficient system, and it worked well and economically, while it was entirely in the hands of British administrators. I can quite understand that it was too rigid and regular to be popular, and, if I had been an Indian, I should have preferred to live in an average Indian State rather than in British India. But the bureaucratic system of the last century, which was based on a mixture of Mogul, British and French forms, can only be justified if it is efficient, and it can only be efficient when it is worked and guided by men who believe in and are born to the system. The Indians dislike the system, and it will break down in their hands. It was possible for the British, without roots in India, without interests and prejudices, to deal with huge Provinces, and to link the Provinces together under the name of British India. But it will be difficult, if not impossible, for Indians, with their sharp traditional and ever-inherent differences, to deal with large Provinces; and, however able, industrious and devoted, they will fail by reason of the inexorable distrust and hatred which are in the very marrow of the religions, races and castes of this infinitely diversified land.

They will fail if they cling to the old system. They

may succeed if they recognise that reform should proceed on indigenous and congenial lines.

There would be a glorious chance then for the Indians to prove their capacity for Home Rule. They could raise the standards and the conditions of the various States into which British India would be gradually divided; there would arise a real and hea thy patriotism for their respective States, and a noble and generous rivalry to make their States the best and the most admired of the United States of India. For purposes of defence, political direction, and for the maintenance of the British connection, a Government of India would be necessary. But its functions would be ana ogous to those which are now discharged by the Viceroy and his Foreign Office in their dealings with the present Indian States.

I have eaten Indian salt, and I wish to see the various countries of India taking their place among the self-respecting nations of the world. I know how dear to all Indians, from the Rája down to the humblest of the village menials, is *Neknámeh*.[1] But I fear that the crude wine of rapid reform may work like poison in the veins of India. There are many lions in the path of the present experiment of reform. Of some the roar is very audible. But there are many others, perhaps the more dangerous because they lurk in silence. It arouses our sympathies when the degradation of the untouchables is mentioned: but what will become of the Bráhman dispensation when the reformers try conclusions with the Hindu castes? And what will happen to the Hindu millions when the keystone of caste has been removed, with its old sanctions and its indefinable influences and social discipline?

We are too ready to cry out on caste, to denounce its hereditary exclusiveness, its rigid obligations. The seeming evil of it is proclaimed, its actual merits ignored. In times of famine and other calamities our Government does its best, but it would be vain were it not for the mutual aid[2]—the

[1] Good name, good repute.

[2] We were always forbidden to make inquiries regarding the income and assets of a village community, and I have never heard or read any account of the income of the various castes. But the aid which is given to the members of a caste in seasons of distress shows that the amounts collected as fines and levies must be considerable. The Bráhman caste has over fourteen millions of members.

essence of caste—which is rendered automatically and unobtrusively. Nothing is to me more miraculous than India's power of recuperation. I have seen a famine district seemingly blotted out and dead—men and cattle all gone. The next year when the rains return, all is smiling—the cattle fairs are humming with life. In 1918 influenza carried off eight to twelve millions of the people: the villages bowed before the storm, but thanks to the caste system they have risen and recovered. One striking example of the power of caste is to be found among the money-lending, shop-keeping caste. There is not much love in business, but the sharp Marwáris will not allow a caste fellow to go bankrupt, and I never heard of a *hundi* [1] being dishonoured. Caste is the one union to which the Hindu can look for strength—his one refuge and his anchor. We may harp on its drawbacks: but it gives cohesion to large communities. It saves Government from Poor-laws and doles, and it has retained for over 2,000 years the support and approval of the Hindu millions, who, when all is said, are best entitled to judge. I certainly cannot imagine what the cleverest contriver can substitute for the caste system in an India which is dislocated in every joint.

I have in places alluded to the bitter hatred which has blazed out of late years between the Hindus and the Moslems; but I have not given great prominence to this regrettable sentiment for two reasons. In the first place, to me India is Hindu, and whatever the picture of "India reformed" may have been in the minds of the imaginative men who made the rough sketch, in the finished work the Bráhman will be the central and the striking figure. In the second place, in the days of the last century, to which my reminiscences relate, our Indian environment was half Hindu, half Moslem. It was a fair system, appreciated by the people, and made for peace. The wicked old Roman prescription "Divide et Impera" was never in our minds. It was never the British way in the times of Queen Victoria; still less is it the British way in this new century. In our domestic life and in our official life the balance was always kept. In the Indian army, class companies were approved by Indians and British

[1] Cf. footnote, p. 30. Chap. ii.

alike, but class regiments were not in favour. There was no talk then of majorities, and the half-and-half arrangement was regarded as fair, and indeed, necessary. I noticed this arrangement in the Indian States, and it always interested and delighted me to see a Moslem Minister in a Hindu State. The *Munshi Sahib*[1] was spoken of with affection by the officials and the people of the State. I cannot remember any case of "communal riots" in an Indian State. In British India, every year in the first month of the Mahomedan lunar year when the Moslems mourn for the martyred Hassan and Hosain, and beat their breasts, marching in procession through the town, shouting with all their lungs: "Shah Hassan, Shah Hassan, Shah Hosain, Shah Hosain!" the British Police Officer would mount his charger and ride at the head of the Procession. In those days it seemed to me that the mourners and the Hindu spectators in the crowded streets looked on the Police Officer rather as an added ornament to the gorgeous *Tazias*[2] which were carried in the Procession than as an agent to prevent "communal riots." The month is known as *Muharram*. It is the holy period in which the minds of the faithful in India turn to the history and the duties of their religion. The pathetic story of Hassan and Hosain seems to have moved the heart of Indian Moslems, Shiah and Sunni alike, and it is well to know something about the *Muharram*, for it will now be a month of anxiety for those who are called upon to keep peace in India. The procession and the bearing of the *Tazias* are so much a part of the lives of the Moslems in India that it is said on high authority that they believe Islám to depend mainly on keeping the memory of the Imáms. Sacred and sad as this custom is to the Moslem, it is equally popular with certain of the Hindu communities, especially the Mahrattas. In Gwalior, a Hindu State, the festival of the *Muharram* is observed with splendid pomp.

It is strange that the month of *Muharram* should be the signal for outbreaks between the two religions, when it is remembered that many of the Hindus themselves observe

[1] A secretary, reader, interpreter, writer. The English use the word for a teacher of languages.

[2] This word, which means "mourning for the dead," is used in India for rich and sometimes gaudy representations of the tombs of Hassan and Hosain.

the festival. I came across many examples of real sympathy between the two great creeds of Indians, examples of what should be, and still may be, if hasty politicians will be content to travel by slow stages. I remember seeing at Baroda an exquisite prayer carpet of pearls, which the Hindu ruler of the State was sending as an offering to Mecca; and one of the strongest and most abiding of friendships between Indians which I ever knew was that of a Hindu Rája and a Moslem Nawáb.

At rare intervals, in my time, there were conflicts between the Moslems and Hindus in British India, and Sir Charles Crosthwaite always told me that outbreaks of this nature were really intended as a demonstration against Government. He was a very wise and experienced Lieutenant-Governor. I wonder what he would have thought of the Communal riots which are now so common and so deadly? Are they a demonstration against the new form of Government? It may be that the increasing bitterness between the Hindus and the Moslems is due to a new problem in Indian life which never presented itself in the last century, the power of numbers and the rule of the majority. As numbers go, it might be thought that in any scheme of Government the Moslems could hold their own in India: but there is a possibility that the Moslem numbers may shrink, and that the Hindu hordes may increase. Both Hindu and Moslem politicians are looking ahead, and the Shuddhi campaign of the former to bring into the fold of Hinduism the "untouchables" includes under this head all those who have in past times left Hinduism for Islám or for Christianity. On the other side there is the Tabligh movement for the conversion of non-Moslems to Islám. Doubtless there are many sincere men on both sides who are working solely for religion. But behind these are men who are racing for the vote. I cannot express an opinion as to the prospects of the Tabligh movement, but I know intimately two large communities converted from Hinduism to Islám, and I am certain that most of these could be whistled back to the fold. They were luke-warm Moslems and had never shaken off some of the old Hindu customs. If the Indian reforms in their present shape are carried to their logical conclusions, and representative government, which Mr. John Morley always told me was out of the question, is established, it will be found that the growing bitterness, which is a curse to India and a disgrace to Hindus and Moslems alike, has taken fresh roots in political rather than in religious soil.

In conclusion, although it is almost contempt of Court to mention the Indian Reforms which come up for judgment in 1929, I am impelled to add that the finest brains in India have been at work on the experiment which is being tried, and in spite of non-co-operation, rebuff and cruel impediment, the Reform Managers have shown courage, faith and patience worthy of all praise. If the experiment known as the Montagu Reform fails, it will not be the fault of the British Officials in India. They have done their best, and with noble and unselfish altruism have met disappointments and difficulties innumerable. But in an India, restless, uncertain and bewildered as she is at present, no scheme of reform, however wisely conceived in England, is sure of success; and in a few years it may be necessary to look around for some other avenue to Swaráj or self-government.

The labour of the last ten years has not been lost if it has shown to men of good-will the limitations and the contradictions which attend democratic experiments in the East.

If the scheme excogitated by an Englishman left to his own devices in the midst of a nerve-racking war breaks down, a better way may be found in calmer times of peace by some great Indian—a way which India can follow securely, and England can declare open without breach of trust.

INDEX

INDEX

INDEX

INDEX

INDEX

INDEX

INDEX

INDEX

INDEX

I

INDEX

INDEX

K

INDEX

INDEX

INDEX

INDEX

N

INDEX

INDEX

INDEX

INDEX

INDEX